THE HIGHLANDS
and
THEIR LEGENDS

THE HIGHLANDS
and
THEIR LEGENDS

OTTA F. SWIRE

OLIVER & BOYD
EDINBURGH AND LONDON

OLIVER AND BOYD LTD

Tweeddale Court
Edinburgh 1

39a Welbeck Street
London W1

First published 1963

Printed in Great Britain by
Robert Cunningham and Sons, Ltd, Alva

INTRODUCTION

I SPENT much of my childhood in the Highlands, chiefly in Easter Ross, Skye and Kingussie but also in long visits to Glen Urquhart, and my girlhood near Inverness. All my life I have loved and collected old stories and legends. The result is this book, which deals mainly with the counties of Inverness, Ross and Cromarty and Sutherland, though Nairn and Forres are included. Caithness has been omitted because it is not 'Highlands', and Argyll and the Hebrides because they are so full of lore and legend that each would require a separate book to do full justice to it.

It would perhaps be well to explain the great difference between the chapters on East and West, which illustrates a difference both in character and way of life. Easter Ross is rich farm land and no man need leave his birthplace (few did), for their livelihood on the land was assured. If a man longed for the sea, he joined the local fishing fleet and might venture as far away as Stornoway or Aberdeen. Fairy tales had died out, for life was serious and busy, but beliefs connected with the earth lived on and were practised and fervently believed in well into this century. In the West, on the other hand, the land was poor and the climate difficult. Almost every man left home as a youth to earn his living elsewhere. Some went to the large cities, more went down to the sea in ships and knew the great ports of the world. They served, too, in every war, whereas in Easter Ross the saying went, 'Only tinkers and fools volunteer; wise men make money. The land's the thing.' And for them it was. The men of the West came home to laugh at old beliefs and superstitions but to listen eagerly to the old people re-telling ancient stories to the children, stories that they too remembered being told in their childhood, and so, despite the Free Church ban on ceilidhs and songs, many of the old tales lived on into this century.

But the two World Wars, with conscription, and also the B.B.C., have changed all this and cut the past from the present. Much that was of beauty and interest is passing into the limbo of forgotten things. This book is an effort to save some of them.

I should like to take this opportunity to thank Mr Stuart Barrie for his delightful line drawings which so ably illustrate the text.

OTTA F. SWIRE

Orbost House
Isle of Skye

CONTENTS

Great were the marvellous stories told
Of Ossian's heroes,
Giants and witches and young men bold,
Seeking adventures.

SHERIFF NICOLSON

I

INVERNESS AND SOUTH

On a hill stood the King of the North, and looked
To the sea, where his proud ships rode;
Then he looked to the shore, where his camp stretched along
And the heroes of Lochlin abode.

Then he turned to the land; and there far away
A terrible hero came,
And above him a banner of Albin's gold
Floated and shone like flame.

'The Banners of the Feinne',
from MacCallum's Collection, 1816.
Translated by Thomas Pattison.

The prospect of ye Town
of Inverness
1690

1

INVERNESS

*As if it were a jewel clasping the folds of
the mountains to the blue zone of the sea.*
RUSKIN

HIGHLAND hospitality has long been famous. Judging
by the number and variety of her visitors Inverness must
have excelled in this respect. Historically her first visitors
were probably Roman legionaries 'exploring', though some say
that before them came Phoenician tin merchants worshipping
their gods at the Clava Stones. But in legend there is no doubt:
Inverness's first visitor of note was Fionn, King of the Féinn.

He came striding down the Great Glen out of the dawn mist, with Grey Dog at his heels, to join his men on the strand. Not much later he was made prisoner by the enchantments of an Irish wizard and handed over to Cormac, the Irish King. Inverness comes in again, for Cormac demanded as Fionn's ransom that two of every bird and beast should be made to pass before him as he sat on the Hill of Tara. Caoilte, who was trying to negotiate Fionn's freedom, hurried to consult Bran (Fionn's own dog) and the Grey Dog, Bran's brother. They said: 'Can do.' But Caoilte feared that if Cormac and his magicians once saw Bran they would never let him leave Ireland, so, being wily, he suggested to Cormac that he would appear a more powerful conqueror if he sat on the hill of Tom-na-hurich in Fionn's own country, there to be served by Fionn's own dogs. Cormac thought that that was so. Bran and the Grey Dog brought a pair of every animal that lived and made them walk round the base of Tom-na-hurich while Cormac sat on the top and looked important. Easy it was for them, great dogs that they were, though mouse preceded cat and rabbit walked with fox; easy it was until they came to the pair of whales. The walking of the whales was a feat worthy of the Great Dogs.

After Fionn and the Romans came Macbeth to murder Duncan, King Duncan to be murdered, and his son to avenge him; the Queen of the Little People to hold revels; Thomas the Rhymer to sleep under Tom-na-hurich; almost all the Kings of Scotland, bringing charters and arms, castles and wars; Michael Scott bringing his demons to build a bridge; the French Comte de St. Pol to watch the shipwrights of Inverness build him a ship for the Crusades; Montrose on his way to execution; Cromwell to restore order and Prince Charles Edward to upset it again; the Brahan Seer to foretell the future; Dr Johnson and Boswell to observe; spirits to inhabit peacocks; Lloyd George to hold a Cabinet meeting; and above all, and towering over all, Inverness's greatest visitor, St. Columba. For Inverness claims the honour of having within its boundaries the first Christian spot in the Highlands of Scotland so naturally St. Columba, his miracles and his monks play a large part in her story.

According to one tradition Inverness was founded in the first century B.C.; certainly Stone Age remains found from time to time indicate a very ancient settlement here. Inverness first positively appears in written history, however, with the coming of St. Columba in A.D. 565. The saint's visit changed the whole life of the Highlands, for it was his first step towards the conversion of the North to Christianity. At this time all this part of the country was under the rule of the Pictish King Brude, who had a chain of vitrified forts on the heights that surround the estuary of the Ness. St. Columba decided that it was his duty to preach the Gospel to the Picts of north and west Scotland, but as a Chief's son himself he knew better than to start converting the followers of another Chief without his consent, so he decided to visit King Brude in person to ask his approval, or at least his permission.

A road (Canal Road) now takes off on the north bank of the Caledonian Canal just across the opening bridge at Muirtown and from it a path leads on up the hillside to the summit of Craig Phadraig. It is here that Saint and King first met, and part of the vitrified ramparts of Brude's old fort, which once crowned the hill, can still be seen, as can the holes in the rock which are believed to have held the bolts of the great gate—that gate which opened of itself. When St. Columba reached Inverness on this important occasion he learned that the King was, at the moment, in this fort on Craig Phadraig, so up the hill St. Columba climbed, accompanied by some of his monks and by Sts. Comgall and Canice who were themselves Irish Picts and therefore, thought St. Columba, more likely to be acceptable to the Pictish king than he, a Scot. As they reached their objective they saw the great gate of the fortress being closed and barred against them. St. Columba knocked and asked permission to enter as he sought speech with the King. This was refused and the gates remained firmly barred. Then, says Adamnan, Columba 'traced the sign of the Lord's Cross on them and, knocking, laid his hands against the doors and immediately the bolts are violently thrust back and the doors open in haste of their own account and, their being thus opened, the Saint thereupon enters with his companions'.

Converted by the miracle, Brude not only gave his consent to the saint's preaching throughout his lands, but he himself and all the garrison of the fort were baptised there and then, and so Craig Phadraig became the first Christian spot on the Highland mainland. Tradition adds two further details. The first is that this was the occasion on which St. Columba and his monks sang Vespers as they climbed the hill and King Brude's Druids tried to drown their voices, both by noise and by magic. But, this being revealed to the saint, he began to sing the 45th Psalm (known in the Celtic Church as the 44th), whereupon his voice, usually low and gentle, was 'lifted up into the air like a terrible thunder, that both King and people were astonished and affrighted with fear intolerable'. The second tradition has it that St. Columba baptised the King and all his men at the root of a young fir tree which, growing in the centre of the fort, made of its branches a shelter for the Saint. (The piece of ground enclosed by the fortifications is of considerable size.) This tree was still growing, one of the finest and largest Scotch firs that ever I saw, when Craig Phadraig was sold to the Forestry Commission in the 1920's and much strong feeling was aroused by their decision to fell it as part of a clearance scheme.

Needless to say, there is no certain evidence as to which of his forts King Brude was actually in on the day of the saint's visit; some believe he was in a small fort on a hillock on the south bank of the River Ness later called St. Michael's Mount, on which now stands the High Church, and give this as the reason for the choice of this site for the Parish Church. And it certainly would be fitting that where Christianity first came to Inverness Christianity should still be preached. Another suggested site is the Crown Hill, where some traces of ancient fortifications have been found, though that is more famous as the site of Macbeth's Castle where, in Shakespeare, Macbeth murdered King Duncan. Strangely enough, so far as I know no one has ever suggested that Tom-na-hurich was Brude's fortress though it looks so obvious, but the Torvean ridge near by has its supporters for the honour, among them the well-known historian Dr Skene, as old fortifications there were clearly seen when the Caledonian Canal was being excavated at its foot. That all these hills were crowned by forts of King Brude's building or garrisoning seems certain—no king claiming overlordship of the North could leave the Great Glen of the Ness unguarded—even if there is some doubt as to which one the King in person was visiting or living in on that eventful day. But Craig Phadraig has always been the favourite site, though obviously unsuited for a Parish Church, and now that the Moderator in person has led a pilgrimage there, its claim seems established.

Tradition usually connects the hill of Torvean, not with King Brude but with Lady Macbeth. Beneath it she is believed to be imprisoned, a sleeper who cannot sleep, for 'Macbeth does murder sleep'. Once a boy, tired of herding goats, lay down on the mound to rest; while his beasts grazed he fell asleep but woke at dusk, terrified to hear beneath him the endless tramp of light footsteps 'like a woman going backwards and forwards, backwards and forwards, inside the hill' he said. It was the sleepless Lady Macbeth. Insomnia that has lasted about a thousand years must indeed be a thing of fear. She is sometimes seen, dressed in a kirtle of natural coloured wool with over it a cloak of deep reddish purple, washing her hands in the River Ness near Torvean. Some say she rubs them with stones taken from the river bed and others have reported her as gathering leaves from a nearby alder tree with which to scrub them. She is reputed to pace slowly up and down the water side, too, on occasion. If she is seen by one person it is a warning of evil to befall him or his, but if her appearance is, so to speak, a public one, then it foretells some national calamity. She is particularly interested in the fortunes of the Royal House and of any of Macbeth's blood. The last time, so far as I know, that she was seen was by some visitors, strangers to Inverness, who mistook her for a film star being 'shot' for a film and were much intrigued. The date was just before Princess Elizabeth and the Duke of Edinburgh were to fly to Africa and, when rumours of 'the Lady's' presence spread, fears for the safety of the royal plane were felt. However, it landed safely, but though Princess Elizabeth flew in safety to East Africa it was Queen Elizabeth who returned.

This ridge of Torvean is said to have been spelt Torbhean as recently as the New Statistical Account of Scotland (1845) and to take its name from one of St. Columba's monks, Bean (Benjamin), who had his cell here and who here prayed and taught the people. Some say that at his death he was buried on the ridge where his cell had stood, others think it held only a cairn to his memory, his body being returned to Iona for burial. The Caledonian Canal now runs along the foot of Torvean Ridge and where the gravelly bank has been cut away a colony of sand-martins have excavated tunnels and taken up their abode. They are the only sand-martins in the vicinity and it is told that 'St. Bean' was permitted to borrow that Gospel which had been 'on St. Martin's bosom 100 years in the earth' and which St. Columba himself had brought back from Tours and given to his beloved monastery of Derry. With St. Martin's Gospel came, of course, St. Martin's birds to guard it, and although the Gospel was duly returned to Ireland some of those martins remained with Bean, and their descendants are here still.

Early traditional history tells of a battle fought here in 1187 between Donald Bane, 'a Hebridean Chief' intent on plunder, and Duncan Mackintosh, son of the Governor of Inverness Castle, who had sallied out with a part of the garrison to meet him. The result of the battle is said to have been the death on the field of both leaders and many of their followers. Mackintosh's men carried home the body of their commander, while Donald's men buried their Chief in a hurriedly dug, shallow grave in the hill's sandy side. When the Canal was being constructed a heavy silver chain 18 inches long and weighing 104 ounces was dug up at the Ridge's foot. It is believed to have been the insignia of Donald Bane and buried with him. So much for tradition, but the real story of Donald Bane is a sad one—one of the many 'misunderstandings' between the South of Scotland and the Highlands.

Malcolm Ceannmor made himself King of Scotland with the help of the Saxons of the southern borderlands and north of England. Under their law of inheritance the eldest son was heir and so, when King Malcolm died in 1093, they immediately desired to place his eldest son Duncan on the throne of his father, and did so. But many of the Highland Maormors (great men) had also supported King Malcolm and their law of inheritance was different. To them the heir to the throne would be the man nearest in blood to the *original* founder of the dynasty, in this case King Malcolm's brother Donald Bane, he being one generation nearer the founder than was his nephew Duncan. When Donald Bane's generation died out, but not until then, the next heir would be, in their eyes, Duncan as the son of the eldest brother. Neither side tried to understand the other's viewpoint. Each side proclaimed their man King and declared the other a usurper, and Scotland was plunged into a war which lasted off and on for about 100 years, the Donald Bane killed at Torvean being the grandson of the original Donald Bane, still battling for his inheritance although in tradition he has become just a plunderer.

Belgium has been called the Cockpit of Europe; Inverness might well be called the Cockpit of the Highlands, sacked, burnt, plundered, beseiged, overrun again and again, she still survives and keeps her clear-cut entity. Brude's forts and defences are the first indication we get of how desirable and how vulnerable she was, though tradition tells of a Roman cohort which reached the sea here and left but little food behind them. On that occasion men, women and children fled to the forest, thence to harry the enemy's march as he turned south again, for further north he dared not go. King David I of Scotland (1124-53) was the first king of whom much is known who took Inverness seriously, and he took her very seriously indeed. It was he who made her a Royal Burgh, one of the oldest in Scotland, and built the first stone castle on the site where the present castle stands. Macbeth's castle is reputed to have been built of wood on the site of an old Dun on the Crown Hill and to have been burnt by Malcolm III in revenge for his father's murder there. That spot is still called 'Auld Castle Hill'. David made Inverness one of the chief towns of his kingdom and the seat of justice for the whole north. King William the Lion turned it into a fortified town during the wars of his reign by causing a great ditch or foss to be dug round it. This was repaired as late as 1689 when the Macdonalds of Keppoch were expected to attack Inverness and did in fact besiege it. Tradition has it that it was William the Lion who granted the town her arms as a reward for the help she gave towards his ransom when he was a prisoner in England. Another story says that the Burgh adopted as 'supporters' the elephant and the dromedary to symbolise her trade with the Mediterranean and the East; a trade consisting largely of timber and furs as wild animals abounded in the huge forest which covered the North in olden times. Alexander III founded a Dominican Priory in Inverness

HTL B

but now all that remain of this once beautiful building are one broken column and the name Friar's Shot Pool on the River Ness near it. Not time but the Parliamentary army are to blame. The old graveyard of the Priory can still be seen off Chapel Street. In it is an ancient carved tombstone, said to mark the grave of the Earl of Mar of barley-brose fame.*

To record the endless wars and rumours of wars which swept the town would be dull. The Highland clans looked on it as representative of the King of Scotland and did not approve of his power having a place in their independent midst. The town was involved in the wars of both Wallace and Bruce, but it was left to the Lord of the Isles, on his way to the Battle of Harlaw in 1410, to destroy not only the whole town, as everyone did, but also its old oak bridge across the Ness. This had been spared in all previous sackings as being a rare and exceptionally fine one and a necessary thing in the life of the North.

James I held a Parliament in Inverness in 1427 and Lloyd George a Cabinet meeting there in 1921 though, as to this last, no one seems to remember why. Everyone remembers why King James held a Parliament here, however, for to it he summoned several disaffected or suspect Highland Chiefs and when they came, unarmed and in peace, he had them all arrested and imprisoned; a piece of treachery which led to endless trouble.

The Castle was repaired and strengthened again and again and the old town crouched beneath its walls. It was in this old town, in a house in Bridge Street known to this day as 'Queen Mary's House', that the ill-fated Queen lodged on her visit to the burgh, the Governor of the Castle (for the Crown) having refused her admittance to 'his' castle. Only the cellars, now a wine merchant's, remain as they were, the house having been greatly altered. The Governor was later executed for treason but on this occasion the town, having sheltered the Queen, went scatheless.

Inverness was for a time the headquarters of the Covenant's army. Cromwell occupied it and his troops built a fortress near the harbour, 'The Citadel', capable of holding 1000 men. They took the stone for its building from Inverness Priory and the Priories of Beauly and Kinloss. Only the clock tower now re-

* See Chapter 15.

mains of this Citadel; in it the clock still works and strikes, 'a brave great clock'. Near Kessock a gunpowder tower built by Cromwell's army still stands. Cromwell's occupation of Inverness is, on the whole, kindly remembered, for he dealt justly and did much for the town.

A fine stone bridge, the first in the Highlands, was built across the Ness in 1681-85. This bridge was built of stones taken from Cromwell's Citadel after that fort had been demolished by order of Charles II 'to please the people'. There was, however, another bridge over the Ness, one which spanned not only the river but also the gap between the destruction of the old oak bridge in 1410 and the completion of the 'New' bridge in 1685. It was, says legend, the Wonder of the North, so great was it. Here is the tale of its building.

Michael Scott, the magician, raised the Devil in the form of three small demons and used them for his own purposes. He then found, as had happened to devil-raisers before him, that he could neither lay them nor satisfy them. 'Work. Give us work. More work,' they chanted. Michael decided to help his friends so when any of them wanted work done, or undertook a contract of any kind, the wizard would pass it on to his demons and it was accomplished without delay or expense. Michael and all his friends grew rich. But at last even Michael Scott's ingenuity gave out and he was reduced to travelling throughout Scotland, ordering his demons to build him a palace in a new place each night and to demolish it in the morning. One of the places he visited on this queer journey was Inverness and here he heard of the town's dilemma—they wished to bridge the Ness but could find no one willing or able to take on a work of such magnitude. Michael immediately went to the Town Council and applied for the job, naming a very moderate fee. Delighted, the Council accepted his offer. He then made one condition; all the burghers and their wives must remain indoors from dark until dawn for three nights. This was agreed. On the first morning, when the curious burghers looked out, there in the river were the piers of a bridge. On the second morning the bridge was half finished. On the third morning the bridge was complete in every detail and poor Michael Scott had to set out on his travels again.

Inverness has what may well be the oldest school in Scotland, certainly in the Highlands. When Alexander III founded his Dominican Priory he included a school for the children of the burgesses. When the Priory fell on evil days the school was re-constituted as a Grammar School and so continued until the Academy was built and the old Grammar School incorporated in it. A life of over 700 years is not bad for any school.

Inverness played her part in both the '15 and the '45. Prince Charles Edward made the town his headquarters for some weeks and Cumberland, after Culloden, occupied it for longer. The Prince blew up the Castle but it is the 'Hanoverian Occupation' which, of all the many evils which have befallen the burgh, takes pride of place. If a half of the stories told are true (and many certainly are) the Germans of 1746 and those of 1945 had much in common. It is pleasant to remember that two English officers surrendered their swords, saying they would prefer to be court-martialled than to obey the Duke's orders, an act which at that time involved the risk of being executed as traitors. A number of other English officers are believed to have said nothing but to have just disobeyed or 'misunderstood' their orders.

The next visitors of note were Dr Johnson and James Boswell. They came when the town was at its lowest ebb; many of the houses then were mere wooden lean-to's clustering below the Castle hill, and the penal laws were still in force. Dr Johnson comments on the 'meanly built' tiny Episcopal church whose service he attended. Probably he did not realise that all Scottish Episcopal churches had been closed and that if a clergyman of that Church held service or prayed with more than four other persons, even members of his own family, he would for the first offence be imprisoned and for the second offence suffer transpor-tation for life. In the poor room which Dr Johnson visited, a Scottish clergyman had been wont to take just such services with his family while, hidden in a loft above the room, his congregation listened through a trap-door. But the clergyman died and his wife, being penniless, left the house which was then used by a Church of England Army chaplain from Fort George who was, of course, exempt from the Penal Laws. It was to hear him that Dr Johnson went. It was these Penal Laws which got the old

Episcopal Church of Scotland its name of 'the English Church'—
a name which still sticks to it in the North—because for long only
Church of England clergymen might hold Episcopal services.
The old Episcopal church in Church Street, being a well built
stone chapel, survived as a building to become in the early part
of the twentieth century 'Chapman's Garage', one of the first
garages in the North.

It was due to the imagination and foresight of a late eighteenth-
century Provost of the Burgh, Provost Inglis, that Inverness received a 'face lift' and became the beautiful town it now is.
Realising the need for a larger centre there, he started building,
but not haphazardly. Instead he employed a good architect to
draw up the plan for a new town with the River Ness as its centre
and main feature, and persuaded all concerned to adhere to it.
A great-grand-daughter of his once told me what a tussle he had
had when it came to destroying unsightly but still usable buildings
or preventing men from rebuilding as they would on their own
land. But he won through and the result is Inverness as we know
it now. It was after him that Inglis Street was named. Another
Inverness street of whose name a story is told is Baron Taylor's
Street. Once this street was full of tailors' shops, seven of them
it is said, and every day at the dinner hour each master tailor sent
his apprentice to buy beer. Seeing hope of a good trade a man
opened a bar in the street among the tailors. It became a most
popular house and soon the explanation that so-and-so was in the
'Bar on Tailors' Street' grew into Baron Taylor's Street, its origin
forgotten and its spelling altered. Another Inverness name whose
origin is uncertain but of which stories are told is 'The Tarry Ile',
an Inn at the corner of Tomnahurich Street just opposite Ross-
leigh's Garage. Some have suggested that its name was once 'The
Tarry Awhile' because drovers on the way to the markets in
Muir of Ord and Dingwall tarried there: others have suggested
some Gaelic name 'gone wrong' or a play on 'tar' (sailor), but the
last is unlikely in the Highlands. Mrs Sangster, the present owner,
tells me that the title deeds yield no clue but that when they
bought the Inn in 1922 Falconer's Stables were beside it and old
houses and 'pens' (narrow, dark passages) ran behind the Inn down
to the river. The old owner told them that smugglers used to

deliver smuggled whisky in tar barrels, bringing it up the 'pens' and, if asked what they had there, would reply 'Ile' (oil), and so the Inn became known among its frequenters as the 'Tarry Ile Inn'.

Thanks to Provost Inglis (himself a great admirer of that city) Inverness has been compared to Edinburgh as the Capital's only rival for beauty in Scotland. Inverness has, of course, nothing to compare with Edinburgh Castle or St. Giles' or the War Memorial Chapel; her castle and her cathedral are both small and modern. But against that, her river with its islands and bridges is a far more beautiful centre for any town than Edinburgh's railway and two railway stations, even though Princes Street's lovely gardens do do much to conceal them.

*   *   *

It is the Tuesday of the Horse Market and an old man with a white beard but young, bright eyes, dressed in archaic clothes, moves among the horses, apparently searching. Here is a chestnut, gallant of head and glossy of coat; she might please any rider. There are a pair of Clydesdales with lovely hairy feet, or a sure-footed Highland pony. The old man barely glances at them and moves on, searching, searching. He is Thomas the Rhymer, Thomas of Ercildown, knight, poet and (some say) magician, who sleeps with his men under Tom-na-hurich, the beautiful hill burial ground of Inverness. He comes out in person to attend all horse sales in the neighbourhood, there to buy horses, but only snow-white beasts with no single coloured hair please him. When he has bought enough to mount all his men he and they will be ready to rise again and save Scotland in her hour of need. As pure white steeds are rare, and yearly growing rarer, it is taking him some time to acquire enough satisfactory mounts. But as the need for him and his men is not expected to arise until Shrove Tuesday and Good Friday change places there is probably no great urgency in the matter. Curiously enough, King Arthur also wanted white horses for his Knights, but he has compromised; in his stable are 100 horses, white, cream, grey and piebald, but none darker. The Rhymer, however, admits of no compromise.

*   *   *

But to return to the Market. Markets in Inverness 'are not

what they were'. Towards the end of the last century Inverness wool market was not only the mart of the Highlands but *the* event of the year. Farmers came from all over the North and West, and buyers, too, from all Scotland. Thousands of pounds changed hands but never an I.O.U., an agreement or any signature. Every bargain was made by word of mouth and kept without legal bond. The first man to ask for a signed agreement is said to have been a Government official in World War I; he probably couldn't help himself but that agreement was the knell of the 'honest' market. The 'Rogues' Market' went on much longer and was not what it sounds. The 'Feeing Market' was held first, in the spring before the May Term, and to it came all the married men in search of a job. Whatever farmer engaged one of them gave him a 'fee' of a shilling as earnest money, whence the name. The next week came the 'Rogues' Market' when Inverness became full to the brim of young single men from all the country round —'the rogues', they being more restless than their elders. It seemed as if every young man in the North changed his job annually, though in fact many came just for fun (after all, good whisky was only 3s. 6d. a bottle then!) and re-engaged with their old masters at the latter end, the event to be pledged in a glass.

Inverness has two unique features, her Islands Park and Tom-na-hurich. Of the former it is told how St. Columba and his monks on their way to visit King Brude reached the spot where Inverness now stands, tired and hungry from their long trek across a wild Scotland. They rested for the night on one of the Ness islands, where they caught a salmon for their supper and then slept undisturbed on beds of leaves and branches. Next day, much refreshed, they prepared to continue their journey, but before leaving their island resting place St. Columba blessed the islands which had sheltered them, praying that they might remain forever green and at peace and that when 'the turbulence of the waters should overcome them it should turn again to their beautifying'. And so it has been. They have escaped the fate which might so easily have been theirs of becoming a housing estate and instead have been made the burgh Park—a place of pleasure and refreshment to many.

Of Tom-na-hurich, the Hill of the Yews, little is known but

much is told. It is a tree-covered, boat-shaped hill rising steep and startlingly alone in the flat land which was, not so long ago, the swamps of the river's mouth. Even now, some parts of the cemetery where it runs on to low ground cannot be used for burials because of the high level of underground water. It is generally assumed to be a core of hard rock which survived alike the glaciers which carved the hills and the flooded river's efforts, and so stands silent, alone and very old. Some, however, believe it to be the work of men's hands, at least in part a dun or fort of some kind; something human, anyhow, and very old. Those who so believed much regretted its present use which has made excavation there impossible for all the foreseeable future. Tradition, too, is divided. Some say it was a Sithein or fairy dwelling and that the Little People are now held prisoners within it. They were not a very kindly folk, the Little People of Tom-na-hurich. They were ruled by a Queen: what she liked she liked, what she wanted she would have. Once her fancy fell upon a young piper, Angus Mor, handsome and of good repute, and she sent her guards to bring him to her. This they accomplished by offering him high pay to play for their mistress, naming no names, who was giving a dance that night so they said. When he arrived before her in the great hall of the Dun of Tom-na-hurich the Fairy told him of her love and her intention of making him her Consort. He refused the honour, as politely as he could but firmly. The Queen pressed him for his reasons. Angus explained that he already had a wife and child whom he loved, awaiting his return in Inverness, and that he desired no other. 'It is no use your returning to them,' said the Queen, 'you will never find them again.' But Angus stuck to his refusal to marry her or to eat the fairy food or to taste the fairy wine which would place him in her power. Instead he drew his skean dhu and at sight of the 'black knife' the frightened fairies let him go.

When he got home he found the fairy queen had been as bad as her wicked word and had carried off his wife and baby son. She was not the only one in whom he inspired affection, however, and a maiden of the Little People decided to give him back his happiness even though it broke her own heart and would lead to her undoing should the Queen discover her work. She waylaid him, therefore, as he set out on what seemed to all a hopeless search for his family and told him that he should go to the entrance of the dun and there sing a certain song which she would teach him, loudly and clearly. It is said to have been a song which reveals many fairy secrets. He was to end it at:

> I know the cat that was in Ulva
> With its tail turned to the fire,
> I know . . .

for at this point, fearing what else he might disclose, the Queen would return his wife and child to him. Memorising the song, Angus hurried off to Tom-na-hurich and, standing on its slope, began to sing. As he reached the last 'I know . . .' the door of the dun was flung open and his wife with her baby in her arms was thrust unceremoniously out of it. They went home together in great haste and happiness.

So much for the Little People of the Dun, but others say that Fionn and his men sleep beneath the hill, while others again know, as we have seen, that it is Thomas of Ercildown (The Rhymer) who rests there with his followers. And very gay they are; there is proof of that. For one day 'about 200 years ago' two fiddlers came to Inverness in search of employment. They met a man who invited them to play that night for him and his friends at a dance and offered them double the usual rates, promising to meet them outside the town at sunset. They duly met and he led them to a small hidden door in Tom-na-hurich. Inside they found a large hall, well appointed, and many knights and fair ladies waiting to dance. They played, as they thought, the night through, re-freshed by pleasant drinks, and at dawn they were paid their double rates and dismissed. Returning to the town they found all changed, shops where no shops had been, new and better houses, and strange people in strange clothes walking the strange paved streets, many no longer speaking Gaelic. Approaching an old man they enquired for the house in which they lodged. He stared. They told him their tale. 'Ay,' he said, 'I remember my grandfather told of two young fiddlers who vanished when he was a lad, a hundred years or more ago. Come, look at your-selves, you have been with the fairies.' They went with him to his house and there saw themselves as old, old men with long white beards. Frightened and strange, they went to the one familiar place, the High Church, where a service was in progress for it was the Sabbath. They slipped quietly into a back pew, not without attracting some curious glances, and sat there until the Minister pronounced the blessing when they crumbled into dust and their fiddles with them.

In Highland fairy tales '200 years ago' seems to be more or less the equivalent of 'once upon a time' or 'long ago'. In this story, for instance, had the fiddlers entered Tom-na-hurich (as stated) 200 years ago they would have come back to Inverness and there turned into two heaps of dust, during morning service in the Parish Church and in full view of the congregation, in Queen Victoria's reign. Such an incident could hardly have passed unnoticed by, say, the *Inverness Courier*.

Once, between the wars, there was an outburst of hooliganism in the cemetery, boys destroying plants and flowers on the graves, defacing monuments and, it was said, hiding in the burial ground at night for no good purpose. Thieves even hid their loot there in the new-made graves. Suddenly, the whole trouble stopped. Why? What had happened? No one knew, but slowly the rumour seeped around that 'Something' was seen, 'Something' that should not be, a 'Something' let loose by the evil and which must never, never, *never* be let loose again. At least from then on the dead in their graves had peace. But men asked again: 'What is Tom-na-hurich?'

It was not only on Tom-na-hurich that something stirred 'in the dark of the moon'. Round the High Church on Hallowe'en a ghostly host can be seen by those who can see. They come up from the river, not through the graveyard but by the paved passage way at its side. In ones and twos they come and pass slowly, silently, and with dignity into the church. No one knows who or what they are. The spirits of those drowned in the river? Perhaps, but though Loch Ness has a bad reputation River Ness has never been found unduly bloodthirsty. Perhaps they are those who fell on Culloden Moor, or, worse, the victims of the useless, wicked pursuit which followed the battle. Whoever they are, they are christened men, certain of their right to enter the church and of their welcome within it.

Some believe the High Church hill to be an old dun, others think it the spot on which St. Columba stood when he first preached to the people of Inverness. In Adamnan's *Life* appears the account of how the Saint and his followers came in their journeyings to the north bank of the River Ness with intent to cross. They found there a great concourse of people weeping and lamenting the death of a young fisherman who had been killed by a savage monster, 'aquatalis Bestia', while fishing in the river, and whom they were about to bury. The Saint, regardless of the crowd's fears, ordered one of his companions to swim across the river and bring back a coble moored on the further bank. The monk began his swim but when he was about halfway across the monster reappeared and, with a roar and an open mouth, rushed at the swimmer. St. Columba thereupon made the sign of the cross in the air and said to the creature: 'Go thou no further, nor touch the man. Go back at once.' The monster fled as if in great fear 'and all the people, barbarous heathen as they were, gave praise to God'. Tradition has it that this was the occasion on which the Saint was going to cross the River Ness after his visit to Brude on the north bank in order to address the people and expound the Gospels to them from the summit of the little hill upon which the Parish Church now stands. This in due course he proceeded to do. It is argued that the monster obviously 'fled' to the sea, from whence it must have come, and as this part of the Ness is tidal it might well have contained a shark. Others, of course, claim the creature as one of 'Nessie's' less remote ancestors strayed from Loch Ness into the river.

Another visitor of note to Inverness was the Brahan Seer, who was born *circa* 1600. He had a great reputation throughout the North, both as a man of unusual wisdom and as a soothsayer. His prophecies covered a large area, indeed most of the Highlands, and will be found in the chapters on the various districts to which they belonged. They concerned, too, many men of note in the North, both of his own day and of later times. He himself was born on Seaforth lands near Strathpeffer and lived his life in Ross-shire, where the legends of his prophetic stone still survive. These and his traditional history will be found in Chapter 9.

Many of his prophecies have been, or are said to have been,

fulfilled. The trouble, of course, as in so many such matters, is, 'Which came first, the hen or the egg?', the prophecy or its fulfilment. But at least one referred to in *The Prophecies of the Brahan Seer*, published at the beginning of this century—that referring to the Seaforth family—was fulfilled years after its publication. His prophecies were originally made in Gaelic and the imagery so usual in Gaelic speech has led to some erroneous conclusions in translations. For instance, the statement which occurs several times, that 'the ravens shall drink their fill of blood' from such and such a stone probably only foretells a skirmish in the district, since a common ending to any tale of fighting was, 'and the ravens drank their fill of the blood of the invaders', or 'of the best blood of the Clan'.

One day 'a gentleman of Inverness' visited the Brahan Seer and, much impressed by his conversation which was very far removed from that of the usual farm worker of the time, invited the Seer to accompany him to Inverness where he would have a clerk record some of the prophecies. The Seer agreed. At first all went well and a number of matters were recorded. Then the Seer said: 'Strange as it may seem to you this day, the time will come, and it is not far off, when a full-rigged ship will be seen sailing eastward and westward by the back of Tom-na-hurich near Inverness, and further . . .', but at this point the 'gentleman' bade the clerk shut his book, explaining that he had been led to believe the Seer a sensible man whose prognostications as to the future might have value, but this was arrant nonsense and not worth recording. So the Seer returned home.

But this prophecy and the then unfinished end of it are said to have been remembered and appeared in the *Inverness Advertiser* in 1859 (I have not seen the actual paper, only a cutting in a 'common-place book'). It said, 'Tomnahurich, the far-famed Fairies' Hill, has been sown with oats. According to tradition, the Brahan Seer prophet, who lived 200 years ago, predicted that ships with unfurled sails would pass and repass Tomnahurich; and further, that it would yet be placed under lock and key. The first part of the prediction was verified by the opening of the Caledonian Canal and we seem to be on the eve of seeing the realisation of the rest by the final closing up of the Fairies' Hill.'

This paragraph was inspired by the fencing off of the hill to protect the crops; that it would later be literally 'under lock and key' as a burial ground was not then expected.

The Brahan Seer remembered Inverness in another prophecy also: 'When two false teachers shall come across the sea who will revolutionise the religion of the land, and *nine* bridges shall span the River Ness, the Highlands will be overrun by ministers without grace and women without shame.' It is claimed that the Ness had eight bridges when the prophecies were published. But tradition gives more spectacular results than this, for the traditional prophecy goes that, 'when *five* bridges cross the Ness (within the burgh) a great flood will destroy the town'. Another gives the prophecy that: 'Whoever shall build a fifth bridge over the Ness *at Inverness* shall live to see enemy troops march over it to sack the town and shall himself perish in the raid.' In consequence all plans to build a fifth bridge have been much opposed. At one moment it would have seemed to the uninitiated that five bridges do span the Ness, plus a temporary one to supplement the main road bridge at the foot of Bridge Street, and when this temporary bridge was put up, shortly before World War II, it caused much alarm, for the wise said that the railway bridge 'did not count' and so this would be the fifth. Now, I understand, the Greig Street and the Infirmary suspension footbridges 'do not count' either, being for foot passengers only, so only three real bridges span the Ness within the burgh and all is well.

Dr Alexander MacBain quotes the Fernaig MS (1690) as containing yet another prophecy of trouble to come for the town: 'There will be a battle in which Macbeth will come forth with sword and armour and the Gael will fall over other on the Bordlands of Tom-na-hurich.' It is a curious wording since 'Bordlands' were usually the precincts of a royal or other castle.

One of the few things that has survived from old Inverness is the Cuddain Stone, or Clach-na-Cuddain, on which the Town Cross stands. It is reputed to be very old indeed. Its name, Stone of the Tubs, is a reminder of the time when the women of the town rested their tubs of water on it on their way back from the river. An ancient 'wise man' was reputed to have used it as his seat and to have learnt his wisdom by asking questions of all

who passed by. He foretold that so long as the stone is preserved
in Inverness the town will flourish. Some have claimed it to be a
large meteorite and thought that on its arrival in this place a
settlement was built by its worshippers, its arrival being hailed as
the coming of a god. Any geologist could presumably settle its
origin.

One of the oldest Inverness industries has been the making of
horn tumblers and spoons, and these can still be bought in the town.
In olden days a horn drinking cup was reputed to protect from
poison and, if set with an amethyst, as they often were, from
intoxication also. Now that is forgotten and many such drinking
vessels are set with cairngorms and other stones lacking in this
protective power. Every baby should be fed at first with a horn
spoon; if fed with a metal one it will not thrive—the Little People
of Tom-na-hurich won't like it. A horn spoon was needed for
the mixing of many simples and healing draughts too, no doubt
a very wise instruction at a time when spoons not of horn (or, for
a rich man, silver) would be made of iron and turn some 'simples'
black. The juice of pears stewed in an iron pot resembles rather
poor quality ink, for instance.

Another more modern industry not entirely free from ancient
beliefs is that of making feather ornaments for hats. Almost every
one contains a jay's blue wing feather. These are lovely things in
themselves but there is more to them than that. As a child I used
to hear 'As much use as looking for a jay on Friday.' The reason
is that when the sun rises to its mid-day height on a Friday every
jay goes underground to visit his master, the Devil, and there
they all stay till dusk, recounting the malicious gossip and news
they have collected since the previous Friday. As they came and
went unharmed, their lovely blue wing feathers were believed
to give safe protection from the Evil One and his servants, and so,
fifty years ago, it was rare to see any feather ornament made
without at least one jay's feather 'for luck'. It seems that peacocks
also have power in their feathers but in reverse. It is very unlucky to be given one or to bring one into the house. Why, I do
not know unless, as some have held, they contain or attract ghosts,
but even the colours 'peacock blue' and 'peacock green' were often
avoided.

INVERNESS 23

During World War I, Inverness was the gateway to the 'Pro-
hibited Area' to the north, which meant a great deal of extra work
and responsibility for many. However tired out they might be
they could not, in the early days, hope for many hours' sleep.
Some of these men, both military and civilian, found that they
were getting hardly any sleep at all because of a garden full of
peacocks who screamed day and night. Had they behaved in a
proper manner and only crowed

> As craw the glittering Peacock should
> When Christ's own star comes over the wood,

no one would have minded—much—but they screamed also before rain and it was a wet year. So at last the wife of one officer
decided that something must be done and wrote a polite request
for the removal of the peafowl. The answer was an invitation to
tea, to discuss 'this very complicated matter'. When she arrived
her hostess explained that she could neither kill nor even remove
the birds, much as she would like to do so as they would give her
no rest either. But unfortunately she knew that one of them
contained the spirit of her late husband and she did not know
which one. Obviously as house and garden were really his she
could not remove him, much less kill him!

2

THE NORTHERN SLOPES
OF THE GRAMPIANS

And laughing and talking wild he was
An' that to a shadow out on the grass,
A shadow that made my blood go chill
For never its like have I seen on the hill.

  ★   ★   ★   ★   ★

And I watched till the death star sank in the moon
And the moon maid fled with her milk-white shoon,
Then the Shadow that was on the moorside there
Rose up and shook its shadowy hair.

FIONA MACLEOD

THE ROAD from Inverness to the south is very new compared with the ancient hills and valleys through which it runs, and so it is that many of the old stories in this chapter belong to hills and lochs some distance from the main road. It is even new as roads go, for before it was made there was General Wade's road which it follows in parts, the 'Via Regia' or 'King's Road' from Tulloch which was made by Alexander II in the thirteenth century, and another old road, the 'Thieves' Road' made by the cattle lifters of Lochaber. Along this road went the droves of cattle rieved from the rich eastern counties; it ran to Lochaber by way of Loch Morlich and Loch Gamhna, the Loch of the Stirk, so called, it is said, because of some cattle thieves. They had paused to rest by the loch side and here they learned that their pursuers were about to overtake them. They promptly drove the cattle, with stones tied to their horns, into the loch, hoping that they would drown and so escape notice. But unfortunately just as they were explaining to the true owners that they themselves were honest men who would never 'lift' so much as a calf, and deploring the prevalence of evildoers in the district, one of the stolen stirks swam ashore.

There was the dream road too, up Glen Feshie, over the pass and down into Dee side. General Wade was the first to dream of it and he sent his engineers to plan it. But he did not build it. Then Queen Victoria wanted it made and once again the matter was looked into, and shelved. The last to dream this dream was the Ministry of Transport. They, too, planned a road here and they, too, dropped the plan. One wonders what the snag is. Obviously there must be one.

The modern South road leaves Inverness by way of Raigmore, turning south shortly after passing close to the Barracks Hill. This was known in Gaelic as Cnoc an Tionail, the Gathering Hill, and was a rallying point for the town in arms or in times of crisis long before the Cameron Barracks were built there. On the left of the road lies Raigmore House and grounds, much of these grounds having now been absorbed by Raigmore Hospital. Like most old Scottish country houses, Raigmore had a large walled garden but this one had a most unusual feature. It was laid out by one of the earlier Mackintoshes of Raigmore as an exact 'to scale' plan of York Minster, which great church he had much admired. Originally, I believe, the flowers in each 'chapel' represented as nearly as might be the colours of the glass in that chapel's windows, those behind the 'altar' the colours of the east window, and so forth. The first village the road passes through is Culcabock, the Nook of the Cheese, a nice name but why? The road begins to climb almost at once for it has a long rise before it, past Drumossie, near which the Culloden Moor road takes off, and Daviot, spiralling its way up to Moy Hall, the seat of the Mackintosh of Mackintosh with its loch and woods (many now cut) and famous grouse shooting. It was one of King George V's favourite places; he shot there several summers as the guest of the Mackintosh.

It was here that the last of the MacCrimmons, the famous pipers, was killed in the '45. Of his death a strange story is told. It is said that before he left Skye he knew he would never return and that as the boat carried him from Boreraig to Dunvegan to join his Chief, Macleod of Macleod, he composed and played the poignant *MacCrimmon's Lament* to which words were later set.

Round Coolin's peak the mist is sailing
The banshee croons her note of wailing

★ ★ ★ ★ ★

No more, no more, no more forever
In war or peace shall return MacCrimmon,
No more, no more, no more forever
Shall love or gold bring back MacCrimmon.
                    Translation by Professor STUART BLACKIE

In due course Macleod's contingent was in action (on the side,
rather surprisingly, of the Government) and MacCrimmon, leading a charge, was taken prisoner by the Prince's men. Here the
first recorded strike in Scotland's history occurred, for since
MacCrimmon was considered to be the greatest piper living all
the Clan pipers with the Prince's army announced that they
would pipe no more until 'their Master' was set free. The matter
was referred to the Prince who immediately ordered MacCrimmon's release. Later, MacLeod's men were involved in a small
skirmish close to Moy Hall. So far as is known no one on either
side was injured at all except MacCrimmon who was killed by a
stray bullet. Some have held that, shocked beyond words at
finding his Chief on 'the wrong side', he found himself faced with
a problem in loyalties and decided that, while his first duty was
to follow his Chief in war, yet he could never return alive to
Skye if he had fought against his King.

In Coire Fhearnag there is said to be a prehistoric burying
place known as the Ciste Mhearad, the Cist (or stone coffin) of
Margaret. Margaret, in legend, was a maiden, jilted by a Mackintosh of Moy, who went mad and wandered through the hills
cursing her false lover and his family until she ultimately died
there.

Between Moy and Inverness there are very fine views across
the Moray Firth to Ben Wyvis in the west and the blue Sutherland
hills in the north. But soon the angle changes and the views are
of the Cairngorms to the south and east. The road passes Tomatin
and over the Slochd, a pass often blocked in winter by drifting
snow or landslides. The road soon reaches Carrbridge where the
picturesque 'old' bridge (not so very old) to which it owes its
name can still be seen.

This bridge is said to have been built originally to carry funerals to Duthil Churchyard in 'The Glen of the Heroes'. In the sixteenth century there lived on the farm of Lurg a very good and holy woman. When she was dying she asked those near her to bury her in Duthil cemetery. They replied that the River Dulnain was in flood as the snows were melting and so it would

The old bridge of Carrbridge

be impossible to carry out her wishes. But she made them promise that they would carry her coffin to the river bank at a certain spot, assuring them that if they would do this the river would divide its waters and let the funeral pass through. They did as they had promised her, the river did divide its waters, and the coffin with its bearers and the head of the procession of mourners passed easily and safely across. Then, alas, a mourner noticed a number of salmon flapping helplessly on the dry river bed. It was too much for him. He bent and picked one up in his arms and in a moment half the mourners had stopped and were scrambling for fish. The river had not been divided for this purpose and it returned to its normal course with a noise like a clap of thunder. Most of the mourners managed to reach the shore, safe but fishless, but several of the greedier members of the party failed to do so. This event is said to have had a profound effect in the district and resulted in the building of this bridge—some 300 years later! —and also the erecting of a memorial stone on the spot near the hill of Tom Biltac. The stone soon came to a bad end and is now broken and lost.

Carrbridge was one of the 'stages' on the road to Inverness in the old coaching days and is now one of the main ski-ing centres of the district.

Not very far from Carrbridge, about a mile from Nethy Bridge, stand the ruins of Castle Roy. It has been claimed as being the oldest castle in Scotland, built in the twelfth century by the Norman Comyns, and is said to show the characteristics of early Norman castle-building. The trouble is that the Comyns are not supposed to have reached Badenoch until the thirteenth century. So which is it, a Norman castle built by the Comyns or a twelfth-century castle built by—whom?

Soon after Carrbridge the road passes by Kinveachy. Near here lived, and presumably still lives, a very bad giant. But, the wicked being wise in their generation, he realised that many would wish to kill him and so he removed his heart, as giants so conveniently can. He concealed it in a stone in Kinveachy Woods, known as the 'Bonnet Stone' because the only way to kill the giant was for a man to lay his bonnet on the Stone, whereupon the heart would die. This sounds easy but in fact it was not, for the giant's heart watched carefully whenever any man wearing or carrying a bonnet approached the Bonnet Stone and promptly hopped out and hid in a different stone. As stones are plentiful hereabouts it is to be feared that the evil giant is still in good health and likely to remain so.

Kincraig is the next place of any size, reputed to be the only place which Queen Victoria expressed regret at having to leave before she could make a sketch of it. Not far off is Avielochan with its ancient barrows. Some of these have been excavated and proved to contain, among other prehistoric funeral furnishings, a number of jet beads and necklaces which, as jet is not found nearer than Yorkshire, seem to imply a very early trade of some sort with the south. One wonders whether jet was even then a specific against the Evil Eye or simply prized as an ornament.

The Moor of Granish, across which the road next runs, had once the reputation of being something quite beyond the ordinary as a sacred place. It is said to have had a large number of stone circles, varying in size from a perfect one of three rings of standing stones one outside the other on the shore of Loch nan Carrigean to some quite small ones consisting of only four or five stones.

Duthil Church in the 'Glen of Heroes'

These standing stones have mostly been taken for use in building or have fallen and broken, so few can now be seen, but a strange feeling is said to be still abroad on the Moor. Here witches met. Here, too, are traces of a number of beehive huts and of tiny 'cells' left by the early saints, as if the first Celtic missionaries had also felt bound to make the Moor a special place apart. Burial in Duthil in the Glen of the Heroes, which is not far from the edge of the Moor, was, as we have seen, much sought after. Here, later, the Chiefs of Clan Grant had their burial place. 'The Men of Duthil' in their day had great renown as a pious sect. It is a curious fact that those places in the Highlands which were particularly revered in pagan times, such as the Moor of Granish, Iona, or Strath in Skye, seem to have retained their sacred character, not only during the days of the Church of Iona whose policy it was to use existing reverence for the greater glory of God, but down to comparatively modern times despite Roman Catholic and Presbyterian disapproval. All over this district, even beyond the Moor of Granish itself, Druid Circles as they were called were once common; usually they were placed on a small hillock near a lake. Every one of the early churches here is said to have been built in or near one, just as the Grampian castles usually stood on old duns. The Wolf of Badenoch himself held his courts of justice inside a Druid Circle, perhaps for his personal safety for inside the ring no demon may venture. We shall hear more of this 'Wolf' later.

It was in the chief circle of standing stones on Granish Moor that the Druids crowned the ancient Pictish kings. The last to be crowned there was King Brude, so the old gardener we had at Kingussie told me. He knew all about it because his grannie belonged to Aviemore and had told him when he was a boy, and *her* grannie had told her, and *her* grannie was a noted 'Wise Woman', i.e. witch, and she *knew*. The gardener's grannie told him that in ancient days when a Pictish king died all who hoped to succeed him went to the priests in the Circle and the priests invoked the Spirits who came and told them which claimant to crown, and other things. When the Demon was called at the death of the 48th King of the Picts he told the priests to crown Brude as King but that he would be the last king they would crown. This they took to mean the overthrow of the Pictish kingdom, so they enquired further on those lines but all the reply they got was 'Living die, dying live' and no one knew what *that* meant. It was the custom when a king was crowned for the priests to raise three spirits or spectres for him to ask each one question. By custom the first question must be 'What of my reign?'. The other two could be whatever the king chose. When Brude enquired 'What of my reign?' he was told that one greater than he should come out of the sea and, by his leave, rule in his kingdom above him and make him great. According to the gardener's chain of grannies there was difficulty over this question—a difficulty of language. It was the custom for the king to decide on his questions and for the priests to call up the necessary spirit; one able to answer was always sent, the king would put his question and the Thing would answer. But on this occasion the Thing which came was the spirit of an Irish champion slain in battle, one of Columba's early battles in Ireland. Being a spectre he could understand the king but as he answered in Gaelic, Brude, who only knew Pictish, could not understand him. Fortunately there was among the Druids one able to translate. According to the gardener's grannie the knowledge of the old ceremonies in the Circle was not lost after the coming of St. Columba but passed down by word of mouth in certain families under oath of secrecy. Later, when the Celtic Church left the Highlands and the Moor was clear of saints, spirits were called up once more by the heads of these families, all the 'real' magicians belonging to one or other of these special families. Here Macbeth came, the gardener said, and it was here that the witches raised for him the 'Bloody Child' and other spectres. As King he had the right to command it. Grannie's grannie herself knew the secret but all she told the gardener's grannie (who was not the heir to it) was that *never* must anyone look directly at a spectre so raised or they would become blind. They must look at, and speak to, its reflection in the moor pool; secondly, those who stood within the triple circle were safe, so within the circle the questioner must remain.

It would seem, therefore, that the Great Circle stood close to a moor pool or loch. Perhaps it was the triple stone circle on the shore of Loch nan Carrigean or perhaps it stood by some tiny peat-black moor pond, a perfect mirror. None of the grannies, it was understood, had had any use at all for 'witches' as we know them, with love philtres and wasting images. They regarded them much as a Harley Street specialist might regard a quack at a village fair. One of the grannies, it is not clear which, also disapproved of Macbeth. He was not told to murder Duncan, he had only to have faith and wait. As it was, he gave power to evil things and Scotland suffered.

My parents discussed these stories with Dr Mackenzie, the
Parish Minister of Kingussie at that time, an old man with a great
knowledge of his people. He and his wife said that the belief that
the Pictish kings were crowned on Granish Moor was widespread
although he thought himself that it was not so much a crowning
as an ordaining or consecrating ceremony, and they both thought
that in times of national stress or crisis spirits were still 'called' on
the Moor with old rites, although of course no one mentioned
such goings-on to them. Still, one cannot spend one's life in a
district and be ignorant of its heartbeats. And the Moor was then,
over fifty years ago, held by many to be a place apart. Dr Mackenzie thought, but was not certain, that there were times when
the Moor should only be visited in company with a member of
certain families; also he thought, but was by no means certain,
that the hidden life of the Moor was held to be controlled by the
moon rather than by the sun. In that connection it is interesting
to see that in many of those old Gaelic incantations and charms
which have been preserved, the moon takes precedence of the
sun. One begins:

> God of the moon, God of the sun,
> God of the globe, God of the stars,
> God of the waters, the land and the skies,
> Who ordained to us the King of promise

Another starts:

> God of the moon, God of the sun,
> Who ordained to us the Son of Mercy
> (Both of these from *Carmina Gadelica*)

It is interesting also that Adamnan in his *Life of St. Columba*
tells how an angel appeared to Columba and told him to ordain
Aedhan as King of Dalriada. Now, the Saint wished to ordain
Aedhan's brother as King and was unconvinced by the angel's
appearance. The angel visited him twice more and showed him
the ordination service for Aedhan in a book of crystal. On the
third night, finding St. Columba still obdurate, the angel struck
him on the side, 'which mark he bore forever'. After these three
consecutive visitations St. Columba agreed to ordain Aedhan,
who arrived in Iona at that time. Obviously the idea of super-

natural guidance for one appointed to ordain the King was recognised at that period.

Dr Mackenzie also told us of a friend of his, a classical don, who held that all normal men and women have born in them the need to recognise and worship something bigger, better and higher than themselves. In primitive times they worshipped anything which they themselves could not do or make—a bubbling spring, obviously a goddess; a mountain, the home of a god; the thunder, the voice of a god; and so forth. As men developed, their worship did too until it reached the highest point the common man understood, then it split; on the one hand were the few, the prophets of the Jews, the top Buddhists, the mystics of Druidism, and on the other hand the many who still worshipped hills and fountains and stones and whose worship tended more and more to degenerate into magic. So far everyone would agree. But he went further. He claimed that the classical religions of Greece and Rome never divided, never provided anything higher for their votaries than the very inferior gods and goddesses of the Greek and Roman pantheons. Men of ideas saw nothing but a ploy for the multitude in their religion and so left it behind and turned to philosophy or to the search for 'the unknown God'. One of the earlier Greek philosophers of note was Pythagoras who is known to have journeyed to many countries, including Egypt, India and perhaps some of the Gaulish lands. There was reason to believe, said the don, that Pythagoras went to the Gaulish Druids and there sat with their wise men arguing such concepts (new to him) as mysticism, earning a soul, transmigration of souls the better to learn and improve, and so forth. But above all he was impressed by the mysticism for which they were famed. His clear Greek brain gave them as much as it gained from them, so they sent him on to Britain to learn more at the fount of Druidism. Pythagoras returned to Greece to found a school among the younger eager Greeks, the most renowned of whom was Plato. Plato went far beyond his Master and ended with his wonderful prophecy of the 'Just Man' and his fate, so closely paralleled in the actual life and death of Jesus. So, this don held, from the Druid hierarchy had come the greatest and clearest foreshadowing of Christ, and therefore Christianity as taught from Iona spread and was accepted in the Highlands at extraordinary speed because it was the logical outcome of the then known, but now forgotten, teaching of the High Druids, many of whom welcomed it. The common Druids simply practised magic, and that many people still do. He held that the teaching of the High Druids on, say, the Moor of Granish was as much a preparation for the coming of Christ as were the writings of the Jewish prophets. How interesting it would be if we knew what the High Druids really taught, or even whether Pythagoras did consult with Druids and, if so, where. To most of us the name of Pythagoras is known only as that of 'the man who invented the square on the hypotenuse' or of the man who was ultimately overtaken and killed by his enemies because he would not cross a bean field for fear of trampling on human souls temporarily inhabiting beans.

It is told how a local farmer took one of the standing stones which formed the Circle on Loch nan Carrigean and made a lintel of it for the door of his byre, but the cattle would not pass under it. Indeed his bull grew so excited that it led him a chase all over three parishes. The farmer then consulted a man known for his wisdom, one of 'The Men of Duthil', who advised that the stone should be returned whence it came and a new stone brought from some other place to be used as a lintel in its stead. This was done and all trouble ceased.

The road next passes Lynwilg Hotel, once an old coaching inn, on the shore of Loch Alvie. Here the picturesque Parish Church of St. Drostan stands on a promontory and is reflected in the loch's waters. When it became necessary to renew the floor of this old church 150 skeletons were found beneath it, no one knew whose. They were reburied in the churchyard with the inscription:

> Who they were, when they lived, how they died
> Tradition notes not
> Their bones are dust, their swords are rust,
> Their souls are with the saints, we trust

Loch Alvie itself is reputed to have taken its name from St. Ailbha (there were several of this name in Iona) who built a little church there in the seventh century and is believed to have converted the district.

There are the remains of innumerable tiny Celtic churches to be seen all over the Highlands. St. Columba's monks built small churches or cells wherever they were sent to preach. Very little is known of the pagan religion which they found among the Picts but it is believed to have been a form of nature worship and very, very old. We know that they found sacred wells, healing wells and demon-infested lochs in quantity. So, too, trees, stones and hills had their spirits, good and bad. Wherever there had been a place of pagan worship, such as a circle or sacred well, there the Celtic Church placed a cell or tiny chapel and left a saint to pray. St. Columba always stressed the need and use of prayer; holy men to live a life of prayer and private prayers in the little churches were alike encouraged, while public services and large congregations were rare until Roman Catholicism took hold and had planned services for the people while direct prayer to God became more a matter for the priests alone. The Celtic Church told the Gospel story very simply, it would seem, and tried by example as well as by precept to spread the vogue for a good life. They taught men agriculture in the same way, by cultivating their own small pieces of land and living off them so that their flock might learn to do likewise. In fact they were a civilising influence which later centuries sadly lacked. Almost every one of the churches had its story if we did but know them. So had some later churches and churchyards.

For instance, a rather tragic story is told of one grave in Kincardine churchyard, close to the Aviemore-Nethy Bridge road. It is the story of a daughter of Cameron of Lochiel who, sent from home to marry a man she did not love, died of home-sickness, and of her husband too, 5th Baron of Kincardine, who loved his gentle wife deeply and truly but could not win her love and could only watch her slowly pine away and die. Her father had asked her what she wanted for her bridal tocher and she replied that as there was nothing in so wild a place upon which to spend money she would like some men of her own Clan to be her guard. Twelve young Camerons therefore accompanied her to her new home; they soon settled down, married local girls and were happy. But Lochiel's daughter pined and died. Her last request to her husband was that she might be buried in Lochaber. He promised. But fighting broke out and it was impossible for the funeral cortege to get through. Then her husband had a large stone-lined grave made for her and sent a party of men with pack horses to bring back Lochaber earth to fill it, that she might at least lie in the earth she loved. But they were attacked and only two returned alive. Then her guard offered to get the earth. They had a plan, they said. So they sent their wives riding pack ponies, unguarded. The women got through and returned, each with her pony's panniers laden with Lochaber soil. In this the Baroness was buried. Each wife is said to have received a farm from the 5th Baron as a reward for her courage. In recent times some repairs to the church necessitated the opening of this grave and it was found to be as tradition had described, a stone-lined chamber filled with earth and containing a woman's skeleton.

At Aviemore the road to Rothiemurchus takes off to the east. The great woods for which it was long famous were mostly cut during the last war but much has been replanted. It is said that about 1764 water was 'put in' to London in pipes made from the long straight trunks of Rothiemurchus pines, bored hollow. The 'Boring House' is still a known name in Rothiemurchus and some of the pine pipes bearing the initials P.G. (Patrick Grant) were only replaced in London within living memory. The Grants of Rothiemurchus were a picturesque family. It is told that once the district belonged to the Shaws but that they, having fallen out with the Government, were 'declared forfeit' and their lands given to others. Rothiemurchus fell to 'Grant of Freuchie' who hastily made a gift of it to his son Patrick in a charter which said he could have it 'gin he could win it'. Patrick won it and kept it. But fighting continued for several generations. At last the last chief of the Shaws was killed in battle by the Grant chief and duly buried, but his body kept coming up from the grave and gave so much trouble that at length Grant had him buried deeply beneath the church floor under his own pew, that he might keep him under his own foot. This Shaw chief was believed to be the same who earlier had ambushed and wiped out a party of Comyns in a hollow near Loch Pityoulish known as the Hollow of the Blaeberries. It is said that since that day no other vegetation will grow there. The blaeberry was the badge of the Comyns.

The original Patrick Grant was succeeded later by another Patrick, a famous character and dispenser of justice. When his wife died he was seventy-eight years old. He at once bethought him of a neighbour who had many daughters and ordered that each in turn should come to be inspected. He asked the eldest, who came first, what she would do if she were given a tocher of gold as big as a mountain. She eagerly told him of the clothes and jewels she would buy. So did all the others till it came to the youngest. She tactfully answered that so much gold would be too great a responsibility for her, she would therefore give it to her husband. Such dutiful docility pleased the old man and he married her. It is to be presumed that she continued to turn him round her finger.

The Rothiemurchus burial ground contains the graves of many a Shaw and Grant. The little church itself is unusual as its ruins show it was set askew. On the grave believed to be that of Ferchar Shaw who led his clan against Clan Davidson in the famous battle on the North Inch at Perth and died in 1405 there lie five stones shaped like cheeses. These are said to have been brought here from the large prehistoric burial mound at The Doune and with them came a prophecy that anyone who removed one would die. A man did so and on his way home the Spey sprang into sudden flood and he was drowned. The Grants would seem not to have been too happy buried so near their old enemies the Shaws; anyhow, one Grant chose to be buried close to the gate of the cemetery so that on the Last Day he could 'make a good getaway' and get his word in first, before the Shaws (buried beyond the church) could arrive with their stories.

Past the present church of Rothiemurchus goes the road to Glenmore and Loch Morlich. This runs through the very heart of the National Park and the Queen's Forest, where some of the fine old pine trees of Rothiemurchus can still be seen, to Loch Morlich and on beyond it to Cairngorm. The old earth road, successor to the Thieves' Road, has now been superseded in its turn by the new ski road open to all and leading to the ski lift. At the further end of the beautiful but formerly little-known Loch Morlich a huge caravan site has been made and already many holiday-makers are sailing and canoe-ing on the

Loch's waters, while children dig castles on its fine sandy beach.

How very trying all this must be for Red Hand, who once owned the sandy shore. Red Hand was the ghost of a gigantic Highland warrior and he marches up and down the sands in full battle array, carrying his drawn sword in his left hand, his right hand being covered in blood—hence his name. He used to issue a challenge to mortal combat to any human unfortunate enough to meet him. If they accepted with apparent pleasure they came to no harm but if they hesitated or showed fear a bad end awaited them. Now, however, Red Hand is reputed to be a reformed character. Even a member of the R.S.P.C.A. perhaps! He spends his time stopping stalkers and poachers and warning both not to leave any maimed or injured beast to die a slow death in the hills, nor to kill too many deer. If they disobey they incur his wrath which is said to be still most potent. Can this change of heart be due to nationalisation? He is, I believe, the only nationalised ghost known.

Not far from Rothiemurchus is a place called the Cats' Den on Kennapole Hill. Here an ancestor of President Grant of the U.S.A. is said to have lived for a time. The Cats' Den is a cleft in the rocks once occupied by wild cats. The trouble began when a younger son of Rothiemurchus created great scandal by setting up house with his housekeeper. His relatives employed one whose alias was Black Sandy to end the liaison. This he did by cutting off the lady's ears. No longer lovely, she was no longer desired. Nevertheless Black Sandy had to fly. He went to Grantown. There he got into a quarrel and, believing he had killed his opponent, fled again. This time to the Cats' Den. But the man was not dead and when he recovered he set about finding Black Sandy, who fled for the third time. This time he went to America, where he did well and became very prosperous. One of his descendants was President Grant.

In the Spey Valley there once lived a very notable white witch, Dame Aliset by name. Indeed if all the stories of her doings are to be believed she must have been an almost complete Welfare State on her own. She could not only predict the weather, like the modern telephonic 'Weather Enquiries', but the future as well; she did not give unemployment pay, it is true, but she could and

often would reveal where hidden or forgotten treasures lay. She
was a complete marriage advice bureau and a most competent
'vet'. But, by far the most important thing of all, she could both
set bones and cure the sick. Consequently her services were in
such demand that she was not at all surprised to be wakened by a
knocking at her door one night. She hurried to light a candle
and open the door. Outside stood a tiny little man, about four
feet high, wearing rather old-fashioned clothes and holding two
ponies. He told her his mistress had sent him to fetch her as her
child was very ill. Dame Aliset quickly dressed, asked a few questions about the child as she packed her basket, and then mounted
the led horse. 'We must stop at the Well of Healing', she said, 'to fill
this flask with its healing water.' The man agreed and when they
reached the spring politely dismounted and filled her flask for her.
While his back was turned Dame Aliset, who had long since
guessed where she was being taken, picked a bunch of rowan
blossom and slipped it inside her bodice. In due course they came,
as she had expected, to the Fairy Dun beside the Spey and she
was led inside. Here the Little People's queen met her and led
her to a bed of furs on which the sick child lay, obviously in high
fever. Dame Aliset prepared a cooling draught from the simples
she had brought and the well water and gave it to the child, then
bade the mother bathe her with more of the precious water. The
fairies did so while the Dame sat and watched. An hour later she
gave a second draught and then later a third; after this the child
fell into a healthy sleep with her skin cool and moist. 'She'll do
now,' said Dame Aliset, and having issued a few practical instructions prepared to leave. The Little People instantly surrounded
her with offers of magnificent gifts of all kinds. But Dame Aliset
smilingly refused them all. She had done little, she said, but what
she would value most, if they really wished to reward her, was
their friendship. This the Little People promised but, feeling
some further gift necessary, they told her that if anyone washed
in the water of the Healing Spring and at the same time so wished,
they should receive their youth again. And so they still do—*if*
they can find the Well.

Some say that this spring or well is the curious 'Boiling Well'
on Rynetten Hill near Tulloch. This is a well of white sand

which contains what appears to be a tiny geyser; this jet of water rises some inches above the surface of the well water as if the well were boiling hard though in fact it is cold. There is no evidence as to whether this is the same spring; if it is, then some special formula must be needed to make clear the 'wish' referred to in the fairies' promise. But more probably the one in question is St. Mary's Well near Orton on Speyside which was famed for its healing powers since time immemorial and was once a place of pilgrimage. This pilgrimage was revived in 1938.

The River Spey not only had a dwelling of the Little People on its banks but also gave house-room to a yellow waterhorse, an unusual one for, though once in the habit of carrying off girls as other waterhorses do, he nowadays never takes any but married couples. He waits till he sees such a couple stopping on the river bank and getting ready to cross, then offers to carry them over. As soon as they mount he vanishes with them into one of the deeper pools. It has been suggested that he was crossed in love and is now interested only in household comfort. He is not the only unusual waterhorse in the Grampians, however. There is one in Loch Pityoulish who takes the form of a white Highland pony with a very ornamental saddle and bridle who specialises in carrying off any children who play near his loch. He has been known to carry off as many as nine at a time.

It is curious that waterhorses almost always wore bridles, some made of gold or inlaid with stones, and this one is noted as having had a saddle as well. While in human form they appeared in good clothes, sometimes even dandified ones, though more often of country homespun, but they were always of an old-fashioned cut. Who makes them, one wonders, especially the bridles which had magic powers? If a woman could get one off and replace it with a cow-shackle she could control the waterhorse forever, while his bridle would bring her good fortune. But only a woman could do it.

It would seem that the people of this part of Scotland were excessively proud of their rivers, for, says an old rhyme:

> The three largest rivers there be
> Are the Tay, the Spey and the Dee

The Spey was held to be somewhat bloodthirsty and to require one life each year. Most Scottish rivers seem to have had this little failing, for old rhymes tell that:

> Bloodthirsty Dee, each year needs three,
> But Bonnie Don, she needs none.

and

> Tweed said to Till
> 'What gars ye rin sae still?'
> Till said to Tweed
> Though ye rin wi' speed
> And I rin slaw
> Yet whar ye droon ae man
> I droon twa.

Evidently Till regarded this as a matter for pride.

Most of the Grampian lochs have their stories. Loch Insh for instance, Loch of the Island (Innis Island), is supposed to take its name not, as one would expect, from the real island in the loch but from a little hillock, Tom Eunan, which is only a true island in times of flood. Tom Eunan was of importance because on it was built the Church of St. Eunan (who is Adamnan, St. Columba's famous biographer) who is believed to have himself spent some time here and warned that after his death his bell must be kept in this church. If removed it would return unaided, for this was its own place. His bell is still preserved in the church, though now much damaged. One day it was stolen and carried away to the south of the Grampians. Some say it was taken as far as Edinburgh, others that it was brought only as far as Perth to cure a sick man there. Wherever it was that it was taken, the bell 'got free' and immediately returned of its own accord to its own church of St. Eunan where it belonged. It came flying through the air over the Grampians, and as it crossed the hills of Drumochter it could be heard ringing out 'Tom Eunan, Tom Eunan'.

In the early Celtic Church every abbot had his handbell with which to summon his monks to prayer or work. This was his badge of office and sometimes his only personal possession. These bells were therefore much sought after as relics. After a saint's death his bell usually became 'dumb', none but he having the right to use it. But no doubt St. Eunan's was an exceptional case.

Tom Eunan's bell was not the only bell in Scotland to use its tongue, however. The Great Bell of Scone, being at the seat of royal justice, was supposed on occasion to ring out 'Touch not what is not thine own'. But few heeded.

Not far from Loch Insh is the hill of Dunachton, undoubtedly meaning Nectan's Fort say historians, but beyond this point they differ. Dr Skene believed it to be the fort of Nectan the Pictish king and thinks that his great battle of Monadh-carno was fought near Loch Insh. Dr MacBain, on the other hand, while agreeing that the name means Nectan's Fort says, 'Badenoch has no claim to the site of Monadh-carno. Loch Dae is now identified with Loch Lochy and Glencarnie is Duthil.' Local tradition ignores all this and holds firmly that a battle *was* fought on the shore of Loch Insh but that the defeated leader was one King Harold, whose grave is on the side of Craig Righ Harailt in the hills behind Dunachton and who sat on the hill of An Suidhe (The Seat) near Kincraig to watch the battle ebb and flow. Who he was, where he came from and when, whom he fought or why, these are forgotten. All that remain are his grave and his name.

Some do claim that Pictish King Nectan fought two battles on the shores of Loch Insh, the first against the Norsemen (led by Harailt?) which he won, the second against the Thane of Fife when he lost both the battle and his life.

Below Dunachton was another old chapel or church, St. Drostan's Chapel, Capella de Nachtan, mentioned in 1380 says Dr MacBain. It is reputed to have been built on the site of an old stone circle by the family of MacNiven who had the Barony of Dunachton and came to a sad end. The last MacNiven had two daughters whom he left as joint heiresses. One of them, Isobel, married one William Mackintosh, cousin of the Chief of Clan Mackintosh. Three weeks later she went alone to bathe in Loch Insh. Here she was drowned by 'evil kinsfolk'. Her sister 'died mysteriously' soon afterwards. The occupational hazards of being an heiress were high.

About a quarter of a mile from the main road near Lynchat is the Cave of Raitts, or of Lynchat, An Maimbr Mhor, the Great Cave. It is usually said to be an old Erd House, or Pict's House and, if so, is the only one known in Badenoch. It is more or less horse-shoe shaped and has been described as 70 feet long, 8 feet broad and 7 feet high. 'The walls gradually contract as they rise and the roof consists of large slabs of stone balanced across the walls.' Like all these Pict houses, its building goes back into the mists of prehistory. Traditionally, it was built by a giant race in a single night. The giantesses dug it out and carried the earth and rubbish down to the River Spey in their aprons. There they dumped it. Meanwhile the giants were quarrying stone in the distant hills. As soon as the excavating was finished they carried down the stones and began to build. The whole was finished before daylight. The first humans whose use of the cave is known were the MacNiven of Dunachton and his nine sons who hid here from their enemies, Clan Macpherson. Some even say that his nine fine sons were the builders of it and that they used the stones of a Druid circle for the purpose and so brought their fate upon themselves, but a more probable explanation is that they built the hut which was known to have stood over the entrance concealing it. The story goes that Robert the Bruce gave the MacNiven lands to the Macphersons, who had supported him, and that when the Macphersons came to take possession the angry MacNivens stole their cattle. The Macphersons, who seem to have been overlords rather than occupiers, desired to avoid a feud with their tenants and sent a daughter to bring back the cattle in peace. But the angry MacNivens illtreated her and finally sent her home in her shift and the bull without its tongue. The Macphersons then moved in the matter. The MacNivens hid in this cave successfully for many months but at last something aroused the suspicion of a Macpherson. That night he came begging to the hut, the woman living there gave him 'a piece' and ordered him off, but he pretended to be ill, too ill to go further, and begged to be allowed to rest. The woman in pity agreed. He pretended to be asleep but watched her continually baking; as each batch of scones was finished she placed them in a wall press and began to bake more. From where he lay the spy could see that each time the cupboard door was opened the cupboard was empty. He suspected the truth. Next night he returned with the Macphersons in strength, they killed the woman who had had pity, pulled down the hut, found the cave, and killed Mac-Niven and his sons. It is pleasing to know that the spy and his descendants have ever since suffered from the disease he pretended to have on that fatal night.

'The Cave' was used with much greater success in later times, especially after the '45 when a number of fugitives are believed to have owed their lives to its shelter.

In the early thirteenth century one 'Gillescop' and his two sons were Lords in Badenoch. They were violent men and had the habit of attacking their neighbours just as frequently and pointlessly as the Wolf of Badenoch himself was wont to do a century later. The King did not bother much what anyone in the North did in those days so long as they kept their wars and forays amongst themselves. But the Gillespies did not. About the year 1228 they came down into the low lands, looting and burning. They burned many of the wooden forts which were supposed to defend Moray from just such attacks, and finally looted and three parts burned the town of Inverness itself. This came to the King's ears and he, feeling bound to do something about it, told Comyn, Chief Justiciar of Scotland, that the protection of Moray was his business and that he could have the lands of Badenoch if he could get rid of the Gillespies. This he proceeded to do—by treachery, it was freely said.

There is, however, another account of these actions which differs sharply from this one. It claims that the Highlands were at that time still more or less in arms against the King of Scots, despite the death of their leader, Donald Bane. Gillespie Mac-Scolaine had become leader of the men of Moray and in 1228 he drove the King's men out of Inverness (always considered a royal stronghold) and burned the town, together with 'certain castles then built of wood', and laid waste the lands of Church and Crown, holding that the former, the Roman Catholic Church introduced by St. Margaret, was as much a foreign despot as the King. The King marched against them without success. But eventually Gillespie and his two sons were treacherously slain by the Justiciar of Scotland, Comyn, who then seized their land.

The Gillespies, though great raiders, had not been unpopular in Badenoch and the Comyns, who were the first to hold the land in 'feudal' tenure as in the South and also to introduce many new laws and customs, were frankly hated.

> While in the wood there is a tree
> A Cumming will deceitful be.

so said Badenoch, and no good was known of them. Their end as Lords of the district is reputed to have come when 'the wicked Lord Walter' was torn to pieces by a pack of eagles when passing through the Gaick Pass, at a spot called Leum nam Feinn, the Fenian Men's Leap. He was supposed to have been on his way to enforce his own evil decree that the women of Ruthven should all go to his harvest fields to work 'unclothed and naked'. His unusual death was held to be supernatural and a judgment on him. 'Walter's fate in Gaick on you' became a favourite ill-wish.

Gaick was an exceptionally wild and lonely district to the east of Dalwhinnie and the idea soon arose that there was more in that part of the hills than met the eye. All sorts of ill luck beset travellers there, so it was said. To be killed by a pack of eagles was unusual but could be natural; to be riding and to lose your horse in a bog, only just saving yourself, as befell another traveller there, could be natural too, only it was queer that no one knew of a bog there or could ever find it again. A man fell over a crag in a hill mist and was killed. Well and good; such things happen. But when a second man fell and lived to tell of a huge figure in the mist who pushed him over, it was queer. In fact if it was not one piece of ill luck it was another, until it was described as 'an unbroken record of dread supernatural doings'.

One Christmas night in the year 1799 Captain Macpherson of Balachroan with four other men were deer-hunting in the Forest of Gaick. They spent the night in a bothy and were all killed by an avalanche of snow which came down upon the bothy and smothered them while they slept. No, Gaick was not lucky. Captain Macpherson, 'the Black Officer', was of course immediately suspected of having sold himself to the Devil. Men who had previously been to the bothy with him claimed to have heard the Devil in the form of something heavy and soft, without bones, clumsily slithering on the roof in its efforts to get in.

Not far from Gaick Galliachus was said to have collected his forces for his attack on Agricola's expedition. That must have been a great occasion for the North and, if they understood at all the odds against them, a terrifying one. Galliachus' name is still remembered in an old rhyme in Berwick:

> Sin the days of Galliachus
> Sin the Romans came to wrack us
> And consume our ancient seed,
> A castle strong has been to back us
> On the top of yon brae head.

The Romans themselves are reputed to have come through the Pass of Gaick on their way back from the Moray Firth. They camped near Pitmain, where traces of the camp have been found.

When in 1813 a stage coach was started between Perth and Inverness thrice weekly, Pitmain was the middle stage with a large staging inn and stables. Hence its Gaelic name meaning Middle Town, anglicised to Pitmain. Below the high hills of Gaick is a chain of small lochs on the River Tromie. The meaning of the name Bhrodain, by which one of them is called, is unknown but tradition claims that Bhrodain was the name of a hound and possibly meant mastiff, or a Great Dog in a superlative sense. Here is the story.

Once a hunter lived near this loch. He was a noted man, but chiefly famed for his 'way with dogs'. One night, hearing a queer scraping noise, he opened his door and found there a Demon come to call upon him. The Demon carried in his arms a litter of exceptionally fine puppies. He explained that for various reasons he could not rear these himself and had therefore brought them to the hunter, to whom he would return for the creatures before they were full grown. The hunter could, added the Demon, keep one for his trouble. The hunter agreed and the Demon then vanished, leaving the puppies behind him. The pups grew up into the finest young dogs the hunter had ever seen. Now, there was said to be a very highly magic and highly desirable white hind living on the slopes of Ben Alder. She was a fairy deer and some said she was Grainne herself, Lady of the Feinn and Fionn's own wife. No living dog could overtake her, it was believed, but when the hunter saw these pups he began to have visions of a pursuit and a capture. However, when they grew old enough to train, their Demon owner reappeared and was about to carry them all off when the hunter reminded him of his promise, whereupon the Demon seized the smallest pup and, breaking its hind leg, flung it down, exclaiming that the hunter need not hope for a dog to vie with his. Such dogs were not for puny mortals. The hunter was furious but he had learnt silence and patience in the hills so he said nothing but as soon as the Demon had gone he took the pup and, bandaging its leg with cooling leaves, tied it up firmly in a basket of willow boughs so that by no means could it stand on the broken leg. In a few weeks the leg healed and the dog became faster than any on earth, but it ran always dot-and-carry-one. The hunter named it Bhrodain and they became inseparable. But one day when they were out together the hunter saw the beautiful white fairy hind grazing near Loch Ericht and he sent Bhrodain after her. Fast as Bhrodain was, the hind was faster, but it seemed by the time they reached Gaick that she was tiring and that Bhrodain would overtake her. She made for the central loch, however, and plunged in, Bhrodain following, and neither of them was ever seen again. The hunter named the loch Bhrodain after his hound. Another story makes the hunter steal the puppy from the Demon in the first place. He was chased, and escaped by the help of a good stallion and much clever strategy connected with the three lochs. Into one of these the Demon was enticed, and he may well be dwelling there yet, cursing and swearing.

Michael Scott the Wizard, as a young man, once came over the Pass of Drumochter accompanied by two friends. As they were nearing the high peaks they were attacked by a huge 'white worm'. The creature seems to have been some sort of dragon. Michael's two friends ran but Michael stood his ground and, after a hard fight, slew the beast. Then he rejoined his friends and they journeyed on to an inn near what is now Dalwhinnie, where they spent the night. The three young men were rather full of their adventure and talked of it. The landlord of the inn then offered them a free reckoning if they would give him the centre portion of the 'worm', which they had cut into three for easier carrying. Michael, as its owner, agreed. The innkeeper gave the portion to his wife and bade her take her largest pot and make broth of it. This she did. Michael, curious to find out what dragon broth would be like, and entirely innocent of any other motive, rubbed his finger on the spoon used for stirring the concoction and sucked it. Instantly he knew all things, the language of bird and beast, how to raise and command the Devil, and much else, including the knowledge that as he had, however unintentionally, stolen the good of the dragon the innkeeper would kill him if he could. So Michael, now the greatest magician in all Scotland, left that place with his friends at some speed.

Many years later Michael, as an old man, returned to the hills. His friends brought a priest, that he might receive the last rites of the Church, but when he learned who Michael was the priest refused to minister to him or even to listen to his confession, saying that for sins such as his there could be no forgiveness: 'To hell you belong; to hell you will go.' The dying man opened his eyes and said to his friends, weakly but clearly: 'Hang my heart from the branch of a fir tree near by, hide and watch. If a raven carries it off you will know the priest spoke truth, but if a dove comes for it you will know that I spoke truth when I said my powers as a magician were used only for good, and that God has forgiven me my sins as a man.' And he died. His friends did as he had asked and, having buried him, hung up his heart. Down swooped a raven, claws out to seize it, when, as it seemed to the watchers, a flash of light passed between the bird and the heart. Something certainly affrighted the raven and it flew hurriedly away. Then there came a dove (or blue rock pigeon, some say) and carried off the magician's heart. Satan, who was reputed to have prepared a bed of white-hot rock in the Grampians for Michael, was much disappointed at the result of the test, his work being all wasted. The priest also was said to be 'somewhat put about'.

3

KINGUSSIE

Mightily rose the cliffs: and mighty trees
Grew on them.
JOHN MASEFIELD

THE NAME Kingussie means Head of the Pine Forest.
Once upon a time, long, long ago the King of Lochlann
(Norway?) visited Sutherland and was immensely impressed by the trees of the Caledonian Forest which once spread
all over Northern Scotland. Very fine trees they must have been
too, judging by the remains of some still found in the peat. Some
of these are said to have measured as much as twelve feet in
circumference, an enormous girth for a fir, and many were
charred by fire. When the King went home to Lochlann he found
he could not forget them but kept comparing the forests of Scotland with his own, to the detriment of the latter. He grew more
and more envious. At length he called up a great monster, said
to have been his Muime (stepmother); she was of enormous size
with the head of a woman, the body of a whale and eagle's wings.
This creature was bidden by the King to destroy the forests of
Scotland that he might rest in peace, owner of the finest forests
in the world. The Muime thought the matter over and decided
that the best way to do it was by fire and the best time the early
summer when the spring winds had dried up the land. So, with
summer came the Muime. She flew far above the clouds, carrying
a huge load of fire which she flung down upon the forests of
Sutherland, then returned to Lochlann for more fire. Meanwhile
the King of Lochlann caused a strong wind to rise, sweeping the
flames on and ever on. Helped where needed by more falling
fire, the blaze spread; south through Sutherland into Ross, down
past the Moray Firth into Inverness and Moray, and up the long
Grampian slopes, not a tree survived in the desert it left behind.
But some of the Grampian woods were saved by a wise man of
Kingussie.

The people of Badenoch were very proud of their pine forest and also believed that without its shelter they and their beasts would be hard put to it to survive a winter on the heights. Much alarmed by the fast approaching fire they met together to discuss the ruin that faced them. 'If you will obey me I'll engage to save the trees,' suddenly said a quiet man, a hunter, whose voice was seldom raised in council. As no one else had any hope to offer, all agreed to do as he might advise. He bade them collect their animals and drive them; the ewes, the cows, the mares to the east of the River Spey, the lambs, the calves, the foals to the west of it. This was done and at once there arose such a bleating, baa-ing, mooing, squealing and neighing from the separated mothers and young as had never before been heard in all Scotland. The noise reached the Muime and she put her head out through her cloud shield to see what went on. This was what the hunter was waiting for; he was ready with a silver bullet, laboriously made by rolling up a silver 'bit', and he shot her through the eye. She came rolling down to earth quite dead. At her death the wind fell and with no fresh fire to feed the flames the blazing woods were soon brought under control by ordinary means. The trees on the high hills were saved.

And what of the Muime? It seemed as if she might prove as great a problem dead as alive, for her body was far too large to bury. But as she lay in the valley it was noted that converging in upon her came streams and streams of small insects, some red, some black, such as had never been noticed there before. They were ants, coming it would seem from all over Britain as news of the feast spread. Soon all that remained of Muime were clean white bones. But that was not all that remained of the ants—for unfortunately they loved the Grampian slopes, the fir woods' shelter and the pine needles from which to build their cities, and there they have stayed. If you walk through any of the fir woods round Kingussie today you will see a wonderful collection of ant kingdoms. Their mounds often look ideal picnic places to the uninitiated, but beware! It is said that every year on the anniversary of the monster's death, from every mound comes forth an army of red warrior ants carefully guarding in their midst a large company of little black slave ants, for without slaves at hand to feed and wash and care for them these very highly specialised warriors die. The armies converge on the spot where once they feasted and when host meets host terrible battles ensue. Not only does army fight army and ant fight ant but when, as often happens, warrior ants are nipped in two at their slim waists the head halves will continue the deadly struggle. The tail halves, equally wishful to continue, will search for each other, ready to sting or to fling formic acid, but seldom find the enemy, being blind. These battles and raids are a strange sight often met with in the woods in summer when robber ants make slave raids on their neighbours' kingdoms. The Gaelic saying, 'That would be rocking an ant to sleep on a gridiron' is said to have had its origin in this district.

The Muime's incendiary raid was by no means the only occasion on which fire threatened the great forests of the Grampians. Tradition has it that Mary, Queen of Scots, the 'Wicked Queen' ever after, ordered them to be set alight because some busybody had told her that 'Huntly' had enquired for the welfare of his forests on his return home, before enquiring for the welfare of his Queen. This so infuriated her that she not only ordered the firing of his woods but came north herself and took up her station on the top of Sron-na-Baruinn, the Queen's Ness, above Glenfeshie and from there watched the burning in person. Fortunately many glens and sheltered nooks escaped.

The forests were burnt yet again in the very dry summer which followed World War I, 1920 I think it was. A friend of mine travelling from Dingwall to Aberdeen by the Grampian line said that the train was never out of sight of smoke from the burning woods from the time it left Muir of Ord (the Black Isle burned for three weeks; the peat ground and even one road 'caught fire' and smouldered till the road had to be closed) until Aberdeen itself was in sight.

Near Kingussie, crowning a small hill in the Spey valley, stand the ruins of Ruthven Castle. Like so many Highland castles, this one has both changed hands and been destroyed and rebuilt several times. The most famous of its occupants was Alexander, a son of King Robert II and generally known as The Wolf of Badenoch, a name based on his evil character. He it was who, having been excommunicated for offences against the Church, proceeded to revenge himself by burning Elgin Cathedral. Sir Thomas Dick Lauder gives an account of the deed in his *Wolfe of Badenoch* and tells how the Wolf rode in to sleeping Elgin one dark night with a guard of armed men and soon the town was as bright as day, lit by the flames of the burning College and Canons' Houses and the Hospital of the Maison Dieu. The terrified burghers, realising who it must be that headed their nocturnal visitors, fled to the woods with their wives and daughters. Some stopped to look back and were, like Lot's wife, frozen in their tracks but this time with horror at the sight of their Cathedral itself blazing, its beautiful Gothic windows a tracery of stone black against the flames. Begun in 1224, Elgin Cathedral was one of the beauties of Scotland, and that any in a Christian country would wantonly destroy it seemed unbelievable. The need to guard against such acts had gone with Danish pirates, or so Elgin had thought.

History tells that Alexander the Wolf had, by order of his father the King, to do penance for his crime at the door of the Church of the Blackfriars in Perth. Then in the presence of the King, his nobles and many Church dignitaries he was finally pardoned and received back into the Church, he having solemnly sworn to make reparation for his ill-deeds. The cause of all the trouble and his feud with the Church in the first place was, it is said, his absolute refusal to leave his mistress, the Lady Mariota Athyn, and live with his wife, the Countess of Ross. Mariota, he pointed out, had borne him five sons whereas the Countess of Ross brought only her land 'and a tight hold on't'. Nevertheless he was *the* scandal of the day. Later, one of Mariota's sons became the first Earl of Mar and another the first Baron of Kincardine.

Tradition makes his repentance but skin-deep. Received back into the Church he may have been, it was said, but repent he did not, for it is well known how a very wicked man—and who but the Wolf was evil enough?—lived on in Castle Ruthven. He and his friends were the terror of the countryside, a band of robbers and murderers by day and dabblers in the Black Arts by night. Not even a priest dare approach them. But little boys can be without fear, and two small friends decided one night to hide near the Castle so as to see what caused the lurid blue light which played round it. They hid and saw the band ride in from hunting, with deer and also a luckless traveller's body across the pack-ponies' saddles. Through a small window they saw them sup and drink and then perform many acts strange to the young watchers. They saw the Castle wall open and a tall thin gentleman, clad in unrelieved black and wearing a black hat and black gloves, step out from the wall. A chessboard was produced and he and the

CASTLE RUTHVEN
"The Castle . . . now but blackened ruins . . . on its hill"

robber chief sat down to a game while the band stood round, apparently sober now. Hour after hour they played and the boys watched, not because they wished to—they wanted to go home—but because they could not move. Nothing moved, not even the night-roaming creatures, not even the moon across the hills; the night stood still. Suddenly the black gentleman moved a piece. 'Check,' he said, 'Checkmate', and rose. All the village saw the storm that followed, thunder and hail and lightning turning night to day, then back to darkest night again. The frightened boys, now free to leave, ran home. At daybreak the village looked out to where the Castle, now but blackened ruins, had yesterday stood proudly on its hill. The men joined together and rather fearfully approached. There, outside the Castle as though killed while running from it, were scattered the dead and blackened bodies of the robber band, all save the Chief. He was found lying in what had been the banqueting hall, his body unharmed and tidy—except for one thing. All the nails in his boots had been torn out.

Two days later a funeral procession started from the Castle; bier after bier was carried out of the door arch. As the last left the ruin the sky grew black again, and again a thunderstorm broke out, with hailstones so large that the bearers were forced to lay down the coffins and seek safety in shelter. It was soon obvious that the storm was centred round the coffins and as long as they lay there it seemed likely to continue and as long as it continued the procession could not re-start. This deadlock was resolved by an old man who came forward and said: 'The first shall be last.' With great courage six men braved the storm and, lifting the coffin of the evil chief, carried it to the back of the cortege. The storm ceased as suddenly as it had begun, the sky cleared and the funeral continued without let or hindrance. But to this day those who approach the ruins on a certain midnight and in a proper frame of mind may see the Devil and the Chieftain sitting within, playing chess for the soul of the latter.

It is strange that while the Devil often carried off his victim in a storm of thunder and hail, a Royal Storm was held to be the highest honour a dying man could receive. I have twice in my life seen what were believed to be Royal Storms. I was in Skye when King George V had his bad illness and one of the worst storms for many years broke out. This was said by some to be a Royal Storm sent specially for him, and when he did not go with it, it was recognised that he would recover as he had sent the storm away, but 'only the truly great may send away a Royal Storm'. The first improvement in the King's condition was in fact announced on the next day. The other I remember was the storm during which H.M.S. *Hampshire* was lost with Lord Kitchener on board. That storm was believed by some to be a storm sent for one who was perhaps the last of the popular warrior heroes and, great though he was, he went with it. These Royal Storms are not thunder storms as a rule, or anyhow not primarily so; they are hurricane-like gales showing to all men the Power and the Wonder.

Castle Ruthven became a royal fortress but was again given to the flames about 1450, this time by John, Lord of the Isles and Earl of Ross, because, he being a minor at his father's death, King James II chose his bride as it was his sovereign right to do and promised John a suitable 'tocher' with her but failed to keep his promise. Reminded of it, it would seem, by the burning of his castle of Ruthven, he soon after made John Keeper of the King's Castle of Urquhart—a coveted prize.

After the rising of the '15 the Government bought Castle Ruthven and turned it into a barracks. It successfully stood siege (garrisoned by an English sergeant and ten men) in 1745 but was eventually taken and burnt by Prince Charles Edward's army in the retreat of 1746. It is said to have taken 4000 men to capture it from the heroic eleven. The ruins remained a shelter and hiding place, however, and after Culloden a number of the Prince's supporters are said to have met there and sent word to the Prince offering to continue the struggle, which offer he refused in his father's name, saying that too much blood had already been shed.

It was near Castle Ruthven that the last green fairy dog was seen, I believe. So far as I know these creatures are now extinct in the Highlands; I never met anyone who claimed to have seen one or to know anyone else who had seen one, though the one near Castle Ruthven was said to have appeared to several people within the memory of those living fifty years ago. These 'green' dogs were not thought to be particularly evil; indeed little was known of them for good or evil except the one terrifying fact. If a fairy dog pursued you long enough to bark three times and near enough to you for you to hear it, then it was a death omen unless you had the courage and presence of mind to turn and stone it at the first bark, when it would vanish, leaving you unharmed. But to hear even one bark brought ill luck. 'Human' dogs howl miserably and flatten themselves to the ground at the approach of the fairy beasts. Some think this may be the origin of the belief that to hear a dog howl without good reason (such as being left behind, tied up, by his master, or baying the moon) is a death omen either for the hearer or for the owner of the dog.

As Longfellow says:

> Dogs howl when, with icy breath
> Great Sammaël, Angel of Death,
> Takes through the town his flight,

so evidently the 'howling' superstition is not only Highland, whereas I think the green dogs are. Here is a fairy dog story I heard in Kingussie as a child. It tells how an old shepherd lived alone in a tiny cottage under the high hills. His only companion was his dog. One night, as he sat by the fire steaming the horn for a crook, he heard a scratching at the door. Believing it to be his dog returned from driving sheep away from the corn land he arose and opened the door. Only the wind entered. 'Come in, hurry can't you,' he exclaimed, 'I'll not be holding the door for you forever,' and there entered a great green hound with 'eyes of gold and ears of crimson' and lay down by the fire. The old man returned to his seat and picked up his work, but he thought not of the crook but of what he should do. A fairy dog is no companion for a lonely night, or indeed any night, yet he had invited it in, unwittingly certainly, but still it was his guest. Without his word it could not have entered, and besides the poor beast seemed cold and tired and gave no sign of the dreaded bark. At last, having thought it over, the old shepherd rose and, muttering fearfully to himself, brought food and water and placed them near the great hound. It raised its head, moved to the water fresh from the burn, and drank eagerly but the food it left untouched. Again came the scratching sound. Again the shepherd rose and opened the door but this time looked carefully before admitting anything. It was his own dog, who, at sight of the stranger, flattened itself in terror to the earth. The green dog raised its head and made a low queer sound in its throat, not a bark, no certainly not a bark, and moved a little to allow the shepherd's dog a sight of the fire. Still fearful but no longer terrified, the collie came to the fire, ate its supper and lay down beneath its master's chair. So sat the three till the dawn clouds gleamed. Then the great green beast arose, shook himself and walked to the door. The shepherd made haste to open it, but before departing the dog put out a tongue, pink and soft as a rose petal, and licked his hand. Then it was gone.

Many months passed and one bitter day of ice and snow the shepherd's dog, following his master down an icy slope, got his foot caught between two stones. His master got him out and carried him home with a crushed paw. This he bandaged with a poultice of dried birch leaves. But that night it snowed, snowed as it can snow in the high hills. At dawn the shepherd set out, crook in hand, in search of his sheep. He looked sadly at his dog, who tried to follow him, then whimpered and lay down. 'Bide still,' he ordered, but added under his breath a doubt that he could do much with no dog. All day he laboured, finding and digging out sheep, but the snow was deep and the wind well iced. The shepherd was an old man and as he ploughed through the snow he found himself growing exhausted. 'If I leave the sheep they'll die; if I lie down my dog will starve,' he kept repeating to himself as he tried to push on. Suddenly there was a blast of wind and a flurry of snow and out of it came the green dog. 'Ay, he knows,' thought the old man, 'but he'd no need to tell me. I know too.' And, too exhausted to run, he waited for the bark. But he heard none. Instead, the dog came to him, again the pink tongue soft as rose petals licked his hand. But with what a difference, for this time there flowed from it into the old man warmth and life. He drew himself erect. The dog flung back its head and bayed (but never a bark) and the moor at once became covered with grey-green dogs with eyes of fire. Backwards and forwards they quartered the ground like eagles hunting a moor; when a dog found a sheep he would stand still until the shepherd noticed, and then begin to dig out the hidden woolly bundle and drive it away. In what seemed no time at all the man found himself half driven half led to a little sheltered corrie free from snow, and there were all his sheep happily grazing with green dogs on guard, and the sheep no wiser than if they'd been collies. Then the big dog took him and before he knew it he was at his door and, for the last time, a rose-pink tongue lingered against his fingers. He bent to pat the great head and there was nothing there, only air and a snow flurry and his own dog whimpering within.

Kingussie is a typical small Highland town, with its main street and the main road one and the same, with the railway to one side and its residential district to the other. The first tiny Celtic church here is said to have been built by St. Columba himself who came to Kingussie on one of his journeys. Much later, in 1490, the Earl of Huntly founded a Priory here in the Saint's honour. A stone tablet in the present churchyard tells of St. Columba. Kingussie has, too, an interesting Folk Museum where, among many other items, can be seen photographs of the old stage coaches which once operated on the North road and between Laggan and Newtonmore. Above Kingussie on the hillside where the Guinach River comes down stands a wool mill which used to make, possibly still does, the most lovely light plaid-shaped rugs in squares of the old vegetable dyes, an art fast dying out, anyhow in the central Highlands. Behind the mill a road follows the river side to Loch Guinach. About a mile from the town, before the loch came into sight, was once a small Wishing Well at the roots of a rowan tree, into which anyone might drop a gift, a pin with a fancy head or even a plain one— the Little People were known to be very partial to pins—a coin or a button, and wish a wish. This the Little People, if they approved the gift that went with it, would grant. Someone once threw in a broken button and his wish was reversed by the angry fairies with disastrous results. In the autumn when fallen rowan berries floated on the water the well could, from the wisdom distilled from them, foretell the future as well as grant wishes. Somewhere near Kingussie, the secret of exactly where has been well kept, there is a spring or well whose waters confer immortality on the lucky finder. If so, immortality must include immediate migration to a different world, for no case of an immortal man living in the district has been noticed. Some, however, have held that the spring was a sacred one and that its gift was not prolonged life on earth but an immortal soul. These claimed that only those fit to be so rewarded had their eyes opened to see the well.

Loch Guinach is one of the many lovely little hill lochs with which Scotland abounds. Standing as it does in the centre of flat marshy ground, the area all round it was a favourite nesting place for green plover and even the shy curlew, while in the rushes round the loch itself a colony of black-headed gulls nested, having come up from the sea for the purpose. Every plover (or peewit or lapwing) contains the soul of a young wife who has died in childbirth which is why they circle round and round their nests, never able to believe in a successful hatching but perpetually crying for the might-have-been. Baby plover and baby curlews are some of the most attractive of all young birds. They hatch out of their very pointed eggs as little balls of nicely marked tabby fluff, mounted on stilts and with their feet and beak almost full grown. My father and I watched a nest of plover near the loch on one occasion. When we arrived one day, of the four eggs one was hatched out and two others cracking. We went on, returning in a little under an hour. All four eggs had hatched and the chicks had left the nest and were not to be seen, but search revealed one a few feet away crouched in a heather root. Some yards further on we found the other three. The eldest tried to run but his feet were so big and clumsy that he fell over them, helped to over-balance by his long beak. Young curlews that we watched left the nest almost as fast but were so clever at hiding by pretending to be stones that we only found one. Both plover and curlew always arrange their eggs all points inwards. We wondered whether it was deliberate, and re-arranged several plovers' nests to see. As soon as the mother returned she pushed them all round with her beak till they were 'points in' again. But if you touch a curlew's nest the birds will leave and never return; if you must lift an egg out to look closer at it, then use a long-handled spoon and wash the spoon in burn water first.

Whether the birds will continue to nest here now that it has become 'forestry' land is doubtful, but I doubt if even the Forestry Commission will be able to dislodge the Devil. When I was young Loch Guinach was a favourite haunt of the Devil who was reputed to spend many months there. When he rose from the water in spring he made a great wave which often flooded out the nests of the black-headed gulls on the loch edge. The Devil was supposed to be far from averse from harming these little gulls because, unlike some larger and fiercer members of their tribe, the black-headed gulls are the messengers of the angels and contain the spirits of those whose good deeds while on earth will enable

them to become at last angels themselves. Meanwhile they expiate
their few evil deeds, shown by their black heads, in the guise of
birds, the angels' messengers.

The Devil was supposed to have first taken up his abode in
this district because 'Kingussie was forgotten when Sodom and
Gomorrah were destroyed and the people who are too bad to live
in Kingussie live in Newtonmore', or so a Kingussie man once
told me. Certain it is that there once lived in Newtonmore a man
who claimed to be able to make men new and better eyes out of
lead. The Devil heard of him and, scenting a rascal, came to call.
The quack, however, was so persuasive that he prevailed upon
the Devil himself to try the new red-hot lead eyes and, so he
claimed, killed him. Little credence was placed in this story, however, it being generally believed that the Evil One is far from dead.

Loch Guinach was also connected in legend with fairy dogs.
There always seems to be some doubt about these dogs, some
holding that they were just a fairy creature, others maintaining
that the fairies were not satisfied with the breed as they had it but
were always trying to obtain really good earth-dogs with which
to cross and so improve their own strain. The Loch Guinach story
which follows, of which unfortunately I do not remember all the
details, seems to uphold the second view.

There was a man who was in great trouble, he and his wife
and his children; indeed the children were crying out with hunger
and nothing he could do to help went right. So he went up to
Loch Guinach to drown himself for he thought that someone
would take pity on his widow and children if they were left alone.
But he stopped to take off his coat and boots that all might know
him dead, as otherwise his sacrifice would be useless. As soon as
he took off his nailed boots he saw between him and the water a
beautiful woman. Soon he was confiding to her his trouble. 'Go
home,' said she, 'and you will find all well if you will agree to
one condition.' 'Any condition,' he answered. 'That is foolish,'
said she, 'but I will not make the more of it. Every wish you have
shall be fulfilled if you promise to meet me here in a year and a
day and give me whatever or whoever first meets you tonight
when you reach your house.' The man, remembering his last
sheep had died that week and that he had tethered its lamb by his

door was sure the lamb would greet him and agreed. But as he approached the house his wife, who had seen him approaching, flung open the door, eager to tell him of food in the pot and other good news. His children also rushed out to greet him, but before they could reach him his dog, which he had left shut in the house, sprang out and, jumping up, licked his face.

A year passed and the man, now a well-to-do small farmer, felt he could not condemn his dog to the fairies and at last confided in his wife. 'We owe as much to her work as to the fairies,' she said indignantly, 'Calum, you must offer back all we have to save her.' So the man and his dog returned to Loch Guinach and there met the fairy, and the dog crouched to the ground in fear. Calum told the fairy how he felt and offered her all his other beasts as ransom for his dog. 'No,' said the fairy, 'your dog is mine.' 'No,' said Calum, 'I will not give you my dog; take back all your gifts.' 'That includes your life, Calum,' said the fairy gently. 'You would be one year dead but for me.' For a moment Calum hesitated, then 'I will not give you my dog,' he repeated stubbornly. But then he saw his dog leave him and go to the fairy, crawling for it could not walk with fear. And the fairy spoke to it in a voice such as, said Calum, he had never heard. 'It would woo the heart from the body,' he said. And the dog rose and came and licked his hand and went back to the fairy. 'Meet me here today year,' said the fairy, and she and the dog vanished.

A year to the day and Calum was there, and there was the fairy and there was his dog and with her the finest pup that ever he saw. The dog came to greet him, bounding and laughing as only a happy dog can. And the fairy smiled and said, 'The dog is mine, Calum, and the best dog in all the world. Only once more shall you see her. When your time comes to die she shall warn you. But the puppy is yours; take it and go home.' So Calum went home, and the puppy to heel, and a good dog it became. It brought some fairy dog characteristics to earth too, it is said, as for instance all its descendants had 'silver eyes' and could see the wind as light-eyed dogs should.

Many, many years later, as Calum went to his sheepfold, he met his old dog and it barked three barks. Then Calum knew what was to be in three days. He said goodbye to his dog, he patted its head and it licked his hand, then he went home to set his affairs in order.

To the south of Kingussie there was till lately a small wood, now cut but which once covered the steep sides of a tiny glen. It was believed to be part of the original Caledonian Forest, though it might perhaps be more accurately described as being formed from seedlings from the original forest. It was always noted for a quite wonderful display of toadstools of every colour, including the scarlet ones with white spots which were very plentiful and made the grass below the trees almost as gorgeous as a field of poppies. These toadstools are specially beloved of witches, for they are powerful alike as a poison and as a love philtre. In consequence the witches from far around used to gather there and hold a special 'coven' in the season of toadstools to gather and preserve them. Do witches bottle toadstools? As it was not known for certain what night they would choose for their meeting—some claimed it would be on All Hallows E'en but others thought this too late in the year—it was as well to avoid both the wood and its neighbourhood as the nights began to draw in. Once a boy, passing the wood very late on some errand, saw the witches 'flighting in' like grey geese. They rode, he said, a variety of steeds, a few real horses (proof that certain horses had been ridden that night was found in their exhausted condition and the hag-knots in their manes, which are witches' stirrups) but most rode cats, broomsticks, ragwort stalks or even straws. Indeed Burns' *Witches of Fife* about describes it:

> Some horses were of the broom cane formit
> And some of the green bay tree
> But mine was made from ane humloke straw
> And a stout stallion was he.

But the most usual mount according to the lad's story was ragwort, long known to have provided horses for the Little People. Indeed in some districts the careful farmer would leave ragwort unharmed round the margins of his fields, outside the fence for it is held to be poisonous, despite its seeding powers as otherwise the Little People would ride his horses at night and the poor beasts would be too exhausted to work next day. The boy who saw the witches in flight was most fortunate not to have been seen by them, as had he been he would surely have lost his tongue.

Not very much further on, just south of Newtonmore, the road to Loch Laggan branches off. Once it was known as Loch Laggan Choinnich, Loch of Kenneth's Hollow, from the tiny church of St. Kenneth whose ruins can still be seen at one end of the water. This was superseded by a new church in a more useful position at Laggan Bridge and the 'Choinnich' has dropped from the name. The St. Choinnich or Cainnech of the old small church is reputed to be that St. Kenneth who one day interrupted the service in his monastery in Ireland by exclaiming that he saw St. Columba in great danger from storm at sea and that they must all pray for him and his companions. An hour later he told them that the saint was now safe and the ordinary life of the monastery could continue. St. Columba and his monks had in fact been in great jeopardy at that moment.

The Grampian slopes are a place of stories, many of them so old that only the names of the kings or heroes preserved by hill or loch or island are remembered—their deeds are often forgotten. In Loch Laggan, for instance, are two islands known as Eilean-na-righ, Isle of the King, and Eilean-nan-con, Isle of the Dogs. Traces of what were reputed to be a palace and large dog kennels are visible there. The palace, all are agreed, was the hunting lodge of 'King Fergus' but who he was no one remembers. The kennels were said by some to have been those of his hunting dogs, but others held that these kennels belonged to the Feinn and once held their world-famous dogs. Who was King Fergus? He does not appear in Scottish history in any recognisable and certain form. Only two kings of that name do appear in Scotland's story at all. The first is called 'The first king of Scotland' and heads the list of legendary prehistory kings. He is reputed to have married Scotia, daughter of the Pharaoh of Red Sea fame, and also to have been a contemporary, some say friend, of Alexander the Great, so he must have had a good long life. He it is, too, who is said to have brought the Stone of Destiny to Scotland. Talking of Alexander the Great, the Highlands knew a different version of his traditional aspiration for more worlds to conquer. ' "It would be something for one man but a small thing for two" as

Alexander the Proud said about the world' is the Gaelic version.

The other King Fergus, Feargus MacErc, was a real person; he even appears in Burke's Peerage. Son of the High King of Ireland, he was blessed by St. Patrick in 493 and led a migration of 'Scots' from Ireland to Alban. He became King of Dalriada; his two brothers, Loarn and Aonghus, who accompanied him, were made sub-kings. But what he would have done with a hunting lodge in Laggan, in or close to the country of his enemies the Picts, it is hard to see.

The story of 'King Fergus' that I was told as a child at Kingussie was that he was a great king and a great hunter. One day he was hunting on the hills and, growing tired, sat down to rest and fell asleep. While he slept the boar he had been following crept close and suddenly charged him. He was unaware of his danger but his dogs alerted instantly and sprang to defend him. This gave him time to wake and draw his sword. Fergus killed the boar and then found that his favourite hound had been gored and lay dying. He called seven of his daughters and ordered them to go quickly and search for a certain herb, the crushed leaves of which might save the dog's life. The girls went off and, after a time, six returned with the required leaves; the seventh came back empty-handed. She had forgotten to enquire what the plant looked like! But all were too late. The dog was dead. Then King Fergus was sad and his huntsman, to cheer him, came to bury it with honour and raise a cairn over its grave. But Fergus said 'No,' his dog was too good to bury. 'Bury a man and his spirit lives on; bury a dog and what have you?' he is reputed to have said. And he placed his hound in the sky, where it became the Dog Star. Annoyed at his daughters' tardiness with the leaves, he set them in the sky also, as a warning to other daughters. They are the Pleiades, six bright and one shining only faintly because on earth she was always so very 'dim'.

Perhaps 'King Fergus' was not a Scottish king at all. One story I used to hear made him 'a King out of Ireland', that Fergus who brought the fateful message to Deirdre and the sons of Uisneath. It has always been known that Deirdre herself, with her woman's intuition, distrusted the King of Ulster and she is said to have persuaded Fergus to remain with them for one year and one day before they left to return to Ireland, that she might have one year and one day of happiness before the curse fell on her and on Ireland and Fergus agreed. So the sons of Uisneath built him a dwelling on this island in Loch Laggan. In this story the kennels have no part.

The kennels have been believed to have been Fiann kennels where the Feinn kept their great dogs. It was in a hollow place near the loch that the 'Great Fight' was held. For you must know that Fionn and his men were once seated round the cooking pot enjoying deer's meat stew when they saw, crossing the hills towards them, a young man in a red garment, by his side a fine black dog. 'His cheek was as the berry's hue, his skin was whiter than moss-cotton' and his hair was black. His head was stately 'like the elk's' and 'on his face fear could not lie'. He greeted Fionn with great courtesy and also the other Feinn. They asked him what he did in their land and he replied that he had heard much of the wonder of the Feinn hounds and had brought his dog to be matched against theirs in fight. For his dog was a pup from the Giants' Isles and there was no dog to beat it in all Scotland. Fionn agreed but refused to allow Bran, his own beloved dog, to be included in the challenge. So for that night the brave young hero and his dog feasted with the Feinn and at dawn the Fiann hunting hounds were brought out and the ground for the fight was set. Every dog sent against him the black dog slew, till he had killed 'three times fifty of the Fiann dogs'. And the Feinn grew angry.

> Then Bran shook his gold chain
> His wailing was loud among the people
> His two eyes kindled in his head
> And he bristled up eager for battle.
> (Translation by Rev. D. MACKINNON
> in *Waifs and Strays of Scottish Tradition*)

At last Fionn was persuaded to allow Bran, the great Bran himself, to be matched against the black dog. They set the dogs 'nose to nose' and there was a long and fierce struggle but at length Bran killed the black dog. Then the young hero lamented greatly the death of his dog and the Feinn lamented with him for the death of the noble beast:

> The shape of my dog was good,
> The joint of his neck was far from his head,
> Broad was his middle and broad his chest,
> Bent was his fore-leg, crooked his hind-leg,

sang the young hero.

> Bran had yellow paws
> Two black flanks and a white belly,
> A green back under which game would lie
> And two sharp, erect red ears
>   (Translations as above)

The Feinn asked the young hero his name and his place. He told them that his name was Eibheinn Oisean and that he came from Innis Torc and his dog came as a pup from the Isle of Giants and its name was For. The Feinn believed it was blood brother to Bran.

> Then the true, generous hero
> Buried his dog in a narrow clay bed
> And the Feinn also buried
> In the mound westward three 50 dogs.

It is interesting to note that in this poem Bran is described as being 'green-backed' like the fairy dogs of the Grampian stories whereas his blood brother from Innis Torc, usually supposed to be the Orkneys, is black, like the Sutherland fairy hound. A Gaelic rhyme tells what points the Feinn required for their ordinary hunting hounds, dogs which, unlike Bran, had no supernatural origin but were, some believe, the ancestors of the old Irish staghound breed from which comes the mascot of the Irish Guards.

> Thus Fingal chose his hounds:
> Eye like sloe, ear like leaf,
> Chest like horse, hough like sickle
> And the tail joint far from the head.

Others think that the Feinn used the ancient Scottish deerhounds which must have been very similar:

> Muzzle like club, ear like leaf,
> Tail to the hough, hough like sickle.

Both are very different from the English greyhound, in which

> A head like a snake, a neck like a drake,
> A back like a beam, a belly like a bream,
> A foot like a cat, a tail like a rat

was what pleased their owners.

One remaining story of King Fergus is curious, however, for it connects King Fergus with the Feinn. This makes Fergus a son of Fionn himself and a brother of Oisean, the Feinn's bard. Now Ossian the Bard was much enjoyed by the Little People and once they made him captive, that they might listen to his tales and songs forever. But Ossian was homesick for the Feinn and desired to escape. His efforts were not successful. Perhaps he was too good a poet to be also of much use in a practical world. At last, however, he did have a really good idea. The fairy mound in which he was held prisoner was on the bank of a river, probably the Spey. With much care he cut slivers from his spear haft and, when the Little People were too busy to notice, floated them down the river as it flowed by the dun. Fergus was out hunting for his missing brother when he saw the slivers and, guessing their meaning, immediately set about rescuing him and brought him in safety to his palace in Logh Laggan where Fergus dwelt as keeper of the Feinns' hounds.

So Ossian survived, to live on for many centuries and to engage in an argument with St. Patrick. But that is another story.

Cumberland Stone, Culloden

4

INVERNESS TO NAIRN
AND FORRES

When the night wind howls in the chimney cowls, and
    the bat in the moonlight flies,
And inky clouds, like funeral shrouds, sail over the
    midnight skies—
When the footpads quail at the night-bird's wail, and
    black dogs bay at the moon,
Then is the spectre's holiday—then is the ghosts'
    high noon!

                       W. S. GILBERT

THE ROAD to Culloden Moor takes off from the main
south road a few miles beyond Inverness. Until the early
years of this century the Moor had changed little since the
Battle of Culloden was fought there in 1746. It had, of course, its
Cairn, its Graves of the Fallen, its Well of the Dead and 'The
Field of the English' where Cumberland's men were buried, but
despite the sunshine usual there and its cloak of heather and other
wild flowers it seemed to remain sombre, brooding on the horrors
it had seen. Standing there, it was easy to believe not only in the

bitterness of the battle itself but also in the frustration and misery and hate in the two armies themselves. Tales are told, such as that of the Macdonalds who are said to have been so enraged at not being placed on the right wing of the Prince's army, their heredi- tary honour, that they would not fight. Neither, however, would they leave the field lest it savour of cowardice, and so they stood, more than half a clan, to be shot down by Cumberland's men as if facing a firing squad. It may not be true but it is exactly true to the Macdonald character. Just such feelings of bitterness and frustration and folly seemed still loose on the Moor.

Now all is changed. The Forestry Commission have taken over much of the battlefield, ploughed up some graves, of which the big Macdonald barrow seems to be one, and planted the land with dark, sombre fir woods—a fitting mourning cloak. The 'Field of the English', too, has not been spared: in what was a part of it now stands a modern villa, built on dead men's bones. Fortunately, about 1950 the Board of Ancient Monuments took charge of the Cairn, the Well and the Clan graves near them. These are now beautifully kept, the short grass on the barrows like velvet and the headstones clearly named. A notice board of their raising asks for respect for the Graves of the Clans, and so in truth the grave of the Highland Clans Culloden was. Truly, civil war is the worst of all wars.

> All over; falls the night on broken men,
> Culloden's sword with blood writes 'Ichabod'.
>
> JOHN M. HAY

After the 1914-18 War a historian, writing a history of the '45, came up to Inverness. He had read all the appropriate books available and now wished to see the lie of the land for himself and take photographs. He was advised to call on an old woman who lived in a cottage on the edge of the Moor. Her grandmother, he was told, had as a child witnessed the battle, hiding with her brothers and sisters to watch. She had taught the whole story to the now elderly grand-daughter who would repay a visit. So off went the historian. He found the old lady at home and more than willing to talk. She took him on to the Moor and began to des- cribe how the Clans were formed up and their order, the personal appearance of each Chief and the Prince and his staff and where each had stood. The historian flipped through his notes; everything was exactly as he knew it to have been and she was able to clear up one or two points which the written accounts left obscure. He purred happily. What a well-spent morning! Then she said: 'And then Cumberland's men came in sight over there,' and pointed.

'Oh, no,' said the historian, 'you've got that wrong. You mean *this* way.'

'That he didn't! My grannie told me they came from over *there*. My grannie knew. She saw it.'

'No, no,' said the historian, sure that she or her 'grannie' had grown confused with the passing of the years. But the old lady stuck to it. 'My grannie said so. She *knew*. She saw it.' At last they parted on terms polite but strained and the historian returned to Inverness and explained to his friends the dangers of believing oral tradition. 'It's most accurate in every detail,' he said, 'and then comes some piece of complete nonsense like that. We know where Cumberland camped the previous night and how he must and did come.' Two or three years later Culloden House was sold. For the first time for many generations every cupboard and chest was emptied and the now well-known 'Culloden Papers' were found, edited and published. The historian held up his book until he had read them, for this was the real thing, the actual reports from men in command. And they proved beyond doubt

Highland
Dress

that Cumberland had swung round (he was undoubtedly a competent general) and come on to the Moor exactly where the old woman's grandmother had told her, and not where the historian, and incidentally the Prince's army, had expected him. The surprise had not helped the Prince's tired troops. The historian returned to the Moor to apologise to the old woman and ask for the rest of the story, but he was too late. She was dead.

So much for oral tradition, but what about film history? About this time an American studio decided to film the story of the '45. They interviewed various high-ups and were promised the help of any Highland regiments in the vicinity and their depots. They came north with a great deal of publicity and began by announcing that they needed men as 'supers' and were willing to pay a daily wage which worked out at nearly twice the local farm wages, and as much again to any man who could bring a horse, 'tinker ponies accepted'. This was during the great unemployment period in the '20s, so the queue when they opened an engagement bureau next day went up that street and down the next, with and without horses. Each man went in beaming and came out glowering. By the end of the morning not one man had signed on. What no one had realised was how strong the feeling in the Highlands was. 'Me to pretend I'm a —— Hanoverian soldier. Not much!' was the general attitude. However, various officials took a hand. Unemployment pay couldn't be

Cumberland's
Soldiers

given to men who refused easy, lucrative work, they pointed out, and after all it was only pretence. Finally 'the Duke's army' was recruited and removed by bus and car and horse trailer to Culloden Moor. The regiments were already there and 'make up' work began in huge tents. The local tinkers became Hanoverian cavalry. Officers of the regiments suddenly sprouted wild hair and red beards to conform to the U.S.A. idea of a Highland Chief's appearance in 1745, and at last the battle was on. The War was but recently over and so the Highland regiments were still composed chiefly of youngsters, there being few older men left. When told to 'charge' they did so with huge enjoyment and the 'English Army' of unemployeds did not await the shock; led by the tinker 'Hanoverian cavalry' they broke and fled, pursued by happy shrieking Highland troops. Indeed everyone was happy, including the cameraman who, knowing nothing of local history, thought he was 'shooting' the best battle scene and pursuit of all time, and filmed madly. Yards and yards of film were spoilt but everyone was finally collected from all over the countryside and it all started again. This time the troops were divided, a stiffening of trained men being used on each side. But no one thought to tell the Director that there was at this time a feud on between the Gordons and the Camerons, so bitter that it was usually deemed inadvisable to put them in the same ward in a hospital, or at least in adjacent beds. When told to 'fix bayonets and charge' they did so with avidity. Six men had to be rushed to hospital by ambulance. It was pointed out later that magazine rifles and bayonets were not the usual Highland arms in the eighteenth century. Then, at last, everyone got down to business and a reasonable sort of battle was fought 'by numbers' and filmed. But again and again yards of film were spoilt by such incidents as the 'English' troops hissing and booing one of their number who happened to have overcome a Highlander. The Duke of Cumberland's proclamation, with its offer of £30,000 for the Prince, alive or dead, was proclaimed by an officer standing in front of Flora Macdonald's statue on Castle Hill in Inverness. As the Prince had not yet been hunted, Flora had not yet helped him to escape; how then did she come to have a statue? But what perhaps amused most of us most when the finished film was shown in the

North was the final scene. The Prince, about to sail for France, was saying goodbye to some of his friends and supporters who had been in hiding in the hills for very many weeks. They had been hungry and wet and exhausted. They had slept in the heather or hidden in caves, forded rivers and climbed mountains, but they all wept into *clean* lace handkerchiefs.

The Brahan Seer once walked across the Moor of Drumossie, as Culloden Moor was then called, and is said to have stopped and exclaimed: 'Oh, Drumossie, thy black moor shall ere many generations have passed away be stained with the best blood of the Highlands. Glad am I that I shall not see that day, for it will be a fearful period; heads will be lopped off by the score and no mercy will be shown or quarter given on either side.'

A great boulder, estimated to weigh about eight tons, for long marked a part of the boundary between the Culloden estate and Moray. It stood well inland, some four or five hundred yards from the coast it is said. On the night of 20th February 1799 this stone was 'mysteriously removed' and was found next day 260 yards out into the sea to the south of the Bay of Petti, where it still lies. No one knows, or has ever known, how it was moved. It was a fearful night of storm. A hurricane was said to have been blowing off the shore, and this, combined with ice, was believed by some to have been the moving force. Others suggested an earthquake. Probably the most popular belief was that it was the work of the Devil, 'His Blackness' (as he was sometimes called by some of his adherents) and his satellites the witches having always been known to favour this part of the country with their presence. The Brahan Seer is said to have foretold the moving of the Stone of Petti also, and its immersion in the sea, adding: 'No one will see it removed or be able to account for its sudden and marvellous transportation.'

In a wood above Culloden House is a spring called St. Mary's Well which was for long a place of pilgrimage on the first Sunday in May (old style). About eighty years ago my mother, as a young girl, was staying with friends near Inverness in May, and the young people decided to make up a party to visit the Well on its day. My mother told me that they arrived at the Well before dawn as it was the custom to drink a draught of its water

just as the sun rose over the hills. She and her friends each drank
the water, wished a wish, threw in a pin or other offering for the
fairies, and then washed their faces in May dew to make them
beautiful; all this with much laughter and merriment. But there
were a number of older people there to whom it seemed a serious
pilgrimage, she said, and who genuinely expected their wishes
to be granted or their ills cured. They drank the water and then
wished their wishes and dropped their offerings into the well,
softly chanting a spell or charm while doing so; my mother was
not clear which but remembered it as a sort of invocation to the
spirit of the well with some saints' names added. Those who
hoped for a cure then tore a small piece of cloth off some garment
which they were wearing; the women usually took braid from
their skirts (the hems of the old long dresses were usually finished
with so-called braid sewn inside the hem and coming just below
it so that it would not show but would keep the skirt's edge clean
and unwrinkled). These pieces of material were then sprinkled
with spring water, rubbed when possible on the wart or rash or
swelling it was desired to remove, and hung on a may-tree near
the well. As the material rotted, so should the illness disappear.
But those who would be cured or wished to receive their hearts'
desire must be very, *very* careful indeed not to look behind them
after they had performed the rites and turned homewards.

Looking back seems to have been considered very dangerous
and the height of folly when engaged in any dealings with other-
world beings. For instance, once Sir Robert of Gordonstoun
wished to drive his coach and four across Loch Spynie, near
Forres, after a single night of frost. He bade his coachman sit
still and, above all, never to look behind. The man obeyed until
they had just reached the further side, when he glanced over his
left shoulder and saw a large black raven flying off the back of
the carriage which, the same instant, sank into the mud but so
near the edge of the water that the horses were able to save it
without the Devil's aid.

When a wise-woman was putting a spell of protection on a
man who was going to war he must go with her to a lonely spot
and, having said his prayers that he might be of a pure and clean
heart, he must stand looking straight before him while she made

her spell. Once a man in Lewis glanced over his left shoulder and
in due course lost his left arm in battle but came, otherwise un-
hurt, through great dangers. So 'not to look back' was obviously
of the greatest importance.

From Culloden (from which we have strayed) the road runs
down to the sea near Nairn, a pleasant seaside and golfing resort as
well as a fishing village. There is a second and more direct road
from Inverness to Nairn by the coast, which runs so level and
straight for much of the way that the Romans might have built
it had they ruled here. It is a great place for speeding, one of the
few possible ones hereabouts in fact. Some three miles before
Nairn a road takes off to the left leading to the attractive little
village of Ardersier and beyond it to Fort George. The Fort was
built in the eighteenth century after the Jacobite troubles and is
still a military station. One of the worst thunderstorms ever remembered in the North took place here one summer afternoon
in the 1920's when the Seaforth Highlanders were holding their
annual Sports Day and At Home. It was a big 'do' with many
cars and a large marquee. This big tent was struck by lightning
and collapsed on top of the unfortunate waitresses who were busy
inside it, and a 'fire-ball' entered the Officers' Mess, settled on the
C.O.'s chair and set it on fire. Guests began to leave hurriedly
and an endless stream of cars took the road to Ardersier. Suddenly
one car in the midst of the line was struck by lightning. Apparently the lightning, having got into the bonnet, could not go on
to earth because of the insulation provided by the tyres, nor get
out again any other way, so it seized the engine and twisted it
round and round into a spiral—an unbelievable sight. The car,
completely ruined, was on show at Macrae and Dick's garage for
some weeks afterwards. No one was hurt.

Not far from Nairn, on the road to Forres, is the old church
of Auldearn with its curious and not very church-like history.
Originally a ring of standing stones occupied the site; later, a
church was built within the circle, but, says local tradition, 'the
evil persists'. The churchyard was long held to be a meeting
place of witches, and then came Issobel Gowdie and her strange
'confessions'. Most of the so-called confessions made by witches
were extorted either by direct torture of the poor old women or

else by such means as allowing them neither food nor sleep until they agreed to every accusation made against them. Not so Issobel Gowdie, the wife of John Gilbert, a farmer of Loch Loy. She appeared of her own free will, saying that she had been already 'too long in the Devil's service' and gave evidence before a Commission of 'reputable gentlemen including four ministers'. She told how she met the Devil by appointment in Auldearn Church and there 'denied her baptism', placing one hand on the top of her head and the other on the sole of her foot and vowing to Satan all that lay between. Then Margaret Brodie (presumably another witch) held her up for the Devil to baptise her, which he did, saying: 'I baptise thee Janet in my own name.' Then he put his mark on her shoulder, sucked her blood and spat it on her head. Issobel Gowdie told much of what they did: how they used toads to plough land with a plough made from the horns of an ox so that the land would become infertile and produce for its owner only briars and thistles while the Devil got the good of it. Of course it had long been believed that only a perfect beast should be used for the plough if you would have a perfect harvest. She told of making clay images and of taking the form of a jack-daw, her friends being a hare and two cats. They had, she said, rhymes for each transmutation, such as:

> I shall go into a hare
> With sorrow and sic muckle care;
> And I shall go in the Devil's name
> Until I come home again.

Instantly they would become the animal they had named. One of their amusements was spoiling a dye vat by taking a thread from it; thereafter it could only dye black. She told, too, how 'about Lammas time in the year 1659' she and some friends visited a fairy dwelling under the Downie hills; a door in the hillside opened and 'we came to a large braw room in the day time. There are great bulls racing and frolicking there at the entry, which frightened me.' But she was not frightened to go by night to catch moles, cut off their feet and place them, with the bones of an unbaptised child, in a small fire-proof bag, one of which was presented to each witch by the Devil when he baptised her. So long as a witch carried moles' feet she would never lack money, said Issobel. Despite her repentance and free confession she was condemned to death.

It is very hard to understand why, knowing the consequences, women should have confessed, unforced, and even boasted of their witchery, the more so as it was generally believed that any woman who became a witch immediately grew wrinkled and tanned, her nose became long and sharp and she grew shifty-eyed —'ugly as a witch' in fact—while men grew beards of coarse goat hair beneath their chins. What did they gain? Prestige?

Between Nairn and Forres, and about two miles from the road, lie the celebrated Culbin Sands. These miles of sand and dunes proved most useful in the last war when they were used as a storage place for high explosive bombs which were collected for the heavy bombers as required. Unfortunately the Culbin Sands, though useful for such diverse things as picnics and bomb storage, won't stay put. The horror of the time when they did get out of control and a sandstorm swept all over the Hay lands, hopelessly burying men and beasts, earth and houses, and producing the Sands as we know them today is not forgotten yet. Those who survived of the Hays, who owned much of the buried district, were said to have been attempting to clear the edges when a battle broke out near by. They seized their ploughshares and rushed to the aid of the King's troops. Their onrush turned the tide in the King's favour and they were rewarded with new lands in the south of Scotland. Another story, however, tells how they struggled on with depleted fortunes until one day one of them got himself into a fight with a Tannasg, or spectre. The ghost threw him and then, kneeling to throttle him, asked: 'Were you ever in so bad a plight?' 'Yes, and worse,' answered Hay. 'What was that?' asked the spectre. 'The worst plight I was ever in was when I was between Hospitality and Want and keeping up Gentility in spite of all.' 'That was hard work,' said the Tannasg, rising to its feet, 'Get up and depart. You'll never meet those two again.' Shortly afterwards the family received fresh lands.

Some years ago the Sands began to move again and a sandstorm, bad enough to block roads, blew for several days; all available road gangs were put to work trying to clear the roads, or, at least, keep them open, but till the wind fell work seemed almost useless. Sand came in as fast as it was swept out, three inches an hour was estimated in some places. Fortunately it has not recurred though at the time considerable anxiety was felt lest the sands be really on the move once more. It is believed that the original sandstorm, with its frightful havoc, was caused by three lean years during which the beasts were only kept alive by eating the bent grass whose matted roots covered and held down the sand dunes. When the grass cover was destroyed the sands 'walked' in the first gale. Some enterprising local landlords of the nineteenth century, the owners of Kincorth, Moy, Dalvey and Brodie, began tree-planting to hold the sands—a huge job. By 1922 the Forestry Commission, which had acquired some land there, began to plant the Culbin Forest which now covers some 7,260 acres and is doing well. As the trees grow, fear of the sands recedes.

The stretch of excellent farm land that runs along the Moray Firth from Inverness to beyond Nairn was always in great demand and much coveted. Those who held it must guard it and the result is a plentiful supply of old and strong castles, from Castle Stewart, not very far from Inverness, with its crown and its quite horribly corkscrewy stone staircase twisting round a central pillar, to the old Castle of Forres. Cawdor is the best known perhaps, partly because it is still the home of the Earls of Cawdor and a live Castle is better than a dead one, and partly because of Shakespeare's 'Hail!, Thane of Cawdor.' At Cawdor and in two other gardens not far away the blue Himalayan poppy, meconopsis, was first grown in Scotland, for Lord Cawdor was a member of the expedition to the Himalayas which brought the first seeds home shortly after World War I. Near Forres is 'Macbeth's Hill' which claims to be the actual site of the witches' greeting to Macbeth, and Macbeth's witches were but the fore-runners of many. Indeed at the time of the witch hunts this district, with Forres as its centre, claimed the proud distinction of having more witches, wizards and other warlocks than any other place of like size in Scotland. Whether this boast was justified I do not know, but it may well have been.

There is a stone near Forres on the West road known as the Witches' Stone. It marks the place where three witches were burnt in the tenth century for attempting the life of King Duffus

(or Donald), grandfather of Lady Macbeth. They were accused
of making an image of the King, roasting it, basting it meanwhile
with a poisonous liquid, and 'by their enchantments did prevent
his sleeping'. They were found guilty and executed, whereupon
the King recovered from his sickness. This part of Scotland, too,
is reputed to have sent its quota of witches to the Armada of 200
Witches which put to sea in riddles and sieves to drown James VI
(James I of England) when he went to meet his Danish bride, or
so the King claimed. The King also accused them of taking two
cats, christening them in proper form with holy water by the
name of Anne of Denmark, his Queen, and then casting them into
the sea, 'that they might drown and the Queen with them'. It
was believed that as they stepped into their sieve boats they
chanted:

> Cummer, go ye before; Cummer, go ye;
> Gif ye will na' go before, Cummer, let me.

to reassure those newly bound to the Devil.

Two celebrated wizards hereabouts were the Earl of Gowrie
and Sir Robert Gordon of Gordonstoun. They studied the black
art in Padua and Salamanca under the Devil himself and claimed
to be the first to become so proficient in it as to lose their shadows.
But this proud claim was also made by the first Lord Reay and
by John Garraford of Skye, both of whom persuaded the Devil
to carry off their shadows instead of themselves. But:

> Who hasna' heard of that man of renown
> The wizard Sir Robert of Gordonstoun,
> The wisest of warlocks, the Morayshire cheil
> The despot of Duffus the friend o' the deil?
> (An old rhyme)

and indeed who in the North has not heard of him for there are
many legends about him and about his end? The best known,
perhaps, is that told of him at Gordonstoun, Prince Philip's old
school and now Prince Charles's which incorporates Sir Robert's
'Round Square'. 'The Square', as the farm buildings on Highland
farms are called, is too common a feature of the Scottish countryside to need comment, but a round 'Square' was indeed an inno-
vation. It is believed that while in Padua Sir Robert came to an

agreement with the Devil that he should have one year of freedom and then be his. But a year seemed all too short a time to
spend in this world full of wonder and he managed to persuade
the Devil, when the year was up, to accept his shadow in his
stead and to give him twenty-five more years of life. Sir Robert
returned to Gordonstoun after his father's death and there he had

The Round Square, Gordonstoun

a furnace—used, it was believed, for many purposes unlikely to
please the Church but also used to make the finest wrought-iron
work in the North. Sir Robert was an inventor of note and
devised, among other things, a sea-pump so good that Samuel
Pepys when Secretary of the Admiralty bought it from him for
use in the Navy. Sir Robert was altogether a man of parts. His
twenty-five years of grace were due to end in November of 1704

and so, growing alarmed as the date approached, he used all his skill and ingenuity to design the round square to be Devil-proof. When the dreaded night arrived he shut himself inside his fortress, protected by many a spell, with one friend—the parson of Duffus —and waited, having first put the clock on an hour. As the clock struck midnight a cloven hoof was seen and the Devil demanded his due but Sir Robert pointed out that the clock was fast; the Devil agreed and said he would wait his hour. Unfortunately at this point the parson's nerve gave out and he begged and entreated Sir Robert to take refuge in that most holy building and sanctuary, the Old Kirk of Birnie. At last Sir Robert fell in with his wishes and set out for Birnie Church. 'The remainder of the story,' says Gordonstoun, 'was told by the Parson of Birnie, the Rev. John McKean, to his wife.' Towards midnight he was returning home when Robert overtook him, breathlessly enquired the way to Birnie Church and fled on. Moments later Mr McKean was over-taken again, this time by a horseman who asked if a man had passed that way. He tried to answer but the truth froze upon his lips; instead, without his own volition, he heard himself saying that he had seen no one. The horseman rode on. All was still. One terrible shriek pierced the silence. Before Mr McKean could even move, the horseman rode by once more; across his saddle-bow lay 'a limp human body and upon either side ran a great hound, and the one nearer to him had its fangs buried in the neck of the corpse'. The Gordonstoun tale ends: 'So the efficiency of the Round Square as a Sanctuary for souls was never proved. Yet those who know the place will have no doubts. It has a singular fascination for all who live and work in it.'

Another version makes the chase last for three days and three nights, through Elgin and all the country round, but in the end the Devil 'got his man'. This old church of Birnie, near Elgin, was long noted for its double font. That is to say, its font had been divided into two by a plate of iron let into the stone so that the water used for the baptism of girls might not mix with that used to baptise boys. The reason being a firm belief that if, at a mixed baptismal service, a girl was accidentally baptised before a boy she would, on reaching maidenhood, grow a large and incurable beard. Nor was that all: the boys baptised after her would have lost their power to grow beards or whiskers, or even, in some cases, to grow hair at all, and girls would take their luck also. This old font was changed for a modern basin early in the nineteenth century.

Witches and wizards were sometimes useful. The story is told of how a young man in the neighbourhood of Nairn got himself into trouble dabbling in politics and was sentenced to transportation to slavery in the Plantations for his crime. His wealthy relatives appealed to one of the district's famous witches. She called up her 'master' and then promised aid. A wax image of the youth was made and this spell chanted over it while appropriate herbs were burnt:

> I hold thee safe in the Devil's name
> Unscathed of water shalt thou remain,
> Unhurt of wind, undrowned in sea,
> Safe so long as it pleases me.

In due course he and many others set sail for the Plantations. A terrible storm arose in the Firth of Forth and the ship was wrecked. The boy was the only survivor and he came quietly home to Moray unnoticed by any outsider except the witch, who, when she saw that the storm had done its work, sang:

> I lay the wind in the Devil's name;
> Let it not rise till I please again.
> May the winds lie, hushed and still,
> And rise no more unless I will.

So the sea ceased to trouble and the wind fell calm.

A less useful type of local witch, however, was that which sometimes took the form of dogs, usually large black dogs, who worried sheep. Their worrying was confined to nights when the moon was dark but which were near their big festivals, May Day and Hallowe'en, so it was easily recognised as being the work of no common dog. Witches were very vulnerable while in dog form and could easily be shot with a silver bullet; then, if some old woman died suddenly, you knew you had killed your witch. This was really a better and safer plan than accusing the suspected witch of being a were-dog or were-wolf because you couldn't kill the wrong woman if you shot her in dog form. Either you killed a witch, if your suspicions were justified, or, if you were wrong, you had killed a sheep-worrying hound, and a good riddance.

When witches took animal form, anyhow in this district, their hands became their front paws, providing the necessary four feet, but as humans have no tail there is nothing that can be turned into one. Hence Shakespeare's 'Like a rat without a tail'. So it was, one would have thought, very easy to know for certain whether the creature seen worrying the sheep was a dog or a were-dog, tailless real dogs being rare in the Highlands. But this was not so. Suspicions were easily aroused and innocent men and women accused. The story is told, for instance, that St. Ronan once visited this part of the country to preach and that the Pictish king, much impressed by his teaching, became his friend and supporter. But one day the accusation that he was a were-wolf was brought against the saint, apparently based on his habit of wandering out at night to pray in lonely places. The King, realising the danger in which the saint stood, immediately arrested him and suggested to his accusers that at a convenient time and place St. Ronan should be brought out for trial by the King's hunting dogs. These dogs, said the King, would immediately tear to pieces any wolf, whether real or 'were', that came within their reach. A day was appointed for the trial. During the intervening period Ronan, by the King's orders, was made to work feeding and caring for the King's dogs. On the day of his trial, great crowds had gathered near the Auldearn Stones to see the sight. A sort of arena was cordoned off and the dogs and Ronan let loose in it. As soon as they saw Ronan the dogs rushed upon him, apparently about to devour him, but instead fawned round his feet and licked his hands and his face. So his accusers decided that Ronan was not a were-wolf but a saint. Few accused were so lucky, however.

The Devil used to take black dog form in the North too. Probably most of us can remember being told as children, if we were cross or naughty, 'There's a little black dog sitting on your shoulder.'

The Clava Stones

5

THE INVERNESS
LAKE DISTRICT

While a hill bird cried and cried
Like a spirit lost
By the grey storm-wind tost.
MARION ANGUS

THE ROAD to the Lakes leaves Inverness up the steep slope to the south and soon reaches the Clava Stones, a group of Standing Stones on the hill side about three miles from the town. Once they were believed to be the remains of a Druid temple and fresh impetus was given to this belief by the finding of a gold rod near them, dug up during a farm drainage scheme. But the name has been translated as The Burial Place of the Town and traces of bronze age burials were found there. Traditionally the Stones mark the family burying ground of

King Brude's family, though Brude himself is said to have been buried in Iona.

Soon after the Stones the road to Errogie crosses the Ness Castle moor and reaches what is generally known as the 'Inverness Lake District'. This consists of a chain of very attractive small moor lochs surrounded by heather-clad hills, with glimpses of Loch Ness in the glen below. Loch Ashie, the nearest to Inverness, is the town's water supply but, as it is no longer sufficient, the next loch, Loch Duntelchaig, is used also when needed, by means of pumps, the two lochs lying very near together. Loch Duntelchaig, Loch of the Fort of the Snail, is said to be so called because, when viewed across Loch Ness from Abriachan, the hill above it bears a close resemblance to that creature. But perhaps real snails abound there also, for it is certainly more than usually popular with every sort of wading bird, some of them rare in Scotland, as well as with a colony of black-headed gulls who nest near by, and many plover. Moreover, when the water of this loch is used for the town strange water beasties, if not actually snails, come out of the taps. Despite these two lochs, Inverness too easily runs out of water. Perhaps it would pay the Town Council to consult the green plover, for once he was a King of the Underworld and he still knows all about subterranean rivers and lakes and can find water under any dry and arid land if he so wishes. He has always kept his kingly crest, too, so one Gaelic name for him is 'bird of the little horn'. Gaelic bird names are often most expressive, 'the weeping, or lamenting, one' for the curlew, for instance, or 'the bird who likes sea-urchins' for the hoodie crow.

"... every sort of wading bird,"...

Close by these two lochs are several cairns and tumuli and a large boulder at the north-western end of Loch Ashie, locally known as King Fingal's Seat. It is said that once a battle took place on this moor between Fionn (or Fingal) and his men on the one hand and the men of Lochlann under their king, called Ashie, on the other. The remains of an ancient stone enclosure near by used to be called the Battle-ford. As far back as tradition runs, it has been claimed that soon after dawn on May Day a ghostly battle can be seen in progress here, the phantom armies being to all appearance as real as the men who see them. In 1870-71 it was very clearly seen on several occasions and was then believed to be some strange mirage of the fighting in France. But the Franco-Prussian War ended and people still saw large bodies of men in close formation, small bodies of cavalry facing an attack from the east, and even wounded men tearing strips from their shirts to bind up their wounds and pulling up sphagnum moss as a dressing for them.

During the First World War the phantom armies were said to have been seen by a cyclist who first saw three men walking ahead of him down the road; they turned a corner and when he reached it there they were in his path, and, to his horror, his bicycle passed right through them. He fell off in amazement and saw, behind and around him, the phantom armies.

A little further along the road, and having passed a rock believed by some to have once been the Castle of the King of the Ocean (whoever he was), one comes to two attractive small lochs beloved of children and trout, Loch an Eom Ruadha (Loch of the Grouse) and Lochan na Curra (Loch of the Heron). If you ever happen to be just below a heron when it rises, you will find it bears an almost terrifying resemblance to a pterodactyl or other prehistoric monster in miniature. One does not wonder that they were reputed to have come from the Underworld, where they were once guardians of the King's Treasure. A road takes off the hill road on the right and runs down past Kindrummond to Loch Ness-side, while another to the left makes for Strath Nairn. Shortly after this cross-roads comes a haunted hollow with a haunted well in it. Here the ghost of a nun was said to be in charge. Who she was or why she was here seems to have been forgotten, but it is remembered that the fortunate do not see her. It was up on these high moors, where the winter snows lie deep and long, that the last wolf in the district is believed to have been killed by a farmer's wife. She went to Dun Cia to borrow a griddle. On the way back she found her steps were being dogged by a wolf, whereupon she turned and hit it as hard as she could on the head with the borrowed griddle. Her blow broke its neck.

The grey loch near by is haunted by 'hobgoblins' and once a man lost in the mist saw the Devil driving his coach across the water. Of the bridge a little further on it is told how a party of travellers were caught there in a bad thunderstorm. All were terrified except one man who, perhaps to hide his fear, boasted that he feared nothing, neither God nor man; nothing could harm him. He was struck by lightning and killed; his companions were unharmed. Once this part was inhabited by a number of noted thieves, the most notorious fraternity in the Highlands. They were reputed particularly clever at causing the blame for their raids to fall on neighbouring clans, and so augmenting clan feuds, that they might fish in the troubled waters. On one occasion a very favourite dun horse was stolen from the farm of Balchraggan near by. No trace of it could be found. But on the following Christmas Eve while the farmer's wife was busy preparing the Christmas fare and hoping the storm which was raging would not interfere with their Christmas dinner, she heard a neigh and exclaimed to her husband: 'If he is alive above the earth that is the neigh of our dun horse.' The farmer went to the door and there stood his dun horse with two ankers of whisky, said to be worth £8 then, on his back and a good stout pony tied to his tail. It was thought that the whisky had been stolen from Ferintosh in the Black Isle and that the loaded horse, passing near, had escaped to its old home. The farmer's Christmas festivities were in no way diminished.

In due course the road reaches Glenfarigaig and one branch of it descends the very steep pass which is reputed to have been one of the deer-drives of the Feinn, its deep gorge seeming well suited to the purpose. Dun Yardil, or Dun Dearduil, perched high on a rock protecting the pass, was traditionally built and dwelt in by Deirdre and the sons of Uisneach. Dr Watson in his

Some Place Names of the North says: 'There is no doubt that
Deirdre's name became Dearduil in Scotland, for it appears so in
poetry.' A description of their dwelling in an ancient Galway
legend tells how 'they settled and made a dwelling for themselves
by the side of Loch Naois (or, maybe, Loch Ness) where they
could kill the salmon of the stream from out their door and the
bounding stag of the grey hills from their window', or perhaps
the other way round, for I have been unable to see the original
of this quotation and of two translations one gives 'Loch Naois'
and the other 'Loch Ness', and the two give the sporting facilities
from the opposite vantage points.

This story of Deirdre and the sons of Uisneach is supposed to
explain the unknown origin of the name Ness by deriving it from
Naois. The starry-eyed Deirdre—Deirdre of the Sorrows—one
associates with Ireland and Argyll but her story has spread here
also. It is said to be here, in the ancient Braoch of Dearduil, that
she dwelt with her husband Naois and his two brothers Aillean
and Ardan, the three sons of Uisneach, after they fled from
Ireland. All know of Deirdre—her hair was black as the raven's
wing, her lips red as the raven's blood, her skin white as snow.
She was the loveliest maiden in all Ireland and it was prophesied
of her that she would ruin Ireland. She was the ward of Conachar,
the elderly King of Ulster, and he planned to marry her and kept
her prisoner in a lonely tower until that day. But Conachar's
three young cousins, the sons of Uisneach came to visit him and
Deirdre's old nurse schemed so that they should see her while
hunting near her tower. Deirdre and Naois loved one another.
They, accompanied by his brothers, fled to Scotland. Conachar
sent Fergus Mac Ro, whom all men trusted, after them with
promises of forgiveness, peace and friendship if they would return
to Ulster. 'The promises of the King were fair but his heart was
false.' Deirdre distrusted him but the three brothers, pining in
exile, longed to believe; also they trusted Fergus. So they accepted
the King's promise, returned to Ireland and were duly murdered,
to the fury of Fergus and the great harm of Ireland. In the Loch
Ness version of the story the bodies of the three brothers were
laid in one grave. Then Deirdre looked into the open grave and
said: 'Let Naois of my love move to one side and let Aillean press

closer to Ardan. If the dead could only hear, you would make room for me.' And the dead heard and made room and she, laying herself down by her husband's side, died. But Conachar was angry and would not have her lie with her husband, even in death, so he had her body moved to the other bank of a near-by stream. Then out of each grave a pine grew and their trunks joined across the stream and they grew into one tree.

Once there was a smithy in this glen and the place where it stood is haunted by a headless creature who is quite friendly and aids travellers in distress, although to meet a man without a head who nevertheless can and will talk is said sometimes to upset very nervous travellers. In this glen, too, is a wishing well.

The left hand branch, or main road, continues along the high ground, past Errogie to the junction with the Loch Ness-side road which comes up to it from Foyers. After the junction it runs on through Whitebridge to Fort Augustus. Away to the left of it lies little Loch Killin near which, say some, Fionn was buried. This small glen is extremely fertile, and for a rather curious reason. There was once a magician who liked to be well supplied with all he needed but did not much care about work, so he decided to steal the fertility of the nine most fertile glens in Scotland and release it all on his own farm. He took the substance from glen after glen, bound it with a withy on his back and passed on to the next. The last he came to was Killin in Stratherrick. Here he met his match, a wizard cleverer than himself. This man took a knife of iron and cut the withy, whereupon the substance of the other eight glens poured out into Glen Killin and it has flowed with milk and honey ever since. Or so say its neighbours.

In the hills above Foyers is the cave where James Fraser of Foyers lay hid for nearly seven years after his escape from Culloden. Many stories are told of the search for him. It is said that a girl was once bringing him food when he, watching from his eyrie, saw that she was being followed by a soldier. He immediately shot him. On another occasion a young boy was going to the cave with a small cask of beer when he was overtaken by some troops who, guessing the destination of the beer cask, ordered the boy to lead them to his master. This he steadfastly refused to do, even when one of them cut off his hand, but he dropped the beer cask and it rolled away, leaping down to the Falls. The spot was long known as the Cask's Leap. It seems a pity that on this occasion 'the Dunbonnet', as the people called James Fraser to avoid naming him, was not looking, but it is pleasant to know that the boy's sacrifice was not in vain. James Fraser survived his long ordeal in the hills and was even among those fortunate ones whose family was not dispossessed of its land, his eldest son Hugh taking 'sasine' of Foyers and Boleskine in 1751 while his father was still a fugitive. Perhaps, as in some other cases, the heir kept aloof from the Rising by secret arrangement so that if it failed he could claim his father's lands and hold them in trust for the family. In due course Hugh's son succeeded him but outlived his only child. So ended the Frasers of Foyers, which place is now the property of Tube Investments Ltd. (once the British Aluminium Company).

It is recorded that when the contents of the mansion house were put up for sale, the family piper, furious that his old master's possessions were to go under the hammer, walked up and down in front of the house playing a pibroch of his own composing, 'Race of dogs, come here and get flesh'.

Not far off is the old churchyard of Boleskine. A notorious wizard, known as 'the Fraser Crowner' and 'the Man of the Devil', did in 1660 by his magic powers raise all the dead bodies in the churchyard: over their souls he had no power. Having raised them he could not lay them again and a horrible scene ensued till the situation was saved by one Thomas Houston who came in haste and laid them all.

II

NORTH OF INVERNESS

At two o'clock in the morning, if you open
your window and listen,
You will hear the feet of the Wind that is
going to call the sun.

RUDYARD KIPLING

Muirtown House

6

INVERNESS TO DINGWALL

Dear spot of my birth, though high swelling ocean
Should part me and cause me far from thee to rove,
While my bosom can beat, I will think with emotion
Of Muirtown, sweet Muirtown, the spot that I love.

by JAMES PATTERSON, born at Green of
Muirtown early in the nineteenth century

THIS CHAPTER begins at Muirtown Bridge, over the
Caledonian Canal. Of course that is all wrong because
this is now a part of Inverness, just as Clachnaharry is, but
it is only very recently a part and one must start somewhere.

Just north of the bridge, on the left, are the gates of Muirtown
with their lion guards. The lions are Italian and are believed to
have brought with them from Italy a southern love of music and
dancing. On Midsummer Night, when all inanimate things have

life, they come down from their pillars and dance together in and out of the trees to a sort of 'Port a Beul' accompaniment of their own loud purring—or should one say growling? Poor things, they were stoned not long ago by one of the Inverness gangs and one lost his tail. ' 'E's a stranger; 'eave 'alf a brick at 'im,' as Mr Punch once remarked. Now they are under official protection but, alas, too late to save a tail.

It was on the Green of Muirtown that the Government representative, Sir Patrick Strathan, held court in October 1718 to assess what many of those 'out' in the '15 should pay as fines and what the confiscated estates were worth. He had an uphill task and found claimants for dowries, pensions, leases and endowments by the dozen on every estate. These people, relatives and close friends of the owners, all had, most surprisingly in a day when such things were rare in the North, documents to prove their rights. Indeed, poor Sir Patrick got comparatively little for the Government while the innumerable 'dowries' and 'rents' were quietly sent over the sea to support 'the rebels'.

In pre-Reformation days Muirtown was a monastery and lazar house. Several places in Scotland, and a number in England also, are said to have been cursed by the outgoing monks when seized from the Roman Catholic Church at the Reformation, curses which in some places are believed to affect all who hold those lands to this day. But Muirtown is the only case I know of which, by tradition, was blessed by the Church for its use by the laity. The story is that the last Roman Catholic Bishop of Moray, Bishop Hepburn, was dying just when the Reformation was getting into its stride. He was a far-sighted man and decided to try to save something from the wreck that was to come, so he made over the Muirtown property, a large one in those days, to his Protestant nephew on his death bed, as though it were his personal property to bequeath; but with this condition. He and his should hold and use the lands with the blessing of Holy Church upon them so long as the Reformed Church held sway in Scotland, but when the Roman Catholic Church came back into power (as he fervently believed it would) the then owner must return the lands to the Church. Should he fail in this trust a terrible curse would fall on him and his. The present house is believed to have been

built on the old foundations of the monastery and is in the form
of a cross. Tradition has it that the present kitchen was once the
monastery chapel. Certainly it would be hard to find a kitchen
less like a kitchen and more like a church. It has a vaulted roof
about 30 feet from the floor, Gothic church windows, a gallery
supported on pillars and a small clock tower which holds a bell
also. Beneath the stone flags of the floor, in front of the spot
where the altar must once have stood, is the Monks' Well, never
known to run dry in the hottest summer.

If anything in the way of a ghost haunts the old house, however, it is not as one would expect in the chapel-kitchen but in the
modern dining room, built on the site of the old refectory less
than a hundred years ago. Here, at 8.20 p.m., a silence falls on all
in the room. I have myself known it to fall both during a formal
dinner party and upon a young, gay ball party chattering like
starlings, as well as on quieter occasions. After the silence has
lasted a few moments (said to be the time taken by the monks
saying grace) the door of the room quietly opens and breaks the
spell. Does it open for the Abbot? Or to let out—what?

The Basin of the Canal near the bridge repays watching; sea-
going ships abound and, tiny though the basin is compared with
a real port, a surprising number of foreign flags can be seen and
strange tongues heard. During the war this was a depot for
various highly explosive materials which were re-shipped here
for the Fleet and other purposes. One direct hit, it was said, and
Inverness would vanish. Enemy planes flew over several times
but never with much real energy, and no harm was done. Inverness, accustomed to being burnt, razed to the ground or blown up
at short intervals for some 900 years, was agreeably surprised.
The next point of interest lies to the left of the road, shortly before
'the awful' Clachnaharry Corner (a bad local 'black spot') is
reached. It is a small spring, now known as Montrose's Well.
The same Duff of Muirtown who shipped the lions home and
made the heart-shaped lawn in front of the house (the heart being
his crest) had this spring housed in a stone shelter on which a Latin
inscription invokes the nymphs of the fountain and grove. It is
said that as Montrose was escorted south on his way to his trial
and execution he complained of thirst. His escort stopped a

passing farmer's boy and asked for water and he directed them to this well, where Montrose was permitted to dismount and drink his fill. It cannot have been a very desirable drink, however, for the spring is a slightly sulphur one and it is pleasant to know that three miles further on the Provost of Inverness had wine waiting for the illustrious prisoner and polite condolences, despite the fact that Montrose in his heyday had bombarded the town 'with two brass cannon'. The old name for the well before Montrose visited it was Fuaran Ault an Ionnlaid, Well of the Anointing Burn. The Anointing Burn, a tiny stream, runs only a few feet from the well. This little burn rises as a spring on the slopes of Craig Phadraig and tradition has it that when St. Columba baptised King Brude and his followers in the fort he used the water of this spring, he and his monks having no font or holy water stoup with them. St. Columba therefore blessed the actual spring and consecrated it, then used the water as it bubbled up. The monks of the Muirtown Monastery were believed always to fill the holy water stoup in their chapel from this burn, holding it to be already consecrated, and also to use it for the good of the patients in their hospital. Some say that some of St. Columba's healing powers were believed to have entered the water and that that was why Muirtown was chosen as the site for a monastic hospital.

Be that as it may, in the nineteenth century the medicinal properties of the well itself were reckoned locally as only second to Strathpeffer's hot springs and it was widely praised as a cure for gout, rheumatism and kindred ailments. The cure consisted in walking to the well before breakfast and again in the evening in all weathers, to drink a draught of fresh water. The water was believed valueless unless drawn bubbling direct from the spring, so perhaps the air and exercise also helped the cure.

Not long ago, between the wars, Inverness got a terrible shock, for the census figures showed that its population was falling so fast that it might soon become smaller than the number of inhabitants necessary to a burgh. Was Inverness to lose its Royal Charter, one of the oldest in Scotland? Not on your life! Steps were taken, and soon Inverness had 'incorporated' Clachnaharry Village and other bits of the surrounding country. The ancient charter was safe but Clachnaharry was not, for that prosperous little village had been wont to house many who worked in Inverness; the trains from north and west stopped there and for a penny ticket you could journey right into the heart of the town. Now the railway saw no point in keeping two stations going in Inverness and so Clachnaharry Station was closed and the inhabitants had to walk to work. Soon, more than half of them had moved 'into town' and it took the village years to recover.

Just beyond Clachnaharry, standing on the hillside above the village, is a small monument. This was erected by a Duff of Muirtown to commemorate a battle fought here between Munros and Mackintoshes. The Munros had been south in force on a cattle raid and were on their way home, driving the captured beasts. Their path led through Mackintosh country; that was unavoidable and the Mackintosh of the day demanded the usual percentage as the price of free passage. But the Munros, though agreeing 'in principle', disputed the amount and a fierce running fight ensued in which both sides claimed the victory. It is reputed to have been the last cattle-raiding fight in this part of the Highlands, hence the monument. Clachnaharry is said to mean either Stone of Repentance or Stone of the Watching. Whichever be the correct interpretation of the name, the stone on which the monument now stands has the reputation of having been one of the Inverness outposts in time of danger and the raising of a monument on it, thereby destroying its old use as a watch point, was felt to be symbolic of the Peace of Scotland. Many of the landing craft for the landings in Normandy in 1944 were anchored in the Firth awaiting 'D' Day, in full view of this Stone of Peace.

The next place of interest, to the right of the road near the sea, is Bunchrew House. This is probably the only house in the world whose drawing room mantelpiece was the subject of litigation which reached the House of Lords. It was in this wise. The fireplace in question was carved with the arms and supporters of Mackenzie of Allangrange; Lord Seaforth and his wife came to tea and noticed it. Lord Seaforth then wrote ordering its removal as he alone, he claimed, was entitled to the supporters. The Fraser-Mackenzies refused and the fight was on. Local gossip had it that Lord Seaforth, believed to be 'a nice quiet man', had been driven to this action by his German wife who, being a German, was unpopular; and when news came that 'Bunchrew' had won there was joy all round. But the fight went on until at last it reached the Lords where not only was the Fraser-Mackenzies' use of the disputed supporters upheld, but Lord Seaforth was warned that *he* had no right to use them. Bunchrew House is now flats.

Almost as far as Beauly the road runs along the shore of the Beauly Firth, through rich farm land. At high tide the firth, with its views of the hills of the West beyond, is beautiful; at low tide it is a mud flat beloved of many kinds of sea and shore birds from swans to smallest sandpipers. Several side roads take off before the Beauly River, famous for its salmon fishing, is reached. All are pleasant but by far the finest and most worth-while is the road to Chisholm's Tooth, Cannich and Affric—Strath Glass in fact— just beyond the Beauly. First, however, the road passes the entrance to Beaufort Castle. This has long been the seat of the Chiefs of Clan Fraser and is famous in both history and legend. Perhaps the best known of its many owners was that old Lord Lovat of the '45 of whom it was said that he had deserved hanging many times over but was eventually executed for a crime of which he was quite innocent. But justice at that period of Highland history was indeed far to seek.

To digress from the main road for a moment; just past Beau- fort Castle the road to Strath Glass takes off to the left, and very fine it is. First comes the small church of Kiltarlity, with its grave- yard almost overhanging the river. More than once, when the high snows melt, the river has overflowed the churchyard and eaten far into its banks. Once a woman passing the church gate after dark on her way to visit a married daughter saw, as she thought, the daughter with her husband and baby waiting to meet her. They seemed in distress. She hurried forward but was unable to get near them; they seemed always just out of reach. Puzzled, she glanced behind her to see how far she had come and, to her horror, there was the young couple behind her. She looked to right and to left and there they were also. She then realised they were ghosts, and fled. A number of others saw them and eventually the Minister himself took notice and waited in the churchyard until midnight, when, seeing a movement, he stepped forward and there they were, weeping and wringing their hands. He asked what was amiss and promised to help 'if it lay within his Christian duty'. The young man then glided to the edge of the graveyard and pointed to the fast-flowing grey river, while the girl, crouching at his feet, sobbed bitterly. At this moment the cock crew and the two seemed to fade away into the grey water where, the Minister thought, an old woman joined them. He had an idea. Hurrying into the church he lit a lamp, got out the church registers and pored over them. Yes, it was as he had thought. In the floods some eighteen months previously a little piece of the graveyard had been washed away. It had contained three graves—those of a mother, her daughter who had died in childbirth and the daughter's young husband, a wood-cutter killed in an accident.

Next day the Minister searched the river bank and also made known what he sought. Soon a small heap of bones, human and (probably) animal, grew in the church porch. A funeral service was held, a new grave dug and a new headstone with three names on it erected, by public subscription for many desired to see the ghosts laid. Thereafter there was peace.

The road runs by the River Beauly through wooded hills and crags, past the famous Chisholm's Tooth rock (for this is Chisholm country) to the village of Crask of Aigus. All the way up the glen the country grows more and more lovely. It passes Aigus House on the right, now an Old People's Home but before that the home of a rich and elderly couple who were Plymouth Brethren. Like most of their Church they held their riches as a trust. When young they had been concerned with carrying the Bible, the actual book, to as many people as possible, and this they continued to do every winter as long as they were able. But in the summer they had other fish to fry. They returned to Aigus, engaged a 'nannie', a governess and a tutor and proceeded to fill the house and the staff's cottages with the children of missionaries of any Christian denomination who had no relatives to take them for the holidays, or families which would otherwise have had to be divided as no one relative could take all. Here the children, with pets, ponies, boats, etc., spent what must often have been the summer of their lives.

In this valley, too, stood the Chisholm Stone, the rallying point of Clan Chisholm in arms, but it is now submerged owing to the hydro-electric dam. Next comes Cannich, with its pleasant little hotel on the Cannich River, and then Affric. Perhaps Glen Affric is the loveliest of all the smaller Highland glens. It has everything—lochs and bare mountains, rivers and islands, birch woods and green land. No wonder that MacBain in his *Place Names of the Highlands and Islands of Scotland* suggests that Affric was once a river goddess. She chose her home well if so. It is now the property of the Hydro-Electric Board but, though much of the low land has been flooded, it is claimed that its beauty is unspoiled. In the Lodge itself are some famous sketches, done direct on to the walls, by Landseer when he stayed there to stalk with pencil and sketchbook.

But even the most beautiful places may not be all they seem. Such creatures as midges and mayfly are plentiful here. Once a woman swallowed a mayfly and immediately became overcome by a desperate, ravening thirst—for this is the vengeance of the mayfly. Indeed an old ill-wish is 'The thirst of the mayfly (or water demon) on thee,' the same word in Gaelic, Lon-Craois, being used both for mayfly and for water demon. The sufferer hastened for help to a wise-woman who lived near by, then hurried home to carry out her instructions. First she prepared and ate a salt herring so that the mayfly, tasting it, would itself be overcome by thirst; then she went to the river side, knelt down, leaning close over the water, and opened her mouth. The sound and scent of the fast-running water was too much for the thirsty mayfly and he at once flew out of her mouth, leaving the woman in peace.

It is time to return to the main road. Beauly, said to take its name from Beaulieu, beautiful place, so christened by the monks, is less than half a mile away. A very typical Highland village, though larger than most, it stands at the head of the Firth of its name, looking out to sea. Once it had a fine Priory, the burying place of the Lovat family, now chiefly a ruin except for the mortuary chapel of the Lovats, over which a strange and baleful light is said to gleam at times. Some say it is a 'death-light' foretelling the arrival of yet another Lovat in the family vault but others hold

that it is seen before the great festivals of the Church such as
Christmas and Easter, and that it does but light:

> All the graves of all the ghosts
> Who rise on Christmas Eve in hosts
> To dance and carol in festivity
> For joy of Jesus Christ's nativity.

★   ★   ★   ★   ★

> Two and two, about, about
> Singing the end of advent out.
>
> MASEFIELD

This is certainly a much pleasanter idea, but whichever is the

Beauly Priory

correct explanation fifty years ago no one would willingly have spent a night in the Priory ruins.

As the Frasers have always remained loyal Roman Catholics it is doubtful whether the Priory would have been left to fall into ruin, as so many were after the Reformation, but for Cromwell. He had large parts of it pulled down and the stones taken to Inverness for the building of his 'Citadel' there. The Priory was founded by John Byset, 'lord of Lovat', in 1230 and the monks were of the Order of Valliscaulians, 'who delighted in gardening'. Hence an old bard of the Mackenzies describes it as Manchainn nan Lios, The Monastery of the Gardens. It is now under the care of the Board of Ancient Monuments and enough of it remains to be well worth a visit. Not far from Beauly is Carn nan Chlarsair, the Cairn of the Harper, believed to be the burying place of the last of the harpers who once provided the music for the Priory services.

Another old church near Beauly, the Church of Kilchriosd now a ruin, is said to have been set on fire, when full of Mackenzies, by the Macdonalds, not a single man escaping. It was reputed haunted and for long no one would approach it at night, but at last a young tailor, sorely needing money to get married, accepted a wager that he would spend as much of the night alone in the old church as was needed 'to sew a pair of hose' (trousers?). He settled himself in one of the pews and, by the light of a tallow candle, began his work. At first all was quiet and the sewing got on well. Then, as the last stroke of midnight tolled from the church clock, the tailor saw, leaning towards him out of the darkness, a fleshless skull with grinning jaws and eye sockets without eyes. In a horrible hoarse voice the skull spoke to him.

'See'st thou the big grey head without food, O Tailor?'

'That I see, but this I sew,' replied the terrified little man and bravely went on sewing.

'See'st thou this long grizzled throat without food, O Tailor?' demanded the Thing.

'That I see, but this I sew,' answered the tailor, and indeed he was now sewing frantically.

'See'st thou this long grizzled trunk without food, O Tailor?'

spoke the Head, but it was drawing nearer and most of its 'body' could now be easily and horribly seen.

'That I see, but this I sew,' said the tailor again as well as he could through chattering teeth.

'See'st thou this long grizzled thigh without food, O Tailor?'

'That I see, but this I sew,' once more said the man doggedly (only three more stitches to do).

'See'st thou this long grizzled arm without food, O Tailor?' And the creature put forth its hand toward him with a low clattering rattle.

Frantically the tailor took his last three stitches, finished off and broke the thread, just as a horrid bony hand was stretched to seize him and the Thing said through its fleshless jaws:

'See'st thou the great grizzled paw without food, O Tailor?'

The tailor sprang to his feet and made for the door of the church (he had had the sense to choose a seat near it) and as he got the door open the skeleton fingers caught at his leg, leaving black bruises on it, but he got out safely and closed the door behind him. Then, as he leant shivering against it, he heard the blind fumblings of the eyeless thing as, failing to find the latch, it began to rattle and bang the wood. Next day the scratches and dents made by its finger bones in the woodwork could be clearly seen; some say they are there still. The tailor won his wager as he well deserved to do, and he and his bride lived happily ever after.

The brave little tailor's reply has become a saying in Gaelic, for one who will not be turned from his object: 'That I see but this I sew.' Another saying was: 'The great grizzled one catch you,' meaning the Devil, whom it was unlucky to name.

It is curious what a large part tailors and smiths played in old stories. Smiths, of course, once had magic powers or at least were associated with 'cold iron' which had, but why tailors? It is re-membered, for instance, that the Devil once wished to become a tailor, so, being a sensible person, he apprenticed himself to a master tailor of repute who tried honestly to teach him his trade. But 'he who doesn't knot his thread will lose his first stitch' is the greatest and most valuable secret in the trade (so it is said) and this the Devil could never learn, since the power to tie a knot had been taken from him at his fall, so he never became a tailor.

Nevertheless, his time as an apprentice was not wasted, since his antics in knot-tying are said to have inspired the well-known reel tune *The De'il amang the Tailors*.

The Devil figures in many Gaelic sayings and proverbs; for instance, the equivalent of England's neat 'Ill-gotten, ill-spent' is 'What's got at the Devil's head will be lost at his tail.' Another is ' "Great cry, little wool", as the Devil said when he sheared a sow', though the story behind that last seems lost.

The story of the tailor and the skeleton is interesting as being the only case I know of the traditional skeleton with rattling bones or clanking chains appearing in the Highlands, though I fancy the clanking of chains may still be heard in certain ancient dungeons, but the ghostly skeleton is missing. (*Can* an inanimate object such as a chain have a ghost? A nice point.) The white shrouded figure of the traditional ghost is equally rare in the North; such white shades as have been reported have varying names in different districts but I know of none classified as a ghost. They might be spirits or fairies or the Highland variety of the Banshee perhaps, but not ghosts. Highland ghosts usually have the semblance of a man or woman who died before their hour, either by accident, murder or suicide, or occasionally from plague or in childbirth, and usually wear the clothes they wore at the time of their death. Anyone whose full time on earth was not accomplished must 'walk' until his proper time came to die, when his ghost usually disappeared. This is held to explain the frequent 'haunts' which are seen regularly for a number of years and then never again.

There is also the rule that anyone who has been drowned walks until a grave is prepared for him; if it is not dug on land to which in life he had a right, this of course including a family burying ground or vault, then the ground must be purchased by a gift of corn or other food laid in the grave, or the ghost cannot rest. Highland ghosts frequently continue in perpetuity their last act on earth. It may well be a fitting punishment for a suicide that not only can he not leave this world at will but that in addition he must continually re-hang himself or lean from a high window about to jump until his appointed hour of death comes to free him; that a murderer might have to continue repeating his crime with all the fear and horror that must surely grow with it might also be just, but what about the innocent victim? Surely he should not have to put up with being continuously murdered until the day on which he should have died brings release. Perhaps only the villain is a ghost, the victim merely an appearance, or one seeking revenge. Or, as I have heard argued, many 'murderees' ask to be murdered by their own folly and so should take at least a part of the blame.

Owing to the ghosts' habit of wearing the clothes in which they died it follows that a new one, i.e. one in modern dress, must be very hard to distinguish from an ordinary person, but there are two definite proofs. One is the sudden feeling of intense cold which heralds their presence and the other, to be practised if you suspect an approaching figure to be supernatural, is to look for a moment at the apparition (if such it be) and then turn your back on it. If you see a man coming from the north and he is still straight in front of you when you turn south, and again due east and due west of you, then you can be sure it is a ghost and should try to learn its need even though it causes you to say, with a Danish friend of mine, 'I was so frightened my hair stood on tiptoe.'

Of course there have always been a few ghosts that could never be laid:

> Woe's me, woe's me
> The acorn's no yet
> Fallen from the tree
> That's to grow to the oak
> That's to make the cradle
> That's to house the babe
> That's to grow to the man
> That's to lay me.

After Beauly the road leaves the water and crosses the Moor of Ord to Muir of Ord village. From the moor one road to the Black Isle takes off. Muir of Ord is itself something of a road centre, for from it roads go south to Inverness, north to Dingwall and beyond, east to the Black Isle, and west to Garve and Strome Ferry. The moor, an unusually flat one, was the subject of one of the Brahan Seer's prophecies: 'When a wood on the Muir of Ord grows to a man's height, regiments of soldiers shall be seen

HTL H

there drawn up in battle order.' A wood grew all right and if airmen count as 'soldiers' perhaps the prophecy may be said to have been fulfilled, for a huge R.A.F. camp covered most of the moor during the last war. But let us hope that another of his prophecies will not be fulfilled. There is a stone, Clach an t' Seasaidh, between Muir of Ord and Beauly at a place called Windhill. It is supposed to be part of what was once a 'Druid's Circle' of standing stones and it is now fallen and broken up but was said to have long stood erect. 'The day will come,' said the Seer, 'when the ravens will, from the top of it, drink their three fills for three successive days of the blood of the Mackenzies.'

Continuing north, the road comes to Conon Bridge, a village on a steep hill which slopes down to the River Conon. It used to be famous locally for its quite lovely cottage gardens, a rarity in the Highlands, but now Dingwall's gardens are the more note-worthy. Watson gives its name as meaning Hound-stream, the old Gaelic name for an otter being water-hound. Otters were animals of great importance in olden days, for among them were certain King Otters and the fortunate man who was able to capture one of these rare creatures would be given the granting of any wish he might frame, as ransom. If, however, he preferred to kill a King Otter and wear its skin, or a piece of it, no sword nor spear nor bullet could harm him. This was not always easy, however, as the King Otter was himself invulnerable except for one tiny white spot, about the size of a half-crown, below the chin. Alexander Carmichael says of them: 'The water-dog is the high king of the black otters (Biast-dubh). He is but rare among creatures of sea and land; there is but one water-dog to every seven black otters. There are always seven black otters along with the Brown Water-Dog, serving him day and night, and Oh! Thou King of Knowledge!, it is themselves that are attentive to him!' If a man put his tongue to the liver of an ordinary black otter his tongue had power to heal burns for the rest of his life. 'The burn will not blister, but be whole in a moment.'

Possibly the common otter had other magic powers now for-gotten. They were certainly beasts of repute. One of the Mac-donalds of the Isles composed a love song for his bride and among the many gifts he offers her in it are 100 otters:

Thou daughter of the King of bright lit mansions
On the night that our wedding is on us,
If living man I be in Duntulm,
I will go bounding to thee with gifts.
Thou wilt get a hundred badgers, dwellers in banks,
A hundred brown otters, natives of streams.

The River Conon was also noted for its waterhorse. A party of villagers were cutting corn by the 'false ford' in the river when their attention was attracted by a movement in the water. It was a huge waterhorse. Just as mid-day struck it drew itself out of the deep water into the shallows and cried out: 'Behold the hour has come, but not the man.' It repeated the cry three times and then disappeared into a pool. A few minutes later the harvesters saw a man, a stranger to them, riding towards the river at a great pace. The men hurried forward to tell him what they had seen and to warn him not to approach the water. But the man laughed at them and would have put his horse at the river and ridden into it had they not seized his bridle. Angry at his refusal to appreciate his danger, and determined not to allow him to ride to what they believed was certain death, the harvesters pulled him from his horse and shut him up in 'the Auld Kirk' nearby. When one o'clock chimed from the church clock they felt the hour was now gone and he could be safely released. But when they entered the church the man was not to be seen. They finally found him, drowned in an old stone trough containing perhaps two inches of water. He had had a fit—or so it was suggested. The waterhorse has not been seen there since.

7

THE BLACK ISLE

The haunted hoosie is down at the end o' the brae
Nae step on its stairs, na e'en the paw o' a poussie.
Alike are the day, the morn and yesterday
To the haunted hoosie.

LEWIS SPENCE

MANY AND VARIED are the reasons given for this name, for, as was once said, 'The Black Isle is neither black nor an island.' The 'Isle' part of the name is easily understood for the peninsula holds to the mainland by so narrow a neck that in the days when water rather than land was the ordinary medium of communication in the Highlands this neck would have little importance. But why 'black'? The most usual explanation is that it was once covered with fir woods. But so was all the North in the days of the Caledonian Forest and as the old farming families of the Black Isle are reputed to go back there almost, if not quite, as far as the Clan names on the mainland, this fine farm land was probably early cleared. The same objection applies to the idea of its being heather-covered. It has been suggested that it was so named because snow never lies. This seems more likely: snow does lie there, of course, after a heavy fall but the peninsula's high back often stands out black or, more frequently, piebald when the adjacent mainland is purest white. Another suggestion is that the Isle remained a pocket of an early dark-haired race little affected by Norse and Celtic invaders.

The road to the Black Isle takes off from the main North-South road near Muir of Ord and, having successfully reached the 'island', splits in two, one going by the south side and the other along the north side of the peninsula, to re-unite at Cromarty. I have heard it argued that both these roads are far more beautiful and rewarding to the tourist than their sister roads along the shores of the two firths. The argument is that whereas the

traveller on the mainland roads sees only tree-bordered fields and
the cultivated Black Isle, the visitor on the peninsula's south side
looks across the Beauly Firth over rich farm land to Inverness with
its spires and to the blue hills beyond, while the northern road
looks over the Cromarty Firth and the Ross-shire moors to Ben
Wyvis itself, 'The Noble or Majestic One', often radiant in a
cloak of snow.

The roads of the Black Isle, however, are not wanting in
beauty and riches of their own. Their banks and hedges vie with
Devon in the profusion of blossom, hawthorn, broom and roses
in their seasons, primrose, bluebells and wood-anemones, and
later the rich pattern of the summer flowers with here and there
sheets of willow-herb setting new cut woodland aflame. Fine
trees offer shade and the Moray Firth can sparkle bluely. At the
hamlet of Tore the road to North Kessock leads off to the right
while the main road continues through Munlochy to Avoch,
Fortrose and Rosemarkie. Not far from here is Redcastle, once
a royal castle founded by William the Lion under the name of
Edirdore, the Place between the Waters, but more often called
Tarradale. It was held for the King for some centuries but eventually fell into ruin and was rebuilt by the Tutor of Kintail, not on
the original site but near it. The Mackenzies of Kintail lost it in
the eighteenth century and then it changed hands many times,
ending up as Redcastle, the property of the Baillies of Dochfour.
The Duke of Windsor, when Prince of Wales, was a guest here.

Nearby is the House of Kilcoy. Both of these old castles have
bad reputations where haunts and curses are concerned. Of
Kilcoy it is told that when this house was planned, and building
was about to begin, an old packman was offered shelter for the
night in a stable there and then was, some say, murdered, while
others say he was buried alive beneath the foundations of the
house. However that may be, he disappeared but owing to his
wandering way of life was not soon missed. Meanwhile Kilcoy
House grew apace and soon was finished and occupied, but the
owners got no peace. Every night the old packman's ghost
appeared and all through the hours of darkness he could be heard
crying in surprisingly loud and strong tones: 'Vengeance, I seek
vengeance.' Despite efforts to conceal the ghost his cries were

heard by many, and at last the authorities moved and his body was discovered beneath the foundations. A trial followed and justice, it is to be supposed, was done as the ghost with his cries for vengeance was never seen or heard again.

But murder and Kilcoy seem to have been close friends, for the story goes that towards the end of the seventeenth century a plague of madness broke out among cattle in the district, whole herds dying in two or three days. Whereupon the proprietors of Redcastle and Kilcoy jointly offered a large reward to anyone able to cure the affected cattle or stop the spread of the plague. An old wizard came forward and said he would stop the plague if, as well as the reward, they would provide a human sacrifice. They agreed, decoyed an old man to a lonely barn and there allowed the wizard to murder him in an unpleasant manner and to make a powder from his heart, liver and other parts from which to make an elixir for the animals. Before he died, the old man cursed them, saying: 'Let the day never come when the family of Redcastle shall be without a female idiot or the family of Kilcoy without a fool.' The Brahan Seer is said to have foretold the murder and the curse and its effects and to have added:

> There are curses on the shedding of blood.
> When the strong castle of Kilcoy
> Shall stand cold and empty,
> Then shall jackdaws and ravens
> Frequent its lone halls.

He also foretold for Rosehaugh in the Black Isle that 'Foolish pride without sense will put in place of the seed of the deer the seed of the goat.' This is said to have come to pass when, as the result of extravagance, the Mackenzies, whose armorial bearings include a stag's head, had to sell to the Fletchers, but why the goat was supposed to represent the Fletchers does not appear.

North Kessock, with its ferry to Inverness, is a pleasant village lying under the shelter of the Ord of Kessock, on which one of the larger of the old vitrified forts once stood. Kessock has given its name to the tiny and most delicious Kessock herrings, caught, it would appear, in no other fishing ground and in my opinion the nicest fish to eat of all in our northern sea. I was told as a child, by 'Old Cookie' who came from this part, that these, and not the full-sized herring, were the fishes created by Our Lord to provide the miraculous draught of fishes, which is why they are sweeter than all other fish. He created them smaller than other herrings because the Sea of Galilee is smaller than other seas. When St. Joseph of Arimathea brought the Stone of Scone to Scotland he brought also, for his voyage, some of these little herrings dried and cured. As they had been his main food supply during his long voyage, the saint was rather tired of them by the time he arrived, and when he landed he threw those that were left into the sea. God granted them life again and they swam searching for a nice quiet inland water such as the one they had left, and decided on the Moray Firth to the great benefit of the Kessock fishing fleet. But there are some who say that St. Kessock rang his bell and ordered them into his waters and that it was they who taught the Highlanders how to kipper herrings.

Having returned to the Cromarty road, the first point of interest we come to is the Black Cairn to the right of the road not far from the Firth itself. It is a steep, grass-covered hill rising almost sheer for about fifty feet. It has been claimed as an early lake dwelling or crannog but seems more probably one of the old duns once so abundant on the Highland seaboard, or it might even be  an unusually fine burial mound. Which it is has never been settled, but it is undoubtedly a hill made with hands and it shares in the belief so widespread in Scotland that the original builders, in the forms of swans, can be seen circling the cairn and watching over it. To this cairn they come in Christmas week; if they circle in silence all is well with the world but if they call as they circle the hill it is a sign of trouble for the district or, some say, a hard winter to come. Because every swan has on its tongue a drop of the Devil's blood which enables it to foresee and to some extent warn of future events, the omen of the swans was a good omen. So says Alexander Carmichael:

Who should be guiding in front?
The queen of luck, the white swan.

All over Scotland there are scattered crannogs and duns and early burial mounds, and legends associate the swan with many of them, it being believed that swans are (or contain) the spirits of the original owners or builders of such places. How widespread this belief really was I do not know but I have come across several cases myself. At Fasnacloich in Argyll, for instance, there is a crannog at the foot of the loch. Swans rarely visit this loch but are said always to appear there, flying or swimming round the mound, before the death of a 'Stewart of Fasnacloich' or any owner of the land, despite the fact that the Stewarts sold the property many years ago. Once when I was staying at Fasnacloich with other guests, a visitor came in from shooting, very apologetic, because, he explained, he did not know his hostess did not like swans to be shot and, seeing a bevy of wild swans on the loch, he had fired before the keeper could stop him. His hostess replied that it was only on account of a local superstition that she protected swans; it did not really matter. 'Swans,' she added, 'are very rarely seen on the loch. These are the first for many years.' In the middle of dinner a telegram was brought to her. It was to say that 'Stewart of Fasnacloich' had died that day and that they were bringing his body to the family graveyard for burial. The undoubted belief in the glen at that time was that the swans were the spirits of the old inhabitants of the land, come to welcome the latest member of their blood to die. The swans, however, belonged to the land, not to any family on it. This particular swan could not be used for food, delicious though they are, so strong was the belief in its spirit origin. Instead, it was discreetly buried. Is it possible that swans, which figure in so many Highland stories, were once goddesses here, or sacred to some early deity? Birds return to the same place year after year from half across the world, and not just to the same district but to the same tree or marshy patch. Is it possible, then, that swans still return to the mounds where once long ago their fathers were worshipped or, more important, fed?

The first place of any size we come to along this south shore road is the small fishing village of Avoch. It is charming, with its

fishing harbour and boats, though certainly it was more picturesque when all or most boats had sails. My mother had maids
from Avoch on several occasions, and very nice girls they were.
But one thing they would not do—they would not burn fish
bones with other rubbish, because:

> Roast me and boil me
> But dinna burn ma bones
> Or then I'll be a stranger
> About your hearth stones,

said the haddock, and if they disregarded the warning their families might catch no more fish. One very nice but very quiet tablemaid my mother had from this district, some fifty years ago,
proved to be a changeling. We, of course, knew nothing of this
until one day a letter carrying bad news for her arrived; her
mother was seriously ill. My mother suggested she should go
home at once and was hurrying to look up rail connections when
the sobbing girl intervened.

'Mother's very ill. I can't go home. I mustn't go home. You
see, I wouldn't be a good person to have in the house if she died.
You see, I am a changeling.'

She was obviously serious and very unhappy. My mother
could only ask with equal seriousness and much sympathy how
she knew she was a changeling and what harm it could do her
mother if she were one. About the latter she was not very clear.
A changeling in the house of death would endanger the soul of
the dying. Why, she did not know. She supposed the fairies who
had sent the changeling might make her steal the soul for them
as it left the body. Or perhaps it was a sin to befriend a changeling
as her mother had always befriended her, and she would rather
die than risk harming her mother.

As to how she knew she was a changeling, that was simple.
As a baby, she said, she was like the others (she was one of eleven
brothers and sisters), fat and fair. Then, she told us, her hair came
in black and she got thin and cried and cried, especially at night.
One night, when she was nearly a year old, and crying 'fit to
raise the roof', her father, 'who's a bit hot tempered like sometimes', picked her up and flung her to the foot of the bed, where
she hit her head on the iron bedpost (cold iron) and lay very still.

All night she lay still and her father and mother thought she was dead and were frightened. But in the morning 'I wasn't dead at all, any more, and I never cried again either, so then they knew I must be a changeling. And when I grew up dark and all of them so fair, then we all knew it. It is lonely being a changeling. I can't ever marry, I'd bring the curse on my husband's home, and I can't ever go to any of my people when they need me. I can't even go to church. It is a lonely thing to be a changeling.'

Changelings are very rare now in the Highlands. Indeed, Margaret may have been the last. But, like most of these old beliefs, the real thing when you meet it is very different from the fairy tales and has all sorts of practical and reasonable repercussions. The 'facts' may be much the same, it is the effect on the ordinary everyday people which is so different. In the changeling 'fairy tales' the tragedy is the mother losing her child and we are all pleased when the wicked changeling is cleverly scored off. In real life the tragedy is the lonely and perhaps frightened changeling itself, for a changeling, having no soul, has no part nor lot with human beings.

Not far from Avoch are the ruins of Ormonde Castle, where the standard was first raised in the Scottish Wars of Independence. After Avoch comes Fortrose, a most charming and attractive small town. Here are the ruins of the Priory, beautiful as these red sandstone ruins always are. The Priory seems to have been usually known as the Chanonry, from a Gaelic name meaning the Place of Canons. It is described by one of the old Mackenzie bards as the Chanonry of the Bells, a nice name. A local story claims that it was not entirely Lady Seaforth who was to blame for the death of the Brahan Seer as set out in the chapter on 'West from Dingwall'. She merely handed him over to the Prior of this Priory as a man having dealings with the Devil. It was the Prior and his monks who condemned him to death for witchcraft. A stone to the right of the monastery path is said to mark the spot where the Seer was burnt and the spot, too, where he uttered his well-known prophecy about the Mackenzies. He is also believed to have told the monks: 'I do not curse you but I see the curse you have brought on yourselves. As you have ruined the homes of others (his family are said to have died of starvation since none

dared help them), so soon shall your home fall. The birds shall
nest and the rabbits burrow where you now defile the House of
God with your folly. Others shall teach in this place the things
which you deny.' The Reformation was, of course, well on the
move by then. The last Roman Catholic Bishop of Ross was
John Leslie, a faithful supporter of Mary Queen of Scots. He is

Fortrose Priory

believed to have written his *History of Scotland* in Fortrose, the
then seat of his diocese, to interest her in her captivity. He died
in exile in 1596. A few books from his once famous library have
survived and are now in the National Library of Scotland.

At Rosehaugh nearby there lived half a century later Sir
George Mackenzie, the famous—or infamous—'Bluidie Mackenzie' of the witch trials, remembered also as Charles II's Lord
Advocate, a relentless persecutor of the Covenanters. Dryden,
however, described him as 'that noble wit of Scotland' and he
founded the National Library of Scotland. Easter Ross was once
famed for its witches; also in olden times in the Highlands people
would keep on raising the Devil without first making any plan for
laying him again, a much more difficult job which required both
skill and forethought. Everyone knew that the Devil has no
power over a christened person unless given it by one who has

himself been baptised or by a man pledging his soul in return for earthly benefits, but many forgot that once that was done Satan's power was infinite. And it is difficult to raise and command the Devil without pawning your soul in the process. This makes things awkward.

There is the tale of the man who wished to rid himself of a rival. He raised the Devil. Satan, knowing what would be required, appeared in the form of a wolf and quickly killed and ate the enemy. The man was delighted. But next night there was the wolf again.

'I am hungry, Master. Whom shall it be?'

So another enemy was liquidated. Next night again the Devil-wolf came for orders. Night by night he ate, first all his master's enemies, then all his acquaintances, and at length all his friends, while the man desperately attempted to lay him with every spell he knew or could hear of. But, having sold his soul to the Devil in the first instance, he was helpless and so at last the wolf ate him also and returned to his own place.

Michael Scott, the great magician, was among those who faced this Devil-laying problem, as appears in the chapter on Inverness, but his devils (he had three) cried, not 'Food, food,' but 'Work, give us work.' So one day he bade them build a causeway of sand to connect Fortrose with Ardersier on the opposite shore of the Moray Firth. The little devils set to work as soon as darkness fell. They divided forces, two working from Fortrose and one from Ardersier, and they were getting on very nicely when a shepherd, out early, happened to pass by just as the dawn began to break. He saw the long new sand bar running out into the sea and the two queer little men working on it. Much alarmed, he called for the blessing of God on it. This put the devils to flight and so the causeway was left unfinished, like two sandspits as we see it today. And it is just as well it was, for had it been completed Inverness and Kessock would have been completely cut off from the sea whereas when the shepherd halted the building there was, and there still is, sufficient room for ships to come and go.

The fairies, however, did not agree with this and, for once trying to live up to their name of 'the Good Folk', decided, out of pity for the people of Fortrose and Rosemarkie toiling round the Firth to Inverness, to build them a bridge across at Chanonry Point. They worked hard and were getting on well, but people *would* come and watch and, though knowing nothing of bridge building, yet *would* give advice, usually foolish. At last this so annoyed the Little People that they exclaimed: 'As you know better than we know, build the bridge yourselves,' and they departed. So that bridge was never finished either.

About two miles beyond Fortrose comes Rosemarkie, till recently a tiny little seaside village with a lovely sandy beach, but at the moment its claim to fame lies in its having been Northern Scotland's first T.V. station. Rosemarkie is supposed to have been founded by a contemporary of St. Columba's, one Mo Luag or Lughaidh, who built several churches, including one here, in the early seventh or perhaps late sixth century. His church at Rosemarkie must have flourished, for by A.D. 697 it had a Bishop Curitan, a cleric of such importance that he, with the Bishop of Iona (Bishop Ceti or Coeddi), were the two clerical sureties from the North for the fulfilment of Adamnan's law forbidding the employment of women in battle. The third surety was Brude, son of Derile, King of the Picts. It is interesting that this law is Adamnan's, for the story goes that the enforcing of such a law was very near to St. Columba's heart.

As a young man in Ireland Columba was a very good and dutiful son and he used to carry his mother on his back wherever she wished to go. One day they passed near where a battle was being fought and saw a woman being dragged from the fight by an iron hook thrust into her breast. His mother demanded to be set down and when he had obeyed she seated herself upon a rock and refused to move, announcing that it was her intention to remain there until Columba promised to stop the practice of using women in war. Knowing her capable of remaining seated there until she died, he dutifully promised.

Later on, in the eighth century, St. Boniface founded a Roman Catholic monastic church at Rosemarkie and the rather startling claim was made for it that the altar stone of this church, on which the saint first celebrated Communion after 'winning' the King of the Picts and his people from the Columban Church to that of Rome, has become the Stone of Destiny. This theory is put

forward, not as one might suppose on the grounds that the legend
of the real Stone of Destiny having been hidden and another stone
similar in size and shape delivered to Edward I in its place was
true, and that this was the substituted stone, but on the grounds
that St. Patrick's stone altar was used as the coronation stone of
the Kings of Munster and so the Scottish Stone of Destiny must
also have been an altar stone. This seems to me a complete *non
sequitur*. However, this is a book of legends and this is a legend,
so it has its place.

Just beyond the village lies the unusual and beautiful glen,
Dell of Eathie. What caused such extraordinary red rock scenery,
I do not know, perhaps earthquake or landslide or mere erosion,
but it is certainly quite unlike anything else in the North and well
worth a visit. Needless to say, local superstition blamed it on the
fairies. Some of them had sinned against their own laws, it was
believed, and so this strange glen was made for their imprisonment. They are held prisoners in the cliff sides and allowed out
only in the dark of the moon, when they cannot dance. This
freedom is given them so that they may visit an old mill near by
to grind their meal. Naturally, the imprisoned fairies are very
angry and bitter about the whole affair and it is dangerous indeed
to meet them trudging to the mill, sacks on backs, for they are
almost certain to ill-wish you. Indeed they might carry you off
altogether as they once did a piper who was so ill-advised as to
play dance music in the glen one dark night for a wager. He was
never seen again but some have heard a sound as of pipes playing
both piteous laments and gay reels, coming, it would seem, from
the heart of the red cliff.

The next place of interest is Cromarty itself, once the county
town of the old County of Cromarty. This county was formed
by a grandson of the Tutor of Kintail, who inherited much of his
grandfather's ability. He became Clerk Register and was then
created Viscount Tarbat and Earl of Cromartie. He then set about
adding to his already substantial estates any odd bits and pieces
he could lay hands on and thought worth annexing, finally getting
the whole raised to the status of County of Cromartie, and so it
remained until it was fused into the present County of Ross and
Cromarty in the nineteenth century. Cromarty has had several

citizens of note, including Hugh Millar, whose statue stands on a hill above the town. Here it looks down on tombstones he carved as a mason before he made his name as an archaeologist and literary man. Also Sir Thomas Urquhart, a noted soldier and author of the classic translation of Rabelais, who is reputed to have died of mirth on hearing of the Restoration of Charles II.

The Cromarty Suitors are too well known to merit description; the two great heads are unmistakable but it is perhaps less well known that on the Last Day the sheep and the goats are to assemble on the moor above the Cromarty Suitor, sheep to the south and goats to the north, for there, on a spot called in Gaelic Neamheidich, Navity (holy or Church land), the Last Judgment will be held. On the Invergordon or Northern Suitor on certain nights a wonderful night-shining jewel can be seen, illuminating the darkness. No one knows what it is or what it portends.

On both the Suitors can be seen the hoof-prints of Michael Scott's horse. Tired of his demon's constant cries of 'Work, give us work!', he fled from them the length of Caithness and Sutherland and across the Kyles and at last leapt from the North Suitor to the Southern One, landing near Cromarty. But it was no good. The demons leapt after him and he had hardly landed and descended from his horse to rest after his hair-raising ride when little voices began again, 'Work, master, more work!' But during his wild night ride Michael had had an idea which, he believed, would keep his demons occupied forever. He ordered them to make a rope of sand long enough and strong enough both to girdle the earth and to bind the moon to the earth as well. Again and again the rope was begun. You may sometimes see lengths of it on sandy beaches still, but always the tide washes it away half done. In Argyll, however, they claim that these sand ropes are spun by the Little People by order of Sir Patrick Duncan of Glenorchy (Black Duncan of the Cowl) who had wondrous powers, and in Sutherland they are made by command of Lord Reay.

The road back from Cromarty to Muir of Ord along the south shore of the Cromarty Firth is on the whole less interesting. However, not far from Cromarty is Poyntzfield, as unexpected a house to find in the Highlands as Foulis Castle itself, and for the same reason. It seems that the Munro of Poyntzfield of the time, being much impressed by the work of the Dutch architect who altered Foulis Castle, invited him to rebuild Poyntzfield in the Dutch manner, which he did. Later, another of the family, having completed the Grand Tour, imported an Italian gardener to lay out the gardens. An avenue of cypress trees leading from the house to a fountain live to tell the tale.

Two small villages in the vicinity have most un-Highland names. They are Jemimaville and Barbaraville, the latter on the north shore of the Firth. They were called after two daughters of Poyntzfield.

Further on, not far from the shore, are the ruins of Castle Craig, once the Palace of the Bishops of Ross. It marked one end of the Ferry of Foulis which it guarded. Then there is Ferintosh, which belonged to Shakespeare's Thane of Cawdor, but by the mid-eighteenth century it was the property of the Lord President Duncan Forbes of Culloden who served the Government so well during the Jacobite 'troubles' that he was rewarded with the privilege (of untold value) of free distillation, with the result that at one time the name Ferintosh was almost synonymous with whisky. The church of Ferintosh is believed by many to have been the subject of the Brahan Seer's prophecy: 'When a magpie shall for three springs have built her nest in the gable of the church of Ferintosh, the church will fall when full of people', though others claim that he must have meant Fearn Church which did so fall. Be that as it may, a magpie did nest for three years in the gable of the church of Ferintosh and a big crack appeared shortly afterwards in one wall of the church. This caused concern and the prophecy was much quoted. One Sunday a famous divine came to preach and the building was crowded to hear him. Seats being insufficient, a builder near lent planks to be laid across the aisle from seat to seat; this being done and every seat and plank occupied, the service began. Suddenly there was a terrible crack, followed by a rending noise and screams as one overweighted bench broke and turned the plank balanced on it into a see-saw, throwing people into the air. Stories of the prophecy recurred to many minds and a panic rush for the door ensued, injuring many. But the church has not fallen—yet!

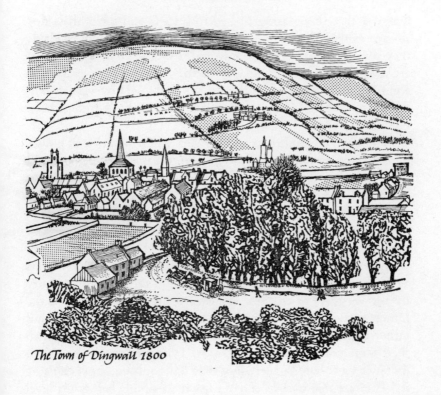

The Town of Dingwall 1800

8

DINGWALL

Gone are the pageant hosts,
And vanished the phantom crowd,
And the old town sleeps by its ancient keeps
Under the midnight cloud.
MURDOCH MACLEAN

AT ONE TIME there was a Spanish ambassador to the court of Scotland who was very fond of boasting. Whatever object cropped up in conversation, Spain always had, according to him, larger and finer ones than those under discussion and more of them. Both King and court grew a little bored.

One day the conversation turned to bridges and the ambassador at once explained what wonderful bridges there were in Madrid; they were built of stone, so large and strong they were, works of art too, and there were *three* of them. 'Only three?' exclaimed King James in tones of courteous sympathy, 'How very trying for the townsfolk. Why, in one of my towns the burghers have forty bridges.'

The town in question was Dingwall, where one row of houses used to stand on the bank of the Boggan Burn and each household had placed its own plank over the rivulet. But Dingwall always has been rather a 'watery' place and claims the first stone bridge in the North, the 'Bridge of Robert de Munro' on the west road. Later rebuilt by a Mackenzie of Seaforth when he was Provost of the town, it still bears the Seaforth arms carved in stone on the arch.

According to a local tradition current in Dingwall fifty years ago, the town was a Dutch one, founded in the sixteenth century by the 'Beggars of the Sea' as Spain contemptuously called the Dutch patriots who, having cut the dykes and flooded Holland rather than let her fall under Spain and the Inquisition, took to their ships and harried the Spaniards. It may be that some Dutch did once settle here but certainly they did not found or even name it. The fact that part of the old town was built below sea level and protected by dykes does give some substance to the idea, since early Highland townships, though often built near the sea or river mouth for ease of transport, were usually sited on rising ground above flood level. But there seems to be no mention anywhere of an historical Dutch settlement at Dingwall. It is possible that the two or three Dutch built 'big houses' in the vicinity gave rise to the legend.

In fact Dingwall was a place of some importance long before 'the Beggars' flooded Holland. Its history in its early days was that of its Castle, a fortress of repute. At a very early time, when the Highlands were ruled by Celtic Maormores or 'Great Men', Dingwall Castle was a seat and stronghold of the Maormores of Moray. Perhaps the best remembered of this family were Finleac, father of Shakespeare's Macbeth, and Macbeth himself who is believed to have been born in the castle. In those days Dingwall was known as Inverpeffer, Mouth of the Peffer, a name dating from Pictish times but still used today in its Gaelic form of Inbhirpheotharain. Finleac was the last of the Maormores to hold Dingwall. By 1034 or thereby all this part of Scotland was in the hands of the Norse Jarls and one of the chief of these, Thorfin, is said to have died of wounds received in fighting for Dingwall Castle against Malcolm Ceannmor, King of Scotland. It is told that King Malcolm, learning of Thorfin's mortal wound, sent an offer of such surgical or other help as was available to ease the injured man. Thorfin replied, asking only for a safe-conduct for his wife Ingebriod after his death. Malcolm immediately promised to be personally responsible for her safe escort to her own people. Now, Ingebriod was a princess whose outstanding beauty has been remembered for over 900 years; she was also probably a cousin of the King's so it is perhaps not surprising that in due and proper season she became Malcolm Ceannmor's first wife.

It was during the Norse occupation that Dingwall got its present name, from the Norse 'Thing-Vollr', Valley of the 'Thing' or Court of Justice. The hill on which the 'Thing' was held can still be seen to the north-west of the town. After a time the Norsemen were driven back into Sutherland and Dingwall became a part of the Kingdom of Scotland once more. In 1225 Alexander II gave it a Royal Charter. Later it became one of the Wick Burghs, five northern towns with the right to send their own Member to Parliament, and it is now the county town of Ross and Cromarty.

After the eviction of the Norsemen the Earls of Ross were Lords of Dingwall and its Castle for some 200 years, then their lands were declared 'forfeit' and the castle became a royal fortress held for the King, to whom the earldom had reverted. Eventually Dingwall Castle fell into ruins but a few remains of its foundations can still be seen in the grounds of the house called the Castle which was built from the stones of the old castle in the early nineteenth century. Dingwall Castle is said to have been built of stone at a date when most neighbouring strongholds were of wood and to have been much used as a meeting place by various chiefs and V.I.P.s—a sort of 'Summit' resort in fact. The number of charters and treaties signed there seems to bear out this idea.

But although its Castle was a strategic point of the first importance, for at Dingwall 'all roads meet', the town itself has for some obscure reason long been felt by its neighbours to be an alien place. Other towns have each their own entity; an 'Invernessian', 'Tain folk', 'Dornoch men', but someone from Dingwall remained just 'a man from Dingwall'. Perhaps this was because of its varied history or because its position as a large market centre made it somewhat cosmopolitan. Certainly Dingwall markets have for long been of prime importance in the Highlands, chiefly a matter of geography of course, but those who believed in 'the Beggars' pointed out how much a little Dutch blood might have helped the burghers to become noteworthy men of business.

Fifty years ago the market held every Wednesday in Dingwall was a sight to be seen. Not only was it the centre of a rich farming area where prize beasts abound, but it was also a centre for the hill farmers of North and West with their herds of pure- or almost pure-bred Highland cattle, so rare now. They were huge-horned, long-haired beasts, very fierce to see but with the gentlest natures and kindest eyes of any breed. Their hairy calves, with eyes almost hidden under their heavy fringes, like great shaggy dogs, were adorable. From early dawn all the roads, east, west, south and north, were filled with droves of cattle and flocks of sheep, with shouting men and barking dogs, as they tried to control their often idiotic charges, with farm carts carrying pigs or perhaps a prize ram, and high dogcarts and traps with the farmers' wives and daughters and their poultry and butter and cheese, for these things were theirs for pin money. But sometimes on a market day Dingwall would see an unforgettable figure. He was a shepherd who brought in his flock from the far hills. Through all the clamour of men and dogs and carts and pigs, the baa-ing of sheep and the lowing of cattle, he walked in silent dignity, leading his flock, and his sheep followed at his heels like well-trained dogs. No fuss and flurry. He picked his way quietly through the mêlée as might a man who walked alone, and always his sheep followed close at his heels as silent and composed as he. This figure, so closely resembling in appearance the conventional representations of The Good Shepherd, was probably the most striking that I ever saw. Incidentally his placid, unhurried sheep always got top prices.

It was a very interesting sight, the market, for everyone came
in who could on Wednesdays. Quite apart from the real business,
it was the week's best shopping day. The baker's cakes would all
be fresh baked for the occasion, fruit, vegetables and farm produce
would have come in fresh, too. The farmers' wives all wearing
jet ornaments, a jet brooch or beads or jet-embroidered jacket, to
avert the Evil Eye—a danger on Market Day when tempers were
short and envy abroad—would have butter and eggs for their
regular customers. In season, children would be selling spiced
apples to keep away moth, dried Scotch lavender (woodruff) to
scent the 'bottom drawer', and bunches of Tottie Grass or
Trembling Jock, because:

> Trembling Jocks i' the house
> And you won't have a mouse.

And then there were the fish-wives in their traditional costumes
with their creels of fresh fish, *really* fresh which had never seen
ice, on their backs, crying their wares. I used to like these best of
all, with their striped petticoats and starched caps.

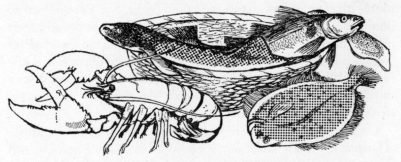

"... with their creels of fresh fish ..."

The particular old fish-wife whose fish my mother usually
bought always had a story or a joke for me. Flounders were a
standing joke. She said they'd made faces once at a rock-cod and
at that moment the wind changed and so the flounder's face stayed
like it now is, 'and so will yours if you make faces and the wind
changes, little lady, so take care, lassie dear. Never make faces.'
Indeed the flounder, according to her, seems to have led an eventful life, for, she said, when the Israelites were crossing the Red

Sea Moses picked up a flounder left flapping on the sea bottom when the sea divided. That night he began to fry it for his supper but he was short of oil and could only fry one side. When he realised that he could not finish cooking it, that nothing might be wasted Moses blessed the half-cooked fish and flung it back into the sea. Here it came to life again and swam away hale and well but bi-coloured, the fried side brown, the other white, and so its descendants have been ever since.

She was genuinely interested in her fish and knew a lot about them. For instance, she told my mother that flounders start life looking like any other fish, with two eyes, one on each side, an ordinary mouth and swimming normally. At a few weeks old they change and begin to swim on one side (which bleaches white quite quickly) instead of upright; soon their eyes change too, the underside eye beginning to move forward until it reaches the edge of the face, so to speak, then upwards and over to join its mate on the upper side. Actually I believe that in some flat fish the eye apparently closes and works its way right through the head and out at the other side, leaving the socket behind for a time—they are called 'three-eyed flounders'. She also claimed to know at a glance where any flounder came from as she said their upper, or dark, side took its colour from the sand or mud on which it lay and so those of every bank or shore differed in shade as also, she and my mother agreed, in flavour. Flounders from a mud shore are muddy to taste—only the flounders from clean rock or sand should be eaten.

Indeed our old fish-wife had stories about most sea creatures. The haddock, she said, was a blessed fish. Our Lord Himself blessed it, for it was haddock that the wee boy had in his basket when Our Lord Christ fed the multitude. He took the fish and blessed them and His finger marks remain on the haddock's sides to this day. All the same she held firmly that no haddock was fit to eat until it had 'drunk three drinks of May water', that is to say had seen three May tides. There was a period in each year when she would not bring haddock to market in her basket. 'Not fit to sell.' The lobster and the skate, on the other hand, were connected with the Devil. The skate, because he once swam to Hell, you can smell the fumes of brimstone off him yet, and so hot was he that, even now, if you hang a skate up by the tail he'll dry and cure himself, clear proof that he once visited the Place of Evil. The fact that the skate does cure itself is well known in the Highlands and these fish can often be seen hung up near a cottage or laid on the roof to dry. They contain so much ammonia that salting is unnecessary. But my old friend assured me that the skate was one of the Devil's spies, always watching and listening and carrying tales; that was the price of his escape from the Bad Place.

The lobster, on the other hand, was, she said, no friend to the Evil One. The Devil liked a lobster for his dinner and at low tide used to search the rocks for them. One day he leaned close to a cranny in the rocks trying to see whether it contained a lobster or a nice fat crab. A lobster was at home. Before the Devil knew what had happened the lobster had him by the nose, and held on. The Devil couldn't get his hands in, for his own head blocked the way, so he could not free himself or pull the lobster out. And the tide began to rise.

'Leb me go,' said the Devil.

The lobster said nothing. He held on.

'Leb me go, or I'll carry you off to the Bad Place,' said the Devil.

The lobster said nothing but he held on, and the tide continued to rise.

'Leb me go, please good lobster,' said the Devil.

The lobster said nothing, but held on, and the tide had risen to Satan's waist.

'Leb me go and you shall be well rewarded,' cried the Devil.

The tide rose to his shoulders and the lobster held silently on.

'Leb me go and you shall have whatever you ask,' cried the desperate Devil, for, though it is not generally known, the Devil, who can be harmed by nothing on land or in the air nor by fire, his own element, is as helpless as a man before the dread power of the sea, and the tide was now up to his chin.

Then at last the lobster spoke.

'Make me safe against all harm and faster than all other creatures of the sea,' he said, 'and I will let you go.'

'I will, I will,' spluttered the Devil through the salt water that had reached his lips.

'Do it now,' said the lobster remorselessly.

So the Devil gave the lobster his hard outer shell then and there, and the lobster let go the Devil's nose and he staggered off to safety, holding his nose with his hands and wishing his eyes would not water so much. Meanwhile the lobster, not quite sure how the Devil would react when he had had time to think, used his newly acquired speed to take himself rapidly out of reach. Hard and fast has he been ever since.

Whiting were bred from the silver beams of the moon. But best of all fish are the herring, for these Our Lord Himself had created in the Sea of Galilee to fill the nets for the miraculous draught of fishes. In daylight they are gleaming silver, pure as their Creator, and at night they shine with a heavenly radiance.

Fifty years ago Dingwall had rather a bad name among the other Highland towns and was apt to be looked down on, chiefly, I think, because of Market Day nights. Drink was *very* cheap and money plentiful on market days and by three o'clock on a Wednesday afternoon the main street of the town would have its gutters full of drunken men and 'lucky if they stayed there'. In the days of horse-drawn traffic most farmers' ponies could and did take their masters safely home but with the coming of cars this useful practice ceased. One curious result of the heavy drinking for which Dingwall was then noted was that when a vote was taken in many Scottish towns between the wars for Prohibition, Restricted Licence or No Change, Dingwall, to the utter horror of most of its inhabitants, 'voted dry', the reason being an excellent turn-out of all prohibitionists with no one else bothering to vote as they considered No Change a foregone conclusion. The result was that though the votes cast were almost unanimously in favour of Prohibition not enough people voted to make the result legal, and all had to be done again. This time, still trembling from shock, almost 100% of the voters turned out and the result was very different.

It would seem that the Devil had heard of Dingwall's reputation and expected to find friends there. Anyhow, one day he visited the old smithy down by the water's edge and, finding the smith very busy shoeing two horses, he sat himself down in a corner and waited politely till they were shod. The smith, not recognising him, then asked him his pleasure and the Devil explained who he was and that he had come there to be shod himself as he felt that iron hoofs might be of frequent use to him. The smith agreed, measured the Devil, blew up his fire and made the shoes. He then began to put them on but the pain was so great that the Devil could not bear it and told him to stop. This the blacksmith refused to do, saying that 'horses were often a bit restive like, too'. The Devil, in agony with the red-hot shoes, now besought him to stop and take them off on any terms. The old smith made him promise that neither he himself nor any of his lesser devils would ever enter a building over the threshold of which a horse-shoe was placed. The Devil, as always, has kept his promise. As soon as he got free of the terrible shoes the Devil fled to cool his burnt feet in the small creek near the Castle. Some claim that it is the horror and terror of this day, and not his enforced promise, that causes the Devil to avoid houses which have horse-shoes guarding them. So hot were his feet that they baked his footsteps in the mud of the creek, so it was said, and anyone able to walk in them would have good fortune. His legs were so long I never heard of anyone able to take the necessary stride.

Entering Dingwall from the south, one of the first things to catch the eye is a somewhat 'home made' looking War Memorial in front of the railway station. Its stem is a crooked fir tree and the arms of the cross are formed of short French scythe blades. This is the monument originally raised to the Seaforth Highlanders at Cambrai in the first World War to commemorate their battles in and around the town and later brought home to Dingwall. Dingwall's main street is still paved with cobbles, rather a rare sight in a Highland town today; it runs past the official War Memorial and on out to the west. Near where the road to the north takes off from it is an ancient churchyard in which Sir Roderick Mackenzie, 'Tutor of Kintail', was buried. The old church was unfortunate, for its thatched roof was set on fire by a man shooting pigeons and the whole church destroyed. Opposite the churchyard is a mound on which is mounted a small obelisk. This is the burial place of a descendant of Sir Roderick's, the first Earl of Cromarty, a distinguished statesman of the late seventeenth century. At his death, it is said, every one of his tenants, man woman and child, came to pass his grave and deposit upon it a basketful of earth. These formed the mound. Originally the mound was topped by an obelisk almost as tall as Cleopatra's Needle but early in this century it became dangerously leaning despite iron supports and the present Countess of Cromarty then erected one of more manageable size in its place.

On a hill above Dingwall stands the tower erected to the memory of Sir Hector Macdonald of Omdurman fame. Born at Ferintosh nearby, he enlisted in the Gordon Highlanders, rose to commissioned rank and ended as a General, a rare feat in those days. His exploits soon made him a local hero and after his death the memorial was erected by his admirers, who were many. Later came tales of mystery about his death. Some said he had committed suicide, others that he had disappeared, yet others had him killed in a duel. But his glory remained untarnished and it is curious to find the usual myth so often told of the great leaders of olden time—King Arthur, Charlemagne, Fionn etc.—told of him also. Just as they did not die but lie hidden awaiting a call in time of need, so Hector did not die either. He was seen here and there throughout the world. I can remember a visitor assuring my mother that her brother-in-law had met him in Ceylon, whereas our gardener's brother had seen and spoken to him in Canada. In 1914 the stories redoubled. He had come over with this or that overseas contingent; he had joined the Seaforths under another name and would lead them in battle; not at all, it was a fact that he was to command the Expeditionary Force. As news from Mons, the Marne, the Aisne, grew worse so did the stories of Sir Hector's coming grow more numerous and more detailed. It was strange to see the old hero-tradition being reborn in modern times.

Yet it was not only about Sir Hector Macdonald. Lord Kitchener, too, could not die. Those of us who are old enough can remember many strange tales after the sinking of the *Hampshire*. When the Admiralty gave out that search was being made

in the area for Kitchener's despatch case and for the bodies of his
Staff, and when various other bodies were found and brought
home for burial but not his and no search for his was mentioned,
the legend grew apace. The Admiralty knew he was alive but a
prisoner, that's why his despatch case only, not his body, was
searched for, was one story. He had had himself smuggled into
Germany to head a rising—the sinking of the *Hampshire* was used
as a blind, he was never in her—was another. The unusually
violent thunderstorm which broke over Eastbourne during his
A.D.C.'s funeral, when the steel gun-carriage, not unnaturally,
became the central focus for the lightning, producing an unforgettable spectacle of coffin and gun-carriage alike outlined in fire,
was held to be a supernatural revelation of foul play somewhere
and gave rise to many conjectures and forebodings. When the
young soldier wrote to his mother in all innocence from a
prisoner-of-war camp 'Your food parcel was most welcome for
though we have plenty of kitchen utensils here we haven't much
to put in them' he was held to have revealed Kitchener's exact
place of imprisonment most cleverly.

Dingwall, like other Highland townships of its day, had its
wise-woman who was consulted on many matters of moment.
Her particular line was interpreting dreams, a very high art indeed. There were certain recognised rules for use in interpretation
but even so it was very difficult, rather like X-ray photographs
now, I fancy. Much is in the eye of the beholder and much
depends on how he reads what is before him. Roughly speaking,
in Highland dream lore dreams go by contraries, as: 'To dream
of the dead is to hear of the living', 'To dream of a living man as
dead foretells his marriage', and so forth. Clans were usually
represented by animals, as a horse for Macleod, a stag for Mackenzie. To dream of broken eggs meant trouble; of dirty water
or clothes to wash, someone 'smearing' the dreamer with lies.
Dingwall's wise-woman lived in a tiny cottage outside the town
and kept hens, as a wise-woman should. Those who wished for
a dream to be read visited her with appropriate gifts, usually tea
or fresh butter. They told her their dream, left the gift (un-
mentioned, of course) on the table and departed, to return at
some specified hour. The wise-woman would then look at the

parcel (it was not 'manners' to open a parcel in the giver's presence) and, catching a hen, she would seat herself by the fire and, if she had plenty of time, stroke the hen rhythmically until both she and it were half hypnotised and seemed unable to move. When she 'woke' she could translate the dream. If speed was very necessary she would, instead, boo into a hen's ear and then, when it had become giddy, draw some sort of omen from its behaviour. One thing was certain; the dreams she was asked to translate, and the translations, were always severely practical in form and meaning and, except at Hallowe'en, were rarely connected with love or marriage. I once saw a 'dream book', a modern one, and it appeared to contain nothing but love, marriage, tall dark men, blondes 'as preferred by gentlemen', and so on—a very great contrast to the old beliefs.

My mother had a cook at one time who was an intense believer in the truth of all dreams. Her firm belief had survived unshaken by uniformed service in the first World War and ordinary life both before and after it. When she came from her island home to be my mother's cook on the mainland, she brought her belief with her. At first it mattered little; indeed it was rather amusing, especially to the younger members of the household. Then one morning when my mother went down to do the housekeeping she was met by an almost hysterical 'Belinda'. 'I must go home. Oh, Mother! My poor mother. I must go home,' she reiterated over and over again. Patient questioning finally elicited the fact that she had dreamt of 'a wee black terrier dog running both ways at once and very agitated'. Now *everyone* knew a 'wee black terrier dog' meant a Macdonald, and her mother was born a Macdonald, and the dog was very excited and so, obviously, had been trying to tell her something was wrong with her mother, and going both ways at once meant that she must follow it home at once. So off she went, in time for the one and only steamer. My mother thought the dream story must be cover for some real worry, something about a young man perhaps, but the other maids assured her that 'Belinda' had gone up to bed perfectly happy and appeared in the morning with her face swelled with crying. Four days passed; then (it was the earliest opportunity) 'Belinda' returned, beaming.

'How did you find your mother? Was anything wrong?' we asked.

'Oh, no!' she beamed, 'Mother was very well and was angry with me for coming home. She says I should have known that "a wee black terrier dog running both ways at once" meant twin lambs for a Macdonald sheep, and one of ours had twinned. Dreams are always true.'

The interpretation of dreams is indeed a high art. I am not sure that the wise people are not the Japanese, who once kept a demon called Baku who, if properly invoked, would come and eat dreams. That settled them.

9

WEST FROM DINGWALL

Oh! for the beautiful sunlight
That smiles on hill and lea,

*   *   *   *   *

The smell of the purple heather,
The myrtle wild, and thyme,
And the balmy fragrant sweetness
Of the autumn's golden prime.
MARY CAMERON

THE ROAD which leaves Dingwall for the West runs through rich arable land for the first five or six miles to Strathpeffer. The Peffer Burn from which the strath takes its name is said to mean 'radiant' or 'beautiful'. On the way the road passes the Fodderty churchyard, in which a ghost wanders nightly among the graves searching, ever searching, for the grave of her faithless lover. She wrings her hands and weeps, poor girl, and those who see her are aware of an eager question in her look as she swiftly approaches them. Those unfortunate enough to see the misty grey figure and foolish enough to bide for questioning are sure to meet with ill fortune, though it is said that if ever one comes who can tell her where her lover's grave was dug he or she will reap great reward.

Near the old church of Fodderty (now a dwelling house) stand three stones. Two are ordinary 'standing stones' but the

The Eagle Stone,
near Strathpeffer

third, known as the Eagle Stone, has an eagle carved on it and is the focus of many legends. It is generally held that the bird is 'The Eagle of Foulis', the crest of Clan Munro, and many think the stone marks the site of the battle between Donald of the Isles and the Munros aided by neighbouring clans, which took place in 1411 when Donald was on his way to Harlaw. Some say it celebrates a Munro victory, others that it once marked the barrow of their dead but was twice thrown down and was then moved near the church to protect it from demons. Yet others claim that it is far older. Some think that the original eagle of Foulis was a real bird to whose eyrie the first Chief climbed to rescue a baby carried off by the bird. He was said to have killed the eagle with his bare hands and thrown it down on to this stone, on which its likeness was later carved by admiring clansmen. Others, again, think it older still. Once there lived in the hills near by a giant of remarkable strength who loved 'putting the stone'; indeed he is reputed to have been the originator of that sport. In those days some of the Feinn lived on Knockfarrel and the giant challenged Fionn to a stone-throwing competition. Fionn refused but offered to match his dwarf against the 'Stoneputter' as he was called. The giant agreed to this. When he and the dwarf took station on Knockfarrel the giant picked up the eagle stone, which three men could not lift, and flung it right across the strath on to this green knoll, where it stuck fast. The dwarf then went up to two huge standing stones, the gate posts of the old fort of Knockfarrel, which seven men could not lift, and hurled first one and then the other to stand upright beside the giant's stone. In proof of the truth of this story the marks of an enormous finger and thumb are shown still visible on one of the stones.

Strathpeffer itself is a strange place, unique in Scotland. Of volcanic origin, it may well be an old crater of which one side blew out. The springs which before the 1914-18 War fed its busy spa produce natural hot, indeed almost boiling, water, both iron and sulphur. Anyone asking to see over the Spa and its pump rooms used to be offered a glass of pure, clear water from a tap, then, before they could drink it, the guide would add: 'Oh! it's not full!' and would fill the glass from a second tap. From this tap also flowed pure, clear water, but as the two waters mixed the glass became filled with an ink-black fluid which (containing sulphur) smelt to high heaven. This natural result of mixing water from an iron spring with that from a sulphur spring gave rise to a legend that Strathpeffer once belonged to the Devil. Now it must be realised that, despite cleanliness being next to godliness, the Devil is a very clean person and has his baths all over the Highlands, any spring which he has used for the purpose being easily recognised by the smell of brimstone from its water ever afterwards. His favourite bathing place was Strathpeffer; here he not only washed frequently, as the very many sulphur springs in the vicinity testify, but also washed his black clothes, producing the curious black water sometimes seen in this district.

Iron springs, on the other hand, were held to be God's especial gift to man and to have healing powers if properly used. But 'proper use' included the fact that the patient must be without sin when he or she approached the water. The faintly irridescent scum which rises on such springs and pools was held to show that a rainbow had touched them, leaving behind God's promise of help. An older tale in the Western Highlands made such springs come from the Blessed Isles, Tir nan Og. The water still reflected the wondrous colours of fruit and flowers in the Isles of the Blest and could give health and even, in some cases, restore youth.

The natural hot baths and waters of Strathpeffer Spa have always been held in very high repute as a cure for rheumatism and like ills. Long before the Syndicate took it over and made it fashionable, older Highlanders and their wives came there to drink the waters and derived much benefit. With them the 'new' spa with its new prices was not over popular, and many tales to its disparagement were told. Perhaps the funniest, which was said to have a tiny basis of fact, was as follows. The hot peat baths, which were emptied by machinery worked from a cellar below tipping them up over a chute, were on one occasion tipped up with a forgotten patient in one of them. She was, said scandal, rescued going out to sea at Cromarty.

Strathpeffer was, of course, very closely connected with the Brahan Seer and figured in many of his prophecies. When St. Anne's Episcopal Church was built about fifty years ago, there was considerable anxiety felt by some who remembered a pro-

phecy of the Seer's that when five spires should rise in Strathpeffer
ships would sail over the village and anchor to its spires. A peti-
tion was presented to Dean Wilson (then Canon Wilson), a main
mover in the matter of the new church, beseeching him to build
a spire-less one for fear the prophecy might be fulfilled. Anyone
who has stood on any of the hills which surround Strathpeffer, or
even walked on the golf links, can see clearly how such a prophecy
could arise. For as you look down from above it is obvious that
the rich valley which leads from Dingwall to Strathpeffer is
simply a continuation of Cromarty Firth itself. Actually the
village does stand a little above sea level but this does not show
from above. It appears to be protected only by Dingwall's small
dyke or embankment. Indeed a part of the valley was a salt
water morass in historic times and when it was finally drained
in the early nineteenth century a whale's skeleton was found
embedded in the soil.

In due course St. Anne's spire rose without mishap but some
people remained worried. Then, soon after the first World War
when flying was still a wonder to many, a small airship attended
the Strathpeffer 'Games', sailed round the spires, and finally, de-
siring to descend, dropped a grapnel which caught in some part
of the building. The prophecy was fulfilled. All was well.

There are, as might be expected, many tales both as to where
the Brahan Seer, Coinneach Odhar, received his stone and as to
how this came about. Most agree, however, that it was a gift to
him in his sleep and was given when someone, usually said to be
his master's wife, planned to poison him. This stone showed him
the poison in his dinner, thereby saving his life. The stone is
usually held to have been blue in colour and to have had a hole
through which the Seer looked and saw things far away in time
or place. The eye with which he saw through the stone was said
to have become blind to things of the present from that day
forward. He is believed to have lived and worked under the
shadow of Brahan Castle, the Great House of the neighbourhood
and at that time the home of the 3rd Earl of Seaforth. Brahan
stands among lovely woods some miles from Strathpeffer. It was
here that the Seer, now famous for his prophecies, was summoned
by the Countess of Seaforth to tell her of the safety or otherwise

HTL K

of her husband, who had been long absent in France. Kenneth looked through his stone and assured her that her Lord was well and happy. Something in his manner betrayed him, however, and the Countess insisted on a detailed account of what had been shown him. Reluctantly he had to admit that what he had seen was the Earl making love to a charming young lady of the French court. The furious Countess thereupon ordered the Seer to be burnt alive on the Castle green to prove that she 'had no belief in his lies'. As he was led to the stake he made a prophecy (or curse) which has become very famous in the Highlands for it is said to have been repeatedly referred to and well known many years before it was fulfilled. The Seer cried out that he saw the line of Seaforth end in extinction and sorrow. He saw: 'A Chief, both deaf and dumb, the father of four fair sons but all shall die before him. The remnant of his possessions, for much will have already gone, will be inherited by a white-coiffed (white hooded) lassie from the East who will kill her sister. And that it may be known when these things shall come to pass, the four great lords Gair-loch, Chisholm, Grant and Raasay shall be one buck-toothed, another a stammerer, one hare-lipped, another half-witted.' The fullest details of this prophecy may be found in Mackenzie's *Prophecies of the Brahan Seer*.

In due course all these things did indeed come to pass. The Lord Seaforth who was the contemporary of the four 'lords' named, was deaf and dumb, survived his four sons and died in 1815. He was succeeded in the lands that remained by his eldest daughter, Lady Hood, who returned from India a newly-made widow wearing the white 'coif' of widowhood. One day while driving her sister in a pony trap she had an accident and her sister died of her injuries. It is a matter of historical knowledge that the four 'lords' in question were in fact afflicted in the four ways foretold by the Seer.

A further prophecy which I heard as early as 1907 in Ross-shire was that 'a bird should plant a rowan tree on the top of the old Tower of Fairburn and that when it reached the thickness of an axle tree the glory of the Seaforths should rise again'. The reason I remember the date is because my father bought his first car, an Arrol-Johnson, in 1907 and one of our first drives in it was to Fairburn where we passed the rowan growing out of the tower, still only a sapling. My mother told my English grandmother, who was with us, the story and, finding me much interested, later bought me a book of the Brahan Seer's prophecies. In 1914 the little rowan had grown big enough to make an axle tree and by the time the 1914-18 War was over Stewart-Mackenzie had been rewarded for his wartime services by the revival of his family's old title and had become Lord Seaforth.

Above Strathpeffer to the south is a hill known as the Cat's Back and on the top of it is Loch Ussie. Like Strathpeffer itself, it must be the crater of an old volcano, its water still barely cold to the touch. The walk to it through woods of larch is beautiful, especially when they are in blossom, their tiny flowers like pink fairy roses; then comes a steep climb and the Loch itself, dark and still. Perhaps because of its volcanic origin and queer position there are many stories about the loch. One makes it the home of an evil spirit. Those who would visit it and return in safety must pay ransom to him of a small piece of money or fancy stone flung into the water. Those who would know the future may call their questions aloud across the loch water. If the answer is 'Yes', silence will reign but if it is 'No', angry ripples and a sound variously described as groaning or as angry snarling will be heard. No fish live in its waters, no birds will alight on them or even fly over the loch. If you visit it after dark (few do) it is said that the voices of girls in great distress and misery can be heard calling for help and lamenting their fate. Once a young man, hearing as he believed the voice of his betrothed among the lamenting chorus, hurried down to a priest and begged him to come and bless the waters. The priest came and listened. Then he said that the voices were not the voices of maids in distress but of demons in torment. If he blessed the water he might release them and that would be wrong. He added that the young man would probably find his betrothed safe and sound at home, which he did.

Loch Ussie, like Strathpeffer, is closely associated with the Brahan Seer. One story tells that the stone called up the lake to hide itself in after the Seer had flung it into a moor pool or, as others say, into a cow's hoof-mark full of water. This story tells that any attempt to find the stone beneath its waters would result in Loch Ussie overflowing its banks and drowning Strathpeffer and the whole valley. Some say that before his execution the Brahan Seer confided the stone to a friend with instructions to hide it carefully and, as soon as opportunity offered, to carry it up to Loch Ussie and throw it in. And so, his dying wish having been faithfully carried out, his powers of prophecy entered the waters. Others again, however, think that the Seer warned his friend not to try himself to use the stone. The friend kept his promise till he reached the loch shore; then, as he took the stone in his hand to cast it into the water, temptation overcame him. He felt he must have one look before the wondrous thing was lost forever, but as he raised it to his eye a bevy of swans suddenly bore down upon him uttering strange cries. The leader seized the stone and bore it up in his beak while his followers drove the foresworn friend away from the Loch waters and down the steep hillside so that he arrived in the valley terrified and exhausted and would never speak of what he saw and heard.

Overlooking Strathpeffer is the old vitrified fort of Knock-farrel. This was said to be one of the three great forts or defence works of the old Pictish kingdom, the other two being Craig Phadraig near Inverness and the Ord of Kessock in the Black Isle. There were, of course, numerous smaller forts. Knockfarrel played its part in Fiann story too. It is said to appear in several Fiann ballads as Bruth Farbairn, the Mansion of Fairbairn, and Tigh Farala and Tigh Fharmail, the House of Farala or Farmal. It is believed to be here that the Fiann women were shut up in a hut and the hut set on fire by one Garadh Mac Morna. The Feinn were hunting in Skye when they saw the flames mount-ing and, fearing harm to their wives and families, they leapt the Strait on their spears and made haste to Knockfarrel, arriving in time to save their wives—but only just. One of the Feinn, Caol Reatha or Rhea, fell short, being rather a small giant, and was drowned in Kyle Rhea, whence its name.

Strathpeffer is, as one might say, the boundary of Eastern Scotland; within a few miles of the village the scenery and vege-tation alike become that of the West. After passing a few fields thicker with stones than seems possible, we reach moor and birch woods and that sign-manual of the West, bog myrtle. A mile or two further on, up a road to the right, are the Falls of Rogie, once a wonderfully beautiful mountain river where one could sit in the heather watching the salmon leaping up the Falls, surrounded by small moor flowers and shaded by wild trees. The little golden bog orchid which grows here first grew when the Virgin Mary, walking over the moor, stopped at some marshy ground to tuck up her robe. As she undid her golden girdle for the purpose it slipped through her fingers into the peat bog and sank out of sight. Where it had fallen the little golden orchids grew, hoping she might make herself a new girdle from their honey-scented heads. Wherever she stepped through the heather the little white star flower of the moor sprang up, emblem of her purity. Now the Falls are a 'Beauty Spot' with a suitable car park and all the latest improvements.

A few miles further and the road passes the Achilty Inn. Down a side road to the left lies Loch Achilty itself, one of the most beautiful, if not the most beautiful, of the small lochs in Scotland, particularly in late autumn when birches and oaks are alike golden. A road goes up the right hand shore of the loch and beyond passes a smaller loch and over moorland to the Conon River and hydro-electric station. Those who at the beginning of this century dipped their fingers in the small lochan found its water warm to their touch and every July it was covered with a thick carpet of white water lilies, whereas in colder Loch Achilty none grew. Now, alas!, the water is no longer noticeably warm and does freeze in winter, a thing it was reputed never to do formerly.

The story told to account for the loch's warmth and beauty was as follows. This small loch was one of Satan's bathing places. He enjoyed the coolness of its waters so much that once he spent a whole night in its refreshing depths, with the result that by dawn its water was steaming hot. Unfortunately on this occasion he had with him a cake of soap which long immersion in the now nearly boiling water melted. The Devil's soap is horrible stuff, made of tallow impregnated with sulphur, ashes of alder wood and the ground-up bones of toads. Soon the whole surface of the loch was covered with soapsuds as if some modern housewife had poured a detergent into it, only worse, for detergent suds are usually white whereas the Devil's suds were the dirty white of tallow, yellow of sulphur and dull green of ancient toads' bones. The result was far from beautiful. But what God has made lovely no creature can permanently defile and so, slowly, the dirty white grew pure as milk, the sulphurous yellow turned to gleaming gold, the green grew fresh and desirable; in short, the little loch was soon covered with a mantle of glorious white waterlilies, their golden hearts open to the sun. But that they might grow the better the loch for long kept some part of the heat it had received from the Devil.

And so, back to the main road. Like most roads to the West this one is lovely all the way. Perhaps the next point of interest is the Raven's Rock, a high crag to the right of the road, nearer the railway really, on which ravens nest. There are, of course, a very large number of Raven's (and Eagle's) Rocks in Scotland since both birds were once not uncommon and favour wild and spectacular nesting places. But this one is rather special because here, it is said, the ravens hold their annual ball. The Dance of the Ravens is a thing to see and once a man *did* see it, despite their precautions, and a wonderful sight it was. He said that they had sentinels posted on every high crag near and another flying over-head, but he lay hidden in bracken and watched until by dawn the birds were tiring and he was able to approach and catch one who seemed the leader, a very fine old bird. The man said that what had impressed him most was the music to which they danced; it was provided in 'a sort of song' by one raven and made even the man in hiding want to join in. So, having captured their leader, he made a bargain with them: he would let him go un-harmed and never betray the secrets he had learnt if they would teach him how to make this 'mouth music'. If not, he would kill his prisoner before the ravens could kill him. He knew, of course, that he could never leave the crag alive unless they permitted it. The ravens agreed to teach him and he proved an apt pupil. What he learnt that night is the origin of our 'mouth music', 'port a beil', today.

One of the Michael Scott stories is attached to this crag, though I think the same tale is told of varying people on similar high points in many districts. Be it known, then, that it was once the custom for each country in Christendom to send an envoy to

Rome every year to ask the Pope the date of Shrove Tuesday, from which all the other dates in the Church's calendar were fixed. The man chosen for this responsible embassy must be a man of substance, serious, trustworthy and of good repute. In fact, one likely to find favour in the eyes of His Holiness. One year the choice in Scotland fell on Michael Scott, for despite, or perhaps because of, his magic powers he was held in high honour throughout Scotland. Michael Scott agreed to take on the job, went home, and, becoming immersed in some problem of high magic, forgot all about his promise until at Candlemas he wanted to know the date of Easter and realised that no one in all Scotland did know and that their ignorance was not only very serious but entirely his fault. Time pressed.

He hurried to the Raven's Rock and there, gazing into the sunset, he summoned the Devil in the form of a horse. A fine young filly appeared.

'What is your will, Master?'

'How fast can you travel?' asked the wizard.

'As fast as the wind travels,' replied the filly.

'That will not do for me,' said Michael and he called again. A larger and stronger horse appeared.

'How fast can you carry me?' asked the wizard.

'So fleet of foot am I that I can outdistance the wind that is behind me and overtake the wind that is before me,' answered the horse.

'You will not do for me,' said the wizard, and he called a third time. Out of the mist below him there rose a great black stallion of enormous power and beauty.

'How fast can you travel?' demanded Michael Scott.

'As fast as the thought that is between man and maid,' thundered the great horse.

'You'll do,' said Michael. 'Carry me to Rome to the palace of the Pope.'

'My right is three questions,' warned the stallion.

'And mine the answers,' retorted the wizard, unperturbed.

Now it was the Devil's right to ask three questions if he wished and his rider must answer them truly. If in the answer he spoke the name of God, the Devil was free of his yoke and could vanish, leaving him wherever they then were, though it were in the midst of the sea. As they were passing over Mull the Devil-horse looked down and saw below a woman with small children.

'What says the good wife to her weans as she tucks them to sleep?' he asked.

'The wind is in my ears. Speak louder,' replied the wizard.

The Devil repeated his question but by now they were over Iona and Michael was able to reply truthfully, 'The blessing of Columkil be upon you and keep you.'

The Devil was silent till they reached the mainland, then he saw some women carrying in peats.

'What say the women of Scotland when they smoor the fire?' asked he.

Michael Scott looked down. There were below them at that moment not godly housewives blessing the house fire but giggling girls.

' "Peat burn, peat smoulder; Bring me luck ere I be older" say the lassies,' he truly replied, but the sweat was on his brow. Then he began to talk to the great horse so fascinatingly that the Devil forgot to ask his third question till Rome was beneath them and, safe in the Pope's palace, the wizard need not answer. Instead he bade the porter summon His Holiness's chamberlain. This worthy came hurrying to enquire what so late a visitor wanted.

'I seek an audience of His Holiness—*now*,' said the wizard.

'Impossible,' replied the chamberlain. 'The Pope is within his chamber. Who are you who arrive in the dark?'

'I am Michael Scott, come from Scotland to ask His Holiness to appoint a day to be Shrove Tuesday.'

'His Holiness did that long since,' answered the chamberlain. 'You are too late.'

'Nevertheless, tell His Holiness I await his pleasure *now*,' replied Michael.

The chamberlain went and soon returned with a jug of wine and a promise that the Pope would see him. In a few moments the Pope entered. He appeared as one but just aroused from sleep who has risen in haste. He was still fastening his fur gown.

'Who are you who disturb me when honest folk are abed?' he demanded.

'I am Michael Scott, sent by your good people of Scotland to ask on what date they should keep Shrove Tuesday,' replied Michael.

'What proof have I of that?'

'This snow on my bonnet is the snow of Scotland.'

'What proof have I of *that*?' repeated the Pope, not unnaturally. 'Tell me something which no other man on earth knows, and I will believe you.'

'Two feet have you,' said the wizard, 'but it is not a match that they are.' The Pope angrily lifted his robe and, behold, on his left foot was a man's shoe but his right was thrust into a woman's slipper.

'I believe you. Get you gone,' cried the Pope.

'Tell me first the date of Shrove Tuesday.'

'It is, as always, the first Tuesday of the first moon in spring,' replied the Pope impatiently. 'Get you gone to Scotland.'

Michael was well pleased with his night's work, for he had learnt what every church longed to know—how the Pope fixed Shrove Tuesday—and so in future Scotland had no need to send a messenger to Rome. His homeward ride was fast and it was silent. By dawn he stood again on the Raven's Rock.

It is said by some that it was on this occasion that Michael Scott discussed hot crows' eggs with the Devil. For Michael had taught his wife all his magic knowledge and now he believed she had gone further than he, and he feared her but could not kill her by any of the means he knew of for her spells guarded her. In the end he killed her by means of grey crows' eggs heated in the fire and put into her armpits, this pleasant murder being counselled by the Devil as the only form of death against which no counter spell had been devised. It is a curious tale, this, and shows the trusted and much respected wizard in a very poor light. It is, however, believed to have given rise to the saying: 'Nothing evil will ever come out of the fire but the grey crow's egg.'

A little further, and Loch Garve comes into sight on the right, a fine loch and, when frozen over and the ice covered with fresh-fallen snow, a wonderful sight. But always there is towards the eastern end of the Loch one black spot which never freezes. This is usually attributed to a large spring set in the loch bottom, but it is really the chimney of the Waterhorse's house. Now water-horses are queer beasts; however much they may resemble men or horses in appearance they are closely akin in reality to fish and have cold blood and, when at home under water, fish's teeth. Consequently they never feel cold, nor do they like cooked food; raw fish or raw water weed with water snails are their idea of a pleasant meal. This is one reason why they find it so hard to get and keep wives and are so often hunting. But on the whole they are kindly creatures and, though they do carry off girls, they try to do what they can to make them happy. They build fine houses for them below the waters of their special loch and keep them well supplied with fresh-caught fish. But the girl this particular waterhorse carried off was not happy. One day he was from home and as he returned to the loch side he heard her crying and sobbing: 'I'm so cold, so cold.' Greatly perturbed, the horse galloped off to a ruined house near by and looked hard at it. Then he went to the village of Garve and ambled down the village street, carefully avoiding any man touching him, until he saw the village mason. He allowed the mason to catch his bridle and even to mount him, but no sooner was the man on his back than the horse was off to Loch Garve. There he persuaded the angry and frightened mason to build him a proper fireplace and a chimney, then returned him unharmed to his house. Now the waterhorse has a warm and contented wife who eats fried fish. As long as he lived the mason had only to go to the Loch side and say 'Fish' of an evening and next day a withy of them would be lying waiting for him on a certain boulder. After he died, another man tried this form of fishing and came to a bad end.

The road goes on past Loch Luichart, where a hydro-electric scheme required a new road, a new railway and a new railway station. Now up over the moors to the watershed, where rivers rise as tiny burns running east and west and where in the winter deer may be seen. Here, too, the roads to Wester Ross take off. The main road runs on by moor and loch, wood and rhododen-drons till it reaches Strome Ferry, 'Closed on Sunday' as most Highland ferries are. Much land thereabouts has been planted with young forests.

It is just over 100 years ago that the railway, which the Brahan

Seer is said to have foretold in the form 'Every stream shall have its bridge, balls of fire will pass rapidly up and down the Strath of Peffery and carriages without horses shall leave Dingwall to cross the country from sea to sea', ran as far as Loch Carron and ended there at Strome Ferry. Its extension to Kyle of Lochalsh was foreshadowed, however, by a ghost train which travellers in the old stage coach saw again and again. The old road and present railway ran on much the same lines for a time and then separated, and people travelling on the coach at night saw and heard a huge black 'locomotive' coming along the road at speed, with blazing lights; at a certain point where road and rail later divided it would turn away and rush into the hills where there was no roadway. After some three years of this it got so much on the coachman's nerves that he refused to drive on this stretch of road after dark and the coach on that stage became 'day only'.

When the Lord God finished making the world He rested on the seventh day. It was a very beautiful day in His new world and He decided to take a Sunday walk through His handiwork. He strolled across the high moors, joying in the clear air and sunshine, and the deer came to meet Him and learn His will. He was pleased and stroked their fine necks and soft noses. Since then their coats have glowed and their noses been soft as velvet. Then the Lord walked on into the woods and all the little wild creatures came to thank Him for creating them, rabbits and hares, stoats and weasels, pine-martens, field mice, tiny shrew-mice, birds, beetles, they all came round Him. But the squirrel could find no place and climbed a tree to get near to Him and God saw her efforts and took her on His shoulder, and while He was talking to the animals He was gently stroking her and fondling her ears. That is why the red squirrel is the loveliest of wild things. Her breast where it touched His robe is pure white. Then God left the woods and stood above the Kyles (where Strome Ferry now crosses), watching the sunset over the Western Isles and sea and hills, and He sighed with content and said, 'It is good.' 'Good,' replied a voice. 'Am I not the First? exclaimed the Lord God in surprise, for never before had a voice echoed through the hills. 'First,' answered the voice. Then God knew that it was an echo from the cliffs and hills across the water and He said: 'As you

were the first of all things in my new earth to praise me, so shall
you have power to help and strengthen the men who seek you.
Teach them to praise me also.' So the hills have strength and the
hillside at Strome Ferry has kept its echo.

10

NORTH FROM DINGWALL—I

Put thy trust in the earth; it never left thee empty.
(Gaelic saying)

DINGWALL TO EVANTON

THIS ROAD which leaves Dingwall for the North branches
soon after the level crossing, a loop takes off up a steep hill
to the left to serve Tulloch Castle, Mountgerald, Foulis
Castle and several farms, then rejoins the main road near Evanton.
Close to where the road divides is one of the most lovely roadside
gardens I have seen. Ross-shire gardens are famous but few are
laid out so unselfishly as this, entirely, it would seem, to give
pleasure to the passer-by.

At the top of the hill is set the main entrance to Tulloch
Castle and the road turns sharp right to avoid it. Tulloch was
also famed for its garden long before the 'opening' and therefore
necessarily the advertising of gardens came into fashion. On its
moor, also, stands a copse of fine firs believed to be a survival from
the original Caledonian Forest, but the Castle was perhaps best
known as the home of that Davidson of Tulloch 'who buried four
wives but the fifth buried him'. One was his daughter-in-law's
younger sister, which, as both sisters had children, led to most
complicated family relationships. Considerable amusement and
interest was aroused when the late Mr Davidson of Tulloch—a
man whose advice was much in demand because of his wise and
balanced outlook on life—sent for a water diviner when he
needed extra water supplies. The diviner with his hazel twig
found water in plenty, which made it worse because in those days
water divining and magic were much of a muchness, and here it
was, actually working.

Not far from Tulloch the road crosses a small, deep burn by a
bridge known as the Bogle's Bridge, being haunted and to be

avoided after dark. The deep banks of the burn were thickly wooded in the early part of the century which doubtless added to its bad reputation. Certainly no girl and few men would pass it after nightfall. There were various stories of the 'haunt'. Some said he had committed suicide as a result of being crossed in love, others that he had been murdered there by a jealous rival, but all were agreed that he was an extremely vicious and dangerous ghost and that young people, especially courting couples, should give the bridge a wide berth. Actually, the present road bridge is comparatively modern; a very much older bridge crossed the burn directly beneath it at water level and between the two bridges, old and new, is a space high enough and wide enough to have held a tiny house. In this space lived our ghost.

The road runs through rich farming country with fine trees. It is a glory of wild flowers in season, its ditches blue with the big water forget-me-not and golden with water ranunculus; gorse and groom and foxgloves clothe its banks and chicory turns the field edges blue, while brambles abound. But woe to the child who used to go blackberrying or nutting on the Sabbath, for the Devil would go with him, 'to hold down the branches'. In many ways this part of the country bears a far closer resemblance to parts of England than to the Highlands. The people, too, are unlike most of their Highland neighbours. When I knew the district well as a child, I seldom heard fairy tales told as in the West; life was too busy for much imagination perhaps, for everyone was farming from morn till night. Superstitious practices long discarded elsewhere, however, still flourished here, for the land was what mattered and the land and its superstitions change very slowly, especially in a place where the young rarely left the farm on which they were born unless to work on a neighbouring one. After all, why leave? What could you gain? You would find no richer farm land and no better climate in all Scotland, although in winter the snow lay sometimes for days on end and the 'Upper Road', as this one was usually called, would be blocked by drifts of from six to twelve feet deep. Push in a stick and twiddle it, and a hole of the deepest, loveliest sea-blue would appear in the pure white snow.

Above this road rich farmland rises to the more distant moors.

Between moor and arable was a narrow band of poor land, used partly for grazing and partly as crofts. In one of these crofts, as late as 1910, lived a white witch, Old Kate. If ever there was a 'wise-woman' it was she. She should, had she had the opportunity, have been a feminist of note. As it was, she did her best. She wore a man's hobnailed boots and thick stockings, a man's tweed jacket, and a man's cap on her head but consulted the proprieties to the extent of wearing a thick shortish skirt in summer (skirts were ankle-length in those days) and two or three tweed skirts of varying length one over the other in winter, the whole topped off by an old sack as an apron. She kept hens and was most successful with them: even when others had no eggs she had plenty. She had no use for men, so it was generally believed that she had been crossed in love, the usual explanation of anyone out of the ordinary.

Old Kate studied the weather and had great success in foretelling it. Few farmers in the district would start cutting hay or corn until their wives had taken a pat of the best butter and called on her. She used to discuss weather signs with my mother, who said that although Kate knew a mass of traditional weather lore she thought most of the old woman's shrewd guesses came from her own close observation of plants and birds. If, for instance, the thistles 'dig in' deep and early it is a sure sign of a hard winter. If plovers stay too long inland, she would say, it is a bad weather sign, as it is also if they stay late on the shore in spring when they should be nesting. 'Geese fly to sea, Good weather be', but if other migratory birds, especially swans and woodcock, come early the winter will be long and hard. But when the first wheatear comes, Old Kate believed, it is safe to sow corn. That may be true on the east coast but certainly is not so on the west.

Much of Old Kate's proverbial lore concerned times and seasons as they affected the farmer: what each month should be like and the awful consequences when it wasn't, such as, 'The snow that comes not at Hallowmas (Christmas) will come thick at Candlemas', and the curious 'If Christmas Day and Sunday meet, Look out for ice and snow and sleet' and 'When Hallowmas falls on a Wednesday all men are uneasy.' This last was supposed to foretell a severe winter. Winter, in her lore, began on Christmas Day and 'Dark, sullen and black the first three days of winter' was a welcome sign of a good year. February, too, *must* be bad:

> February fill the dyke
> Either with the black or the white
> But if it's white, the better to like.

Also, 'All the months of the year curse a fair February.' (In England too, weather lore is equally aware of the evils of a 'fair February'. 'The hind would as soon see his wife on her bier as that Candlemas Day should be pleasant and clear.') Old Kate held that March should come in with serpent's head and peacock's tail (cold and sunny), for 'Whatever the weather be, sow your seed in March. Let the first Tuesday pass, let the second pass if need be, but on the third Tuesday sow your seed though you couldn't throw a stone against the north wind, for he who won't sow in cold won't reap in heat.' One night's growth in March was held to equal three days' later. Sowing should never be begun on a Monday, why I don't know, nor a journey on a Saturday, for 'Saturday flitting, short sitting.'

Old Kate always warned that all her farming proverbs belonged to the 'real' dates, i.e. before the calendar was altered, so that her May 1st would be our May 12th and so forth. What she would have made of Summer Time I don't know. Probably she would have gone all modern and quoted, 'The clocks "spring" forward and "fall" back.' She believed, too, that the weather and the moon were as closely connected as the moon and the tides. Change of weather could, she said, be expected with a new moon and was modified by the quarters. The change began one to two days before the actual moment of the new moon. But, 'One Saturday's moon is enough in a king's reign,' and a late-in-the-day change was better than an early one. She shared the widespread belief, too, that certain plants and vegetables should be sown in the wane of the moon and others in the increase, that timber should be cut in the wane that it may be firm and lasting, and that sheep should be killed when the moon is new or the meat will shrink unduly in the cooking.

Old Kate was wise over the ills of man and beast though some of her cures would horrify us today. She believed, for instance, that if a sick man were laid on bare earth the earth would give him of its own strength and he would recover. She always preached, too, that children should *never* be allowed to share a bed with the old. This was a very common practice in the cottages of that day. She held that the old 'grannie' would draw strength and vitality from the child and live longer and stronger at the child's expense, and she firmly believed that 'a green winter makes a full churchyard'. She taught me that the best cure for a cut or scrape was sea-water or plain earth to stop the bleeding. 'Earth and sea are not greedy for blood,' she would say, 'and never hurt honest folk.' It certainly worked so as a child, if grown-ups were not about, I always used one or other, usually rich, well-manured garden earth, for cuts, as being the easiest to get. Many years later I cut my hand seriously on rusty metal. Later again, discussing old cures with the doctor, I mentioned the panacea for all wounds of my childhood—garden earth. 'Ah,' he said, 'that probably accounts for your hand healing so easily: you must have inoculated yourself against all known germs!' 'But,' he added severely, 'you should have got tetanus.'

Old Kate sometimes cured cattle with herb drinks after the 'Vet' gave them up: more often he was not consulted. Once there was a cattle sickness of some sort on the farms and also measles in the school. I had a French governess from Brittany then who was friends with a farmer's wife near, and we were often invited to visit a new calf or foal. This day we were asked up and found two big bonfires blazing on a small hillock with only a narrow strip of ground between them. One of the farm children told me we were too late: we had missed seeing the old shepherd lighting them by rubbing sticks together. Now that the fires were burning well, big branches of fresh-cut rowan and yew were thrown on them and all the cattle on the farm were driven through the smoke. After that, we children were told to run through it, between the fires, to keep away the measles. The oftener we ran through, the longer we would be free of the measles, we were told, so we did it several times. I did not get measles until I was over forty! Afterwards we were given bits of a queer oaten bannock to eat. So were the cows. Later, Mademoiselle told my mother that the 'need fire' was 'just like in Brittany', that the farmer had said 'Nonsense' and gone off to market leaving his wife to arrange it, 'just like in Brittany', and that the bannock was made from a recipe of Old Kate's; oatmeal ground by hand and winnowed by fire, eggs from a hen that never saw a cock, butter made from a cow's first milk (that had had to be borrowed), and honey of wild bees dug from the ground, all mixed with water from a running brook, a boundary burn for choice.

On the right of the road, about three miles from Dingwall, the Mountgerald avenue takes off. Mountgerald, which my parents rented for some years, was reputed to be haunted by the ghost of a workman killed in its building in the early eighteenth century and buried as a sacrifice for the house beneath the foundations. The story went that, by order of the owner, one wall was built up first, then a block of stone from the top of it was dropped upon one of the workmen (a vindictive man disliked by his fellows being chosen for the role of sacrifice) and his body buried beneath the foundations. He is reputed to haunt the place where he was killed, a cellar at the bottom of the basement stairs, and to this spot he is bound except for five nights of the year—New Year, Midsummer, the Spring and Autumn Solstices and the anniversary of his death, in mid-August. On these five nights his ghost is free to roam where he will and to do harm or good as he chooses, his supernatural power being greatest in August. Vindictive in life, vindictive in death, he is believed to wreak all the vengeance he is capable of on those nights on anyone sleeping in the house. Curiously enough, an old friend of my parents who was staying with us, shooting with my father, died suddenly on the evening of the August anniversary. For the remainder of our time there, nine or ten years, the excuses made by some of our maids to go home for a day or two that week were fearful and wonderful. For Easter Ross before the first World War was superstitious beyond belief.

Perhaps to say 'was before the first World War' is misleading, for I have the following story on very good and reliable authority, though the place must not be named for obvious reasons. In a certain Highland glen, 'East of the Sun and West of the Moon', there was after the 1939-45 War a great shortage of houses. The Local Authority was approached and agreed to erect some 'prefabs'. This, in due course, was done, a number of families applied for them and those to whom they were allotted were in high delight at their luck. But some of the old folk disapproved strongly and, 'Prefabricated houses! That's no way to build! "They" won't like it,' was widely quoted among them, some even trying to dissuade their grandchildren from applying for them. After the families moved in bad luck seemed to settle on the 'lucky' ones. Illness and accident became the rule. At first of little importance, the accidents grew more and more serious until a man died after a car crash, a child was burnt to death, a baby was still-born and its mother rushed to hospital, there to fight for her life. It was then that the Minister's wife, a kind and sensible person from the South, called to offer help and sympathy to the husband left with a small child on his hands. To her surprise she found the doorstep and kitchen floor blood-stained but thought only that he was evidently no housekeeper and passed on to a neighbouring house to assure herself that the child could continue in their care. Here too were blood-stains. She then noted them on other doorsteps. Puzzled and worried, she hurried home to the Manse to consult her husband, who 'belonged'. He seemed worried but not surprised. 'The County Council omitted to bury anything under the new houses,' he explained. 'It caused a lot of worry at the time and naturally all these accidents are blamed on that omission. I was afraid this was bound to come. What are they doing? Sacrificing cocks, of course. No doubt one was killed in each house today and the doorstep sprinkled with blood. It is as old as the hills. "He shall lay the foundations thereof in his firstborn and in his youngest son shall he set up the gates of it." Let us be thankful that nowadays it's only cocks.' Now all goes well with those pre-fabs.

This idea of a 'sacrifice' for a house sounds to us barbarous and stupid. But our ancestors were hard-headed sensible people; if they had not been they could not have survived and we should not be here. By them it would seem to have been considered just honesty and common sense, because 'before the gods that made the gods had drunk at dawn their fill' the Highlands belonged not to men or giants or even the old pagan gods and goddesses but to something far older and more fearful—some primeval Spirit of Earth. His name, if he ever had one, is forgotten (the more fear-

ful things are often nameless) and so are his deeds but it is known
that he lived deep in the earth's heart, owned the soil and resented
its disturbance by man. It seemed obvious that he was a Great
One and much feared. Little bits of his worship still survive in
odd corners, such as this matter of burying a cock as a propitiation
before inhabiting a new house. Foolish would anyone be who
neglected such a necessary act. No honest man would expect to
live rent free in a house he neither owned nor had built, nor
would he expect to build a house on another's land without paying feu duty or rent to the landlord. If the owner of the house
and the owner of the land have both the right to be paid, how
can we expect the owner of the subsoil to demand no recompense? The first two, if ignored, can and probably will take the
squatter to court but "They" who live below the earth will judge
and punish him by their own laws. And though the mills of the
earth gods grind slowly they were certainly believed to grind
most exceeding small, so it is better not to start them turning.

At the time of the death at Mountgerald previously referred
to, I, being a child, and so somewhat in the maids' confidence,
heard much of death lights and death fires being seen. Three
'death watch fires' were said to have been seen hovering on the
outer wall of the house just below the window of the room in
which the death took place on three separate occasions shortly
before the event, and I was shown the fire marks on the harled
wall. Three brown marks like scorches there undoubtedly were
and I, anyhow, had never seen them before. But when I asked
my parents—needless to say without giving the reason—what
caused such marks I was told they were probably rust marks
caused by some iron stanchion or nails in the wall, and, 'how
quick of you to notice them; we never did'.

From the Mountgerald entrance a little wood, sweet with the
scent of woodruff in early summer, runs beside the road as far as
a burn. Beside the road bridge here the local smithy used to stand,
a most important and fascinating gathering place. But, small as
it is, this burn had in my childhood its own importance also, for
it had cut deep into the rich soil and become the boundary between two properties, Mountgerald and Lumlair. In those early
days of this century the Evil Eye was still a potent force firmly

believed in. There were those who could 'take off' the Eye and even, if you were lucky, turn it back on the sender, his or her family and their beasts, and these 'wise-women' needed the water from a boundary burn in their art. If one bank of the burn bounded Church land, so much the better, but any two properties would do. The exorcist must fill a bucket from such a burn with her bare hands, drop by drop, wash the bewitched person

Mountgerald

or cow with the water while repeating the proper formulae, and then throw what remained on to some large stone. If the exorcism had been a success the evil and the curse would recoil on the sender, but if the person bewitched had deserved the bewitchment of himself or his beasts, then the most he could hope for was that the evil would leave him and fall upon the stone, in which case it usually burst into pieces. This type of 'cure' was expensive and there were some people even then who thought that those who were highly paid for removing the curse might be those who had put it on in the first place, on the principle of 'he who hides can find'. But that the Evil Eye and 'over-looking' were themselves real, few doubted.

Further on, on the left of the 'Upper Road', stand the gates of Foulis Castle. Until recently the two stone pillars of the gateway were crowned by eagles—the Eagles (or Fowls) of Foulis. There were many stories about these more than life-sized birds in my childhood. They flew free, of course, on Midsummer Night as do all statues, and it was said that the attitudes they took up on their return to their perches foretold the good or evil fortune of the Clan for the coming year, for Foulis Castle was the seat of the Chief of Clan Munro. On their presence hung the glory of the Clan: an old prophecy was said to run, 'When the Eagles leave Foulis the Munros will leave Scotland.' The birds have now gone from their place on the gate pillars and the owner of Foulis Castle is no longer the heir male and Chief of the Clan.

In the year 1590 Katherine Ross, Lady of Foulis, was tried for the attempted murder of her stepson, Robert Munro, and her sister-in-law, Margery Campbell of Balnagown. Several of her fellow-conspirators confessed the whole plot and it is said to have been proved that her old nurse, having accidentally tasted ale that the Lady of Foulis had prepared for her stepson, dropped dead. She was also accused of making 'images of butter and pictures of clay' and shooting elf darts at them. She was acquitted, however, and Hector Munro, who prosecuted her in the case, was himself tried for witchcraft on that same day, on the grounds that, being ill, he did summon a witch to cure him. She gave him three draughts and said that she could only save him if the principal man of his blood would die in his stead. This was Lady Katherine's eldest son, George Munro. That night the witch dug a grave on a spot where the lands of King and Bishop met, placed the sick man in it wrapped in a blanket and replaced the green turf over him. Then one of the participants ran round the grave nine times, came close to the grave and asked the witch her choice. She replied, 'Hector to live and George to die.' So Hector was carried home to bed and recovered. He was tried for 'the cruel, odious slaughter of George Munro, as he took from you the sickness from which he died'. Hector, too, was acquitted but it does seem to have been a quite first class family row.

Some generations ago a Munro of Foulis married a Dutch girl and she, rather horrified by the stark grey stone buildings of the North, persuaded her husband to employ a Dutch architect when alterations were planned for the Castle. The result was that Foulis Castle soon bore a far greater resemblance to a traditional Dutch house than to an ancient Highland castle. Nevertheless, it is an old Clan stronghold and the rent payable to the King of Scotland was 'one snowball, payable at whatever time of year it may be demanded'. This was easy for the owner of Ben Wyvis, as the old Hag Winter keeps Spring's bride a prisoner in a cave on this mountain until the girl washes a brown fleece white, and the Hag takes care to see that the maiden is always surrounded with snow and ice so that Spring can get no foothold.

Sir Hector Munro of Foulis was one of the many who lost son and heir in World War I. This seemed particularly tragic because he was killed not long before Armistice Day. By 1918 it was said that not one direct male heir was left to any property between Beauly and Invergordon. The Highlands have never been backward in war.

The Upper and Lower Roads join at the village of Evanton. The 'Lower Road' as it is often called is the direct route from Dingwall to Tain and the north and hugs the shore of Cromarty Firth. This firth is for the first four or five miles a mud flat at low tide and is the only sea-loch I know of where a strong wind may override the tides and keep perpetual high or perpetual low water for days on end. The Conon River runs out through the centre and so shallow is the sea water and so little salt does it carry into the Conon's bed that both sea-trout and salmon could be caught with a fly in the river channel at low tide three or four miles below Dingwall. It was a somewhat dangerous sport, however, for two reasons. The first is that those mud flats are for a large part quicksands, only narrow paths where the small burns run out to sea being safe to walk on. It is needful to know the paths out to the central sandbanks well, for a false step might mean death, and an unpleasant one. Having reached the sandbanks, the fisherman is safe enough unless the second peril intervenes—the local rifle range. When this was in use and any bad shot missed the targets completely, bullets would suddenly whizz past your head or ricochet along the sand at your feet. Then the wise man left in haste, salmon or no salmon.

During the hard winter of 1914-15 the firth froze hard, men walked across on the ice as near the open sea as Evanton and a man drove a horse and cart across. Another had planned to drive his car across next day but thaw set in. The ice froze in huge rough blocks so that even to walk across was a job. It was the hardest frost ever remembered in the district, 33 degrees of frost, but it did not last long.

About three miles from Dingwall a stone building stands in a small field by the shore of the firth. This was once a chapel, the field its graveyard, but later it became the Mountgerald boat-house. It is now a dwelling-house and the graveyard has disappeared, though at the turn of the century many old grave stones could be seen half buried in the grass. Even then most of them were too old and worn to be deciphered, the most modern still legible being eighteenth century. The little church was built by the Mackenzies of Findon as their chapel when they owned the two properties, Mountgerald and Findon, facing each other across the water which provided in those days the easiest means of communication.

The last of the Mackenzies of Mountgerald was a keen Roman Catholic. He and his two sons attended a banquet in Dingwall being given in honour of twelve priests who were visiting the district. Unfortunately the cook mistook a root of hemlock for horse-radish and made a sauce of it. The whole of the party except one priest ate it and all but he died within twenty-four hours. So ended that family of Mackenzies and the little chapel fell on evil days.

The night before the priests' fatal banquet a girl had slipped into the woods by the shore to meet her lover. As they talked together in the shelter of the trees they became aware of a low, unhappy keening. The girl was frightened but the young man said it was a beast in distress and they must find it. They went towards the shore and saw the surface of the firth covered with lights, low blue lights moving softly in groups of three, two at the head and one at the foot as death lights would. Both were now frankly terrified and made for safety to the little chapel by the shore, not then dismantled of course. Here the worst shock of all awaited them. Light flowed out of the chapel windows and when the young couple opened the door, expecting to find the peace and safety of an evening service, they saw instead three coffins laid out in due order with lights at head and foot, and by each coffin knelt a nun, rapt in prayer as a few days later would be seen in the flesh.

It is said that even though the direct line of Mackenzie of Findon is now extinct, before any of the blood died the old chapel would be seen lit up. If anyone approached and peered through the chinks of the now boarded-up windows the semblance of a funeral would appear within and from the size of the coffin the person for whom the preparation was made might be guessed. In August 1914, on the evening before war was declared, a man and a girl, strolling along the shore, saw the old church, which by then had long been converted into a boat-house, fully lit up and when they went closer they saw that a funeral service, as they thought, was in progress. Surprised at such a service late at night and unaware of any local death, they went to the nearest house to enquire. The owners had not heard of any funeral either and did not even know that the boat-house had been a consecrated building. They laughed at the idea but the son of the house agreed to come and see for himself. When they reached the building all was as the young couple had described, except that there was no coffin. The new member of the party recognised the service, of which he heard a part, as a Requiem Mass. Questioned later, all three agreed that the chapel seemed properly furnished and in order. Next morning it was once more a boat-house. It would be interesting to know whether anything similar will ever be seen again now that the building has been turned into an occupied dwelling-house.

Not far beyond the chapel point the Mountgerald boundary burn comes out to sea. It comes down through one of the loveliest small valleys imaginable, thickly starred in spring with primroses and wood-anemones and, here and there, a blue drift of violets. Overhead the sky can be seen through a lattice of gean (wild cherry) boughs white with blossom. Trees and banks are alive with small nesting birds, wagtails and stonechats by the stream, robins, linnets, pippins and finches, while blue-tits hang upside down among the cherry blossom ready to snap up an unwary bee. There are rarer birds too sometimes, crossbills and firetails, even waxwings, and in June the bullfinch flaunts his beauty. All this part of Ross-shire is a birds' paradise and the dawn song there is unbelievably beautiful.

Where small birds nest there will, of course, be cuckoos. All over the Highlands the cuckoo is held to be a 'queer' bird, in touch with unseen powers and possessing illicit knowledge, for it always winters in the Underworld. Its call heralds the spring and in the Islands to hear the first cuckoo call in the spring before you have eaten is most unlucky—in some parts a death omen. In some places girls ask the cuckoo, 'How soon shall I marry?', while the old people ask, 'How long shall I live?' The cuckoo answers with a clear 'Cuckoo' for each year. But in Easter Ross girls went further and used to ask the cuckoo many questions and especially what colour they should wear, because lucky colours, particularly at the time of courting, were held very important there. The procedure was as follows. The girl would go into a wood where she thought a cuckoo was and would wait quietly until she saw or heard him; then she would say,

> Cuckoo calling on the tree
> Tell me what brings luck to me.

after which she would ask her question, whatever it might be, in a form requiring Yes or No for an answer. For instance, not 'What is my lucky colour?' but 'Cuckoo, cuckoo, is it blue I should wear?' If the cuckoo replies with one call he means No and the girl must try again, 'Cuckoo, cuckoo, is it red?' and so on until he calls several times in succession, meaning Yes, or That's right.

In another mile Ardully Point runs out into the firth. This was a great wintering place for East Coast fishing boats, especially sailing ones: sometimes fifty or sixty at a time would be laid up there and they were always worth a visit, if only to read their names. The majority, of course, bore girls' names after sweethearts and wives, or even daughters, but some were more imaginative, *Wind's Daughter*, *Silver Herring*, *Dream*, *Man's Desire*, *Foam Lover*, and some more unexpected, *Parallelepiped* for instance, and *Pax Vobiscum*, *The Ass* and *The Hexagon*.

Near here a tragedy occurred before the 1914 War. The Ardully shooting tenant (Ardully was the Foulis dower-house and when not so required was let as a shooting lodge) brought some of his staff with him from England, including a young footman. This boy was much teased by the other servants. One day he announced his intention of walking across the firth. In all seriousness the local men warned him of the grave danger of the quicksands but he, believing it just another leg-pull, set off and was sucked down a few yards from the shore. A cyclist heard his cries for help and went for assistance but it came too late.

11

NORTH FROM DINGWALL—II

A story I heard on the cliffs of the West
That oft thro' the breaker's dividing
A city is seen on the ocean's wild breast
In turreted majesty riding.
But brief is that glimpse of that phantom so bright;
Soon close the white waters to screen it
And the bodement, they say, of this wonderful sight
Is death to the eyes that have seen it.

EVANTON TO TAIN

AFTER re-uniting at Evanton, a pleasant village, the Upper and Lower roads soon fork once more, the lower branch continuing by the shore, the upper or left branch (which we shall follow first) running through wooded glens and by hair-pin bends up on to the heather-clad moors until it reaches the famous Struie Hill where it twists down steeply amid breath-taking views over the Kyles of Sutherland to Ardguy and Bonar Bridge. The A.A. has erected an 'indicator' at a view point near the hill top, naming all the mountains, towns and villages visible on a clear day, and it is a spot indeed worth visiting.

Down below in the valley can be seen Fearn House, a charming house standing on the Ross-shire shore of the Kyles near the village of Wester Fearn. When my grandfather rented Fearn late in the last century there was a family, noted for their water-manship and success with the fishing, living near by. He was told that the reason for their success was that they were descended from a merman. Mermen and mermaids were believed in Easter Ross to wear belts, in which belts lay the secret of their amphibious nature. If anyone could steal such a belt the merman—or mer-maid—to whom it belonged would become his prisoner on dry land, unable to return to the sea. A Fearn girl found just such a belt on the shore of the Kyles and took it home. Its merman owner came in search of it and they fell in love. Soon they were married and lived most happily, says tradition, and had a family, but, just to be on the safe side, the wife kept her husband's belt well hidden. On her deathbed she told him the hiding place. After her death he gave to their children 'the only gift he had to give', that they should be free of the sea and no one of them nor of their descendants should ever drown or be harmed by the sea. Then he put on his belt and was never seen again. So the family naturally became noted fishers.

Close to the Kyles stands a small green hillock. Here in late autumn the wild geese flight in, this being their first 'stand', and sometimes many hundreds can be seen there, resting for an hour and turning the hill grey. Some years, none visit the hillock at all and none seem ever to care to remain there. A firm belief in Ross-shire before the Wars was that when geese flight in in winter, if the first skein to arrive contains more geese than ganders more girls than boys will be born that year in the district, and vice-versa. Also, if a goose or a gander was seen near the home of an expectant mother, the child's sex would be that of the bird seen. An interested watch for the first arrivals was always kept.

Now to return to the lower or shore road. This passes through the small village of Alness, reputed to have made a fortune out of Naval wives and families in the first World War by charging unbelievable prices for everything, even the smallest attic rooms. This, Alness denies indignantly. The road passes by the woods of Novar, the mansion house of which was lent as an hotel for naval wives in that same war, to Invergordon itself. Here the Grand Fleet then had a base and here one Christmas H.M.S. *Natal* sank at her moorings with incredible speed, pinning down her returning 'liberty boat' under her mast as she turned over and so taking it down with her. The Captain and officers had been giving a children's party on board and the story swept over the county that half the children of Ross and Cromarty had gone down with the ship, but actually the last boatload of small guests had already reached the shore in safety. Invergordon was a great centre of rumours in those days. The extraordinary 'Russian Soldiers' myth had one of its many beginnings here. On the same day, all over England and Scotland, this story burst forth. Someone,

never the actual narrator, but someone 'reliable', had seen trains
full of Russian troops passing through the local station. Some
were even seen changing trains. A division, it was said, was on its
way to France and an Army Corps would shortly follow. In
Invergordon our gamekeeper's sister 'saw them herself' and was
told they came from Archangel by ship and were entraining here
for London. In England, trains brought them from Scotland.
Everyone everywhere knew of them being seen on the same day.
Yet there were none. Was it an elaborate hoax? Some curious
propaganda effort? A cloak for something quite different? No
one ever really knew, for those who 'were in the know' and had
'certain information' never could agree.

In 1914 the railway north of Perth was a single-line track and
this made supplying the Grand Fleet in northern waters almost
impossible. It was the railwaymen themselves who solved the
problem. They offered to give up completely, for goods traffic,
the very necessary safety rule of fifteen minutes between trains
and, at those times when the line was clear of passengers, trains
followed each other at four-minute intervals, looking like a
parade of caterpillars nose to tail. Thanks to them the Fleet never
went short of food, coal or munitions of war.

Invergordon in peace is a small and pleasant seaside resort. Its
most noticeable feature is probably the monument, a copy of the
gates of Seringapatam, erected by Sir Hector Munro of Novar on
Fyrish Hill behind the town when he returned from his Indian
campaigns. The monument can be seen (though its origin is
usually forgotten) for many miles round and an enterprising
young naval gunnery officer once offered £5 if he might lay his
guns on it and have three shots. The country inland from the sea
hereabouts is very lovely, especially the wooded glens in spring
and autumn. But many years ago there was a summer when no
trees, from the woods of Novar as far west as the Great Glen,
became green. They came into leaf as usual but the leaves came
out in varying shades of yellow and brown. The woods looked
like an under-exposed colour photograph of autumn colouring.
Everyone in the Highlands knew the belief that if the trees wither
or turn colour out of season on any one property it is a death
omen for the owner, and if all over a district it presages some

great disaster to the country as a whole or the death of the King. But few had ever known or heard of its happenings on such a scale as this and thought it on a par with such sayings as 'When I find a cuckoo's nest' or 'When you build a tower of mosquitoes' teeth' —just never, in fact. There was considerable nervousness in some parts as to what it might portend and when, in the autumn, King George V had his serious illness many believed that the trees had foretold it. What causes this rare discoloration no one seems to know. If a late frost, different species of tree would be at different stages, so all should not be hit. A drought perhaps, but in this case there was not one, at least not memorably so. There certainly was not a caterpillar plague such as sometimes withers foliage. The queer mis-coloured leaves seemed perfect in shape and substance and un-nibbled.

The road from Invergordon carries on by the shore as far as Barbaraville, giving excellent views of that fine pair of cliff headlands the Cromarty Suitors. These were once giant brothers who, having offended against some primeval law, were changed into these great cliff guardians of the low lands behind. On the right of the road lie the Sands of Nigg and Nigg Bay itself. Once, says tradition, many centuries ago what is now sea and sand was a low-lying and very fertile valley. But a great storm arose and swept the sea in between the Suitors, all the fields were submerged and later buried in sand, while a small village there and its church were covered by the sea. My mother, when I was a child, sometimes had maids from Port Mahomack on the north of the peninsula, the daughters of fishermen. One of them told me that her father had sailed as a boy on a boat with an old man who always 'listened' before setting out, saying that if danger threatened the fishing fleet the submerged church bells of Nigg would sound a warning. He said that when *he* was a boy, on still, clear days signs of buildings beneath the sea could still be seen, also great stones, but all were shrouded in sand then and had now disappeared. He also, this old man, told how as a young boy he had been on a boat when a man on board heard the warning. The man said it sounded not like bells but like great horns blowing and that it came, not from the church but from the Stones. Be that as it may, the boat put back into port at once, all believing it a death omen for the man who heard it. He was duly drowned three days later. This belief in drowned villages wherein it is a death omen to see the image of their village riding on the waves, and whose church bells sound storm warnings, is very widespread in Britain, particularly in the West, but Port Mahomack had many other 'sea' beliefs.

Blue was lucky, for instance, and if a member of a boat's crew died, the boat would have a blue 'mourning' line painted round her. It is unwise to turn a boat anti-clockwise; if you do, she may be 'smashed on the hidden rocks of the sea'. Worse still, turning widdershins puts you in the power of the Evil One. An old ill-wish there was, 'The left-about unlucky turn to you.' Mermen or some such sea-creatures have been known to seize the prow of a ship in storm and try to turn her against the sun so as to put her crew outside the protection of God. Another thing no boat owner must do is to take to sea anything made of rowan wood if he has already on board anything made of juniper, for these two woods have a 'hate' for one another so strong that it may split the boat and cause it to sink. Be careful, too, that no haunted tree, the home of ghost or spirit, is used in the building of your ship, for if it is you will find that the ghost has come to sea with its tree. 'The boat builder who knows his trade must place a crooked sixpence in the keel of every boat' and if she is fair enough to be coveted her owner should try to start on his first sail without spectators lest their coveting of her does harm. Nets should always be let down on the right-hand side for a good catch, for that is what St. Peter did. A maiden's hair, just a single strand of hair, woven into a rope more than doubles its strength. All this I was told.

Then, too, if a man's hair won't burn he should never put to sea, and no woman should burn her hair combings when anyone of her blood is at sea if she cares for his safe return. Neither should you put to sea fasting, nor carry a coffin or a minister in your boat if it can be avoided. Be sure, too, that no white stone has got on board, even among the ballast. Cats should always be well watched: if they frolic it is for joy that a storm is coming up, for your cat may well be a witch. Certain it is that she can bring wind by whipping water with her paw, but usually when you want her to she won't. If a cat washes behind her ears it will bring rain. But, above all, *watch* the ship's cat. As long as she busies herself on deck or below all is well; she may be just a cat with excellent intentions with regard to rats. But if she is seen climbing the rigging, beware! She is undoubtedly a witch and will cause the ship to be cast away. It is most unlucky to kill a swan, a teal duck or a porpoise.

Once, porpoise meat was a valued food in the Highlands, anyhow on the west coast, as was whale meat and seal meat. Like seal meat, porpoise could be eaten in Roman Catholic times on Fridays and in Lent, even by a priest, counting as fish. Porpoise eating was not very well thought of round the Moray Firth and the Kyles of Sutherland when I was a child, and this was the reason said the daughter of Port Mahomack. Once a ship was in need of fresh food, so a sailor tried to harpoon a porpoise. He flung his knife and hit the creature but it immediately dived and so escaped, taking the sailor's knife with it but leaving upon the sea water an ominous stain. Instantly the wind dropped and the ship found herself becalmed. Round her the sea lay frowning, oily and heavy as the doldrums. Then the black waters parted and out of them stepped a handsome young Chief with a host of armed retainers. They walked across the glassy water and the Chief hailed the ship, demanding to speak with her captain. Much alarmed, the captain came forward, to be met with a peremptory order to hand over immediately that member of his crew who had recently wounded a porpoise. The captain refused.

'You would be wiser to obey,' said the young Chief in reasonable tones, 'for if you do not I shall drown your ship and all aboard her.'

At this point the sailor, seeing no help for it, came forward and expressed himself as willing to go with the strangers to save the ship. He climbed over the side and found himself sinking through the water at breath-taking speed. Indeed he could hardly breathe at all but as he believed himself drowning this did not surprise him. What did surprise him was to find his feet shortly set upon sand and the young Chief's hand on his arm guiding him, and he himself still with power to walk. He was led into a comfortably furnished house and to a seat in it and there was bidden to rest for a few moments until he should recover from his swift descent. He was left alone and soon found himself breathing comfortably. Shortly, the young Chief returned and, telling the sailor to follow him, led him into another room where lay a handsome young man with his eyes closed and the pallor of death on his face.

'This is my brother whom you wounded,' said the Chief sternly, 'there is the knife in his side. Draw out your knife, place your hand upon the wound to close it and wish with all your heart that you both may live.'

The sailor, much frightened but also genuinely regretting his action, did as he was bidden. Soon the young man's eyes opened, his colour returned, and within an hour he rose to his feet cured.

'Now we will dine,' said his victim to the astonished sailor, 'and then my brother and I will return you to your ship, but first you must promise me two things: that you will never again harm or allow others in your presence to harm a porpoise, and that you will tell this story to all who will listen, that they also may extend to us the protection we consider our due since we harm none.'

The sailor promised and after a good dinner was once more returned, very breathless, to the surface. His astonished friends eagerly pulled him aboard and the voyage proceeded well, with a school of porpoises playing about the ship as if guiding her.

Dogfish were believed in the Dornoch Firth area to grow into 'caa-ing whales' (porpoises) or else into sharks. But dogfish unlike the true porpoise, must be killed. If you catch a dogfish, whether in net or on line, no matter how hard it is to kill it (and it *is* very hard) nor how much it goes flapping round the boat bottom refusing to die, you must never throw it back into the sea alive. If you do it will grow into a shark, become a man-eater and hunt the boats, for that is how man-eating sharks are made. Whales should always be treated with respect—remember Jonah! So, to some extent, should haddock. It was a good sign if haddock came to your net because the haddock was the fish which St. Peter caught in the Sea of Galilee and which contained the tribute money. The two black marks or smudges on its sides are the prints of the Saint's fingers.

How large a part sea and fish played in the life of the North can be seen by the number of English proverbs whose Highland counterparts are concerned with the sea, as:

Make hay while the sun shines = Get bait while the tide is out.

As fat as butter = As fat as a seal.

Carrying coals to Newcastle = Putting salt in the sea.

Blind as a bat = Blind as a dogfish.

As swift as the wind = As swift as the wave tops.

A man without a gun sees fine birds = A hammerless woman sees many limpets.

As dead as a doornail = As dead as a herring. (Herrings were reputed to die more quickly out of water than any other fish.)

Don't count your chickens before they are hatched = Never count your fish till they're out of the sea.

As brave as a lion = As brave as a salmon.

As white as a lily = White as sea-foam.

And finally, one for which I know no English equivalent, 'Marriage is a bag of eels with one flounder in it.'

Actually the main road does not touch Port Mahomack but swings inland across the isthmus, passing Balchraggan where a road to the right leads to Fearn Parish Church, a church with an interesting history. Fearn Abbey and its abbey church are believed to have been founded early in the seventh century by one St. Aeddan, nicknamed Maidoc or Madwg 'the Beneficent'. He seems to have caught the imagination of the Celtic world and the name Maidoc became very widespread both in Ireland and in Wales as well as in the North. Tradition has it that a Prince of North Wales came to study in the abbey and took a form of the founder's name, Maidowe, but he was not a monk at heart but rather an explorer. One night he dreamed that an angel appeared to him and ordered him to take a ship and sail west and west and west until he should reach a country of gold and of sun and of heat such as he could not imagine, a country of vast temples and of a people who spoke a strange tongue, wore strange clothes and worshipped strange gods. Here he was to preach and leave his bones. Having dreamt this three times, he approached the Abbot, who was unsympathetic. That night the Abbot also dreamed the same dream except that in his dream, having shown him the strange land, the angel bade him let Maidowe go there with his blessing. So the Abbot arose and sent for Maidowe. Maidowe returned to Wales, got a ship from his Princedom and sailed into the west. Traditionally he is the teacher who, in Aztec legend, is remembered as having come out of the east in a vessel with sails 'white as the sun's rays' and taught the people of Mexico. Perhaps he was a better teacher than the angel was navigator, for had he strictly followed his instructions he should have fetched up at the St. Lawrence River, not Mexico!

To return to Fearn, the Abbey fell into ruin but was refounded by Alexander II for the White Friars. A terrible accident overtook their church, however, in 1742. Here is an account of it from the Journal of Bishop Forbes who visited the Diocese of Ross some years after it had happened:

The roof of flagstones, with part of a side wall, was beat down in an instant by thunder and lightning on Sunday, October 10th 1742, and so crushed and bruised forty that they were scarcely to be discovered who or what they were, and therefore were buried promiscuously, without any manner of distinction.

Fortunately this was the first Sunday on which a rival Presbyterian service had been held near by, and the Presbyterian congregation hurried to the spot and saved many of the wounded. Had the church been as full as on previous Sundays, it was estimated that over 100 persons would have lost their lives. A part of the church, the nave and the choir, survived and is now this Parish Church.

After Balchraggan the road continues across the flat green dune land to Tain—a most ancient and attractive old town, once the county town of Ross and later one of the Wick Burghs. It is a place of churches. Its 'old' church still boasts an hour glass in the pulpit (one hour and ten minutes was its timing for the sermon, I am told!) and what must surely be an unique east window, for the five lights each illustrate a flower mentioned in the Bible, such as the Lilies of the Field and the Rose of Sharon. Tain's old Gaelic name was Baile Dubhthaid, Duthus's Town, and the ruins of the ancient Church of St. Duthus stand in its graveyard near the Tain Links, a lovely ivy-clad ruin. Once it was one of the most important churches in the north. St. Duthus' relics were held in high repute as miracle workers and many made pilgrimage to visit them, including King James IV who made a pilgrimage to 'the shrine where he was born'. This 'he' was long supposed to have referred to St. Duthus but it is now known that the saint was born in Ireland, and as it is also known that Queen Margaret, James IV's mother, was in the north at about the right time (17th March 1472-3) it is believed that the 'he' really referred to King James himself and that he was born in a small chapel nearby in the churchyard, some ruins of which are still visible. Local tradition has it that Queen Margaret, at last expecting a child after some

The ancient Church of St. Duthus

years of a childless marriage, made this pilgrimage to beseech St. Duthus that her baby should be a son, and that while she was in Tain James was born. Whatever the reason, the shrine was highly thought of in royal circles, for not only did James IV visit it more than once, it is said, and such a journey can have been no light task in those days, but his son James V is reputed to have come to its ruins as a barefoot pilgrim in 1527. If so he was only about fifteen at the time and one wonders what brought him at that early age and whether his visit had any connection with the burning at the stake of the Martyr Abbot of Fearn in the following year. This Church of St. Duthus was one of the two great Sanctuaries of the North—The Garth of Tain—its sanctuary area carefully marked out with stone crosses, now destroyed.

There is an old belief in the Highlands that swallows, while seeking man's company and befriending him, will never presume to alight on or build their nests in a church. At Tain, where swallows are common, they were said never to enter the Garth which was once sanctuary. Among those who sought sanctuary here in its heyday were the wife and daughter of Robert the Bruce, but safety was not for them and the Earl of Ross unhesitatingly violated sanctuary, carried them off, and delivered them both prisoner to Edward I of England. Later he changed sides and led the men of Ross to fight for Bruce at Bannockburn. As King, the Bruce must have welcomed so powerful a vassal but one wonders what he thought as a man and how much he trusted one who came to him as a renegade from the service of both the King and the God whom he had vowed to serve.

The road from Tain continues up the shore of the Kyles of Sutherland to Ardguy, once famous for its heather honey, and so across Bonar Bridge into Sutherland.

12

SUTHERLAND

Through fields where the ghosts
Of the marsh and the moorland
Still ride the old marches,
Despising the plough.

     *   *   *   *   *

The marsh and the moorland
Are not to be banished.

SIR ALEXANDER GRAY

IN SUTHERLAND, unlike those in *1066 And All That*, all roads lead not 'to Rome' but 'from Lairg'. Why, I don't know, they just do.

Lairg itself is a pleasant township on the southern end of Loch Shin. In this excessively long though narrow loch, a yellow waterhorse has its home. It is a rather lonely, unhappy beast, poor thing. Most Highland supernatural creatures were very much concerned about their souls if they had any, or gaining a soul if they had not. They loved theological discussions, too, and were interested in all Church matters. The waterhorse in Loch Shin was no exception to this rule.

He was a golden horse, of course; almost all those in the North and East were, the black waterhorses belonging to the West coast only. In the early days of Christianity in the Highlands this waterhorse held long discussions with the local priest on theological matters and finally agreed to help him to build a church if thereby he might win a soul. Knowing of a conveniently situated dun nearby, the horse took stones from it and carried them on his back, across the loch, to a suitable site for a church. The dun, however, was a fairy dwelling and the Little People were, perhaps not unnaturally, displeased. Since then the poor waterhorse has not been well received in the best fairy circles, while the priest, having had his labour, made little effort to get him a soul. Waterhorses *were* stupid.

I wonder whether waterhorses once needed to hide and, if so, from what. Certainly they seem to have been pioneers of protective colouring, for it is noticeable that here in Sutherland, as also in the Great Glen, where golden bracken with red deer-grass in winter and early spring would make a yellow horse very inconspicuous for most of the year the waterhorses are almost always described as 'golden'. Whereas in the West and the Hebrides, where the hillsides are dark with heather and peat hags, black waterhorses, who would merge well into that background, are the fashion.

In the early days of Scottish history, Caithness and Sutherland formed the Province of Cat (or Cataobh), one of the seven Provinces of Pictland, probably meaning 'the land of the Cat tribe' for the Duke of Sutherland's Gaelic title is Moruir Chat— 'The Great Man of the Cats' or 'The Noble Cat'. As its place-names and stories alike show, Sutherland was once more Scandinavian than Highland. It was made a shire in 1631, the south part of it belonging to the Earl of Sutherland but the heart of the county, northward to Cape Wrath and the coast, belonged then to the Mackays. Later the Sutherland family were able to purchase the Mackay lands. Now much has been re-sold and there are many owners. But we have gone too far, and a long way from our road.

The main North road crosses the Kyles of Sutherland at Bonar Bridge, where the road to Cape Wrath and Lairg takes off. Once across the Kyles, the scene changes, as do the people. Apart from a belt of wood and farmland near the Kyles and other parts of the coast, and in one or two river valleys, Sutherland is a county of endless, sparsely populated moors and mountains, studded with so many moor lochs, large and small, that it appears to have almost more water than land surface. Geologists say that before human history began much of Sutherland and Caithness was covered by a huge lake which they have called Loch Orkadie. The moor lochs of today may be all that remains of it. Certainly Sutherland is 'grand for the fishing'.

The road to Lairg runs up the lovely valley of the Shin. On the left, Carbisdale Castle is to be seen on its hill. When it is reflected in the quiet waters at its foot it looks far too lovely to

have been built in hate by a Duchess of Sutherland who wished
to annoy her ducal husband with whom she had quarrelled, but
so it was. It is now a Youth Hostel. The road divides into two
near Invershin, one going up each side of the Shin River, that on
the west bank being the more beautiful and interesting, and from
it the Shin Falls can be visited. The Shin, with its steep banks
covered with birches, bracken and a myriad moor flowers and
its peat-brown pools and gleaming white waterfalls, is indeed
lovely. So, it is said, Christ thought. The River Shin never
freezes, a fact well known to fishermen. Legend gives this reason.
Christ, who loves all the world but especially the little Highland
glens and brown peat rivers, sometimes visits them. He usually
comes in the winter, when there are few human beings about and
He can watch the fish and birds and beasts who come to greet
Him. One wonderful clear winter night, bright almost as day
with the full moon's light, when every tree and grass blade
sparkled with the silver frost, Christ came to the River Shin and
rejoiced in the beauty of it. Then He noticed the fish, heavy,
busy and preoccupied, obviously in trouble. He called a large
salmon to Him and asked what was wrong in so beautiful a world.
'Oh, yes, it may be beautiful,' said the salmon impatiently, 'but
it isn't going to last. We can smell a real freeze coming, real black
frost, and then the river may freeze too. That is the one danger
against which we are helpless.' And Christ had pity on the
salmon. He stretched out His hand and blessed the River Shin
and said to the salmon 'You need no longer be afraid. The
waters of this river will never freeze again.' And they never have.

To sit and watch the salmon leaping up the Shin falls when
there is plenty of water in the river is fascinating, but even more
interesting is it to watch their manoeuvres when water is scarce,
the care with which they regulate their leaps so as to land for a
second on any ledge where the water may be deep enough to give
their tail the impulse it needs for the next leap, the care also with
which they pick the best line at the moment, perhaps mid-stream
or perhaps close to a bank, and their endless patience and deter-
mination. Over and over again a fish may fall or be thrown back.
Up it comes again. It goes on until exhausted, then rests and
tries yet again. When the river is in spate the big salmon usually

attempt to reach the deep brown water above the broken white of the falls in one leap, while the small trout struggle to attain the little shallow pools among the rocks near the bank and so to edge their way up unnoticed by the flood.

The road runs on to Lairg, where both the river and Loch Shin are dammed by the North of Scotland Hydro-Electric Board but the dams are far from eyesores; indeed when lit up and reflected in the waters of the loch they are well worth looking at. After Lairg the road to Durness and the West runs up the east shore of Loch Shin, past West Shiness, and on along the banks of Loch Merkland and Loch Mora beneath the startling frown of Ben Stack and with the Reay (deer) Forest towering above them. Among the mountains in the Reay Forest is Foinne Bheinn, about which it is said that the Brahan Seer once prophesied that 'the day will come when a raven, attired in plaid and bonnet, will drink its fill of human blood on Foinne Bheinn three times a day for three days'. It is hard to think of anything less likely to come true. However, this lonely mountainous country is well supplied with ravens, who once were most important people in the North: 'Bird of Odin' and 'Battle Bird', they guided the Valkyries, the Choosers of the Slain, to the field of battle, because ravens can smell war and death afar off. There were, too, memories in the Scandinavian lands of the famous ravens on the banner of the Sons of Ragnar, which flapped their wings and barked before victory, drooped head and wings before defeat.

But among the Highlanders it was far otherwise; the raven to them was a bird of ill omen. An old Gaelic verse is:

> Nest at Brigit (St. Bride's Day), egg at Shrove,
>   chick at Easter,
> If the raven has not that he will have death.
>   (from *Carmina Gadelica*)

To see two ravens quartering the sky, hunting, is unlucky. Obviously they hunt something or someone; it may be you. If a raven flies close to a house it is a sign of ill luck. If one settles on a house where someone is ill, they will die. I have heard this last argued as being not a superstition at all but a plain fact. Ravens are very wild birds and would never settle on a house unless attracted by the smell of death; Q.E.D. I have also been told, with at least equal authority, that owing to the construction of their beaks no bird can smell at all, good or bad. It would be interesting to know more of this matter of smell. The speed with which a raven will find a dead sheep and the cruel way he kills the latter if he arrives too soon certainly excuse a certain antipathy for the creatures. Anyhow, an old 'ill-wish' was 'The raven's death to you', ravens being believed to kill their parents on Easter Sunday. If a baby be given its first drink from a raven's skull it will know all wisdom and understand the speech of birds.

Seagulls, too, were battle birds but in a different sense. They were the spirits of men killed in action, ever wary, ever on guard, the bright red spots on their beaks the symbol of their wounds. On nights of the full moon birds gather together:

> Sea-mews pied black and white are there,
> On every forehead a blood-spot clear.

Sutherland is a great place for birds of all sorts, sea fowl, wading birds and birds of moor and mountain.

After Loch Mora comes Loch Stack and many a smaller loch besides. Loch Stack contains a fairy dog of very large size and fierce appearance. Just as in the case of waterhorses the colour differs in different places, so fairy dogs are different here too; for one thing they are black and not green and their business was usually guarding hidden treasure, perhaps because of huge Garmr (or Gurme) who in Scandinavian myth guards the entrance to the lower world. It is one of these black beasts who guards a Viking treasure of gold which was hidden by its owner beneath the waters of Loch Stack. He awaits the lawful command of one of the rightful blood, whom he will then allow to remove the golden hoard, but until the true owner arrives to free him from his trust woe betide any who approach the water with burglarious intent.

Through wonderful wild country the road runs down to the sea-loch of Laxford at Laxford Bridge. Here two roads meet (or should it be divide?), one, a most excellent road, going to Durness and on to Tongue and the north, the other south-west by Scourie and Assynt. At first the road to Durness passes through a pleasant country of innumerable small lochans, many with tiny islands, generally connected to one another by singing brown peat streams of varying size. Small birds frequent the water's edge or hop about the stones. Probably all have their stories. In about two miles comes the sea again, this time the sea-loch of Inchard with at its head Rhiconich Inn. This is a strange and lonely place to find a wide modern road with concrete fencing, but for two or three miles one does find just that. The road rises near Guillain to the strangest plateau I have ever seen. It is almost entirely outcrops of rocks with tiny pools in their uneven surface, just like a west-coast rocky sea shore. This curious configuration must cover several square miles. From it rise barren stony hills.

This part of Sutherland was once the home of the giants. Here they amused themselves by playing a primitive kind of ball game on the mountain tops. Some believe it to have been a form of skittles while others think it to have been the forerunner of shinty. Be that as it may, the young giants, like human boys, never bothered to tidy up behind them, and the boulders they used as balls can still be seen left carelessly on the summit of every mountain ridge.

It may have been in this wild upland country that the Norse giants once built their Hall of Feasts. It was certainly somewhere in the wilder part of Sutherland. In the olden days it was not unusual for a man, while going about his business, to meet one or more of the ancient Norse gods in human form, for they often visited the earth in the guise of men, but their incognito was not so good as it might have been, owing to their custom of wearing cloaks of a wonderful deep blue, the blue of the night sky, which colour no dyer on earth could achieve. Thor in particular often visited the giants in Utgard. It was said to have been on one such visit that he, well known as a cat-lover, was introduced to the worm Jormungand in the form of a cat, and desired to lift and play with him. But within the cat was the whole weight of the world. Nevertheless, so powerful was Thor that he almost succeeded. This was held to have given the gods much food for thought as they planned their strategy for the last great battle of all.

It was somewhere in this same wild upland country that the Keeper of the Winds lived. She was a witch well known for selling winds to sailors who had need of them, and probably other less innocent things also. It is strange how widespread this traffic in winds was, both by wise-women and by witches; presumably it was one of the easier forms of magic. No one could be a wise-woman, if virtuous, or a witch, if evil (the line between was often extremely thin), unless she was both observant and quick-witted. Such a one would recognise calm before storm and, if she knew also of boats awaiting a breeze, would expect customers and watch the sky. If wind clouds gathered and scudded lightly over the blue, she would mark their path and be ready to oblige customers who desired that particular wind, but refuse, for some plausible excuse, to oblige others. Then all that was needed was a knotted cord and instructions, most impressively delivered, to 'untie the knot' at 'the exact moment the sun sinks below the sea' or at 'the precise moment the sun rises over the hills', coupled with a promise of a wind from the desired quarter that day.

The road goes on through the strange and now lonely country, though it would seem from the number of Picts' houses and other such remains found here that it may have been busier in Pictish times than now, along the shore of the Kyle of Durness to the township of that name. Near here a passenger ferry will take those who desire it across the sea's arm to the Cape Wrath peninsula at the Kyle of Keoldale. Cape Wrath, as its name implies (though some claim that it merely means the turning point!), is no placid headland. It is perhaps the wildest place left on the mainland of Britain and has enormously high cliffs and, of course, a lighthouse, but no roads. This great headland of Parth stands lonely and awe-inspiring. It is a place of many stories. People have always known that somewhere on Sutherland's bleaker moors (and where so bleak as here?) one may meet that terrible monster the Cu-Saeng, of whom nothing is known because those who are believed to have crossed his path, whether on the Moor of Rannoch, the Grampian slopes, or the Sutherland hills, have never lived to describe him. But once a man saw, or thought he saw, the shadow of the Cu-Saeng on a hillside. If he did, the creature has two heads.

Other shadows have been seen here too. On winter nights, when the wind howls round the cliffs, the sea-birds' crying is stilled as a huge dark form blots out the light for a moment, then passes silently on. And whose are the footprints of enormous size which mar the otherwise unruffled snow? It does indeed take brave men, say some, to tend the Cape Wrath Light.

From Durness the road continues along the coast to Tongue, passing not far from the celebrated Smoo Cave. It was here that the first Lord Reay had an encounter with the Devil who was supported by a pack of witches. This first Lord Reay was a man of note in his day, highly intellectual and a keen soldier. He served under Gustavus Adolphus in his wars and while on the Continent he met the Devil. They found they had much in common. The upshot was that Satan invited Lord Reay to join a school he had just opened near Padua for students of the Black Art. His Lordship accepted and was enrolled. Now, it was the rule of the School that at the end of each session the pupils should run and that the last through the door of the Great Hall would be carried off by the Devil. This worried Lord Reay and he gave much consideration to the subject, realising that some day he might be the last. Sure enough, he was. But he was ready for his master and as the Devil seized him he looked over his shoulder and, pointing to his shadow, exclaimed: 'De'il tak' the hindmost.' The Devil, confused for the moment, let him go and carried off his unprotesting shadow instead. When Lord Reay returned to his home near Tongue his friends and tenants noted that he had no shadow and he told them how it was that he had lost it.

The Devil pursued him to Sutherland and there on the moor they had a stand-up fight with fists. Lord Reay, who was noted for his great strength, gave the Devil a beating and got from him as a ransom a horde of little demons who did all his work, ploughed, harvested, threshed his corn etc. until at last, to cure local unemployment, he sent them to make ropes of sand on the sea-shore. These can still sometimes be seen. After their fight Lord Reay and the Devil became fast friends for a while; on one occasion, for instance, when Lord Reay was journeying into Caithness, the Devil met him at the county boundary and while Lord Reay sat upon the boundary stone, an old megalithic monument, to eat his lunch Satan walked up and down playing the bagpipes to him. Then they continued in company. Neverthe-

less the Devil, though he seemed so friendly, had definitely lost
face over the fight and is believed to have been plotting vengeance.
He learned that on a certain day Lord Reay was going to explore
that natural curiosity the Smoo Cave, in the cliffs near Tongue.
This cave has three caverns, one leading to the next, and when
Lord Reay had got as far as the second his dog, which had raced
ahead into the third, returned 'howling and hairless'. This showed
Lord Reay who awaited him in the third cavern and he brought
all his hard-won knowledge and native wit to the circumvention
of the Evil One. But before the matter could come to a head a
cock crew and the Devil, with three witches who accompanied
him, realising that their hour was past, blew holes in the roof of
the cave and so departed rather than face Lord Reay in the outer
cavern. This is the origin of the holes through which the Smoo
Burn enters the caverns.

As far as is known, Lord Reay lived to a ripe old age and died
in the odour of sanctity.

But to return now to Laxford Bridge and from there follow
the road which goes left to Scourie, Kylesku and Assynt. It is a
very beautiful but narrow and twisty road which runs through
the hills as far as Scourie. Scourie was the birthplace of General
Hugh Mackay, a famous soldier of the seventeenth century who
ultimately met defeat at Killiecrankie. Not far away is the Island
of Handa, now a bird sanctuary but once supporting seven families and their 'queen' who ruled them. Its chief title to fame is its
claim that Iain Beag who assassinated Judge Morrison in the reign
of James VI and I was a Handa man. It has strange basalt for-
mations.

After Scourie the road, as the Guide to Sutherland aptly remarks, 'writhes' for ten miles to Kylesku. It is a most beautiful
ten miles of hill and sea, islands and lochs, *if*, but it is a big 'if', you
can take your eyes off the next corner long enough to look at them.
Especially beautiful is the curiously named Badcall Bay with its
islands, not that that is any more curious a name than Coldbackie.

The Kylesku ferry itself is both free and efficient and the
country beyond it well worth a visit. The mountains of Sutherland are of such varied and strange shapes—look for instance at
the Quinag, Suilven (the Sugar Loaf) and the Stack—that it is

easy to believe the story that when the world was new and soft and malleable the Norse gods came here to practise mountain-modelling. They then returned and modelled Norway with more experienced hands.

In due course the road reaches Loch Assynt and there again divides, one branch going on to Glen Oykell and the other to

Ardvreck Castle

Loch Inver. We are now in the country of the Macleods of Assynt and everywhere one finds traces of that Clan. Among the mountains to the west lie small hill lochs with such names as Loch à Leoid and Loch Feà-Leod, and there is Ben Leod. In Loch Assynt itself are the ruins of the Castle of Ardvreck standing well out into the water on its narrow and easily defended peninsula; this was the Macleod stronghold. The Devil is reputed to have had much to do with the building of this Castle of Ardvreck and also with its fate.

The first MacLeod of Assynt received the district with the MacNicol heiress whom he married. Macleod greatly desired to be lord of a castle as proud and as strong as Dunvegan. The Devil of course knew this, as he knows all things that may be of use to him. Taking the form of a handsome dark man he visited Macleod and offered to build him such a castle as he desired in return for his soul, explaining of course who he was and that he had power to make good his side of the bargain. Macleod was, obviously, sore tempted but after giving the matter some thought he refused the offer, explaining that he felt it would be foolish to put himself into the Devil's hands for ever in return for only a comparatively short period in which to enjoy his castle. If the Devil would offer him immortality, perhaps? The Devil would not. Matters had reached a deadlock, it seemed, when the door opened and Macleod's young and beautiful daughter brought wine to her father and his guest. She smiled sweetly at the handsome dark stranger and was thrilled by his answering glance. As soon as she left them the Devil formally asked Macleod for the child's hand in marriage, adding that he would of course be anxious to oblige his father-in-law in any little matter such as the building of a castle suitable for his bride's father. Macleod agreed, not apparently realising that in so doing he undoubtedly gave the Devil a very good chance of becoming possessed of his soul. The marriage was duly celebrated and the castle built. The Devil's bride was never seen again in the flesh, but a childish form, weeping bitterly, is said sometimes to be seen wandering in the ruins on nights of storm. After this unnatural deed little good was ever recounted of the Assynt family, nor any good fortune. They seem to have been frequently divided as a clan and warring one against the other.

Perhaps they are best remembered for the part they played in one of the mysteries of Scottish history—the capture of Montrose. Local tradition claims, and is reinforced by such writers of note as John Buchan, that Niall Macleod of Assynt sold Montrose who, starved and hunted, had accepted his protection, to his enemies for £20,000 (Scots) and £5,000 worth of meal but adds that Macleod never got the money and that the meal, which he did get, was sour. This accusation against the Assynt family of gross treachery may well have been most unfair. There seems little doubt that Macleod of Assynt did 'sell' Montrose to his executioners: on the other hand, Scotland at that time was sharply divided and Macleod of Assynt does not seem ever to have declared himself for Montrose; on the contrary, in the earlier civil wars of Charles I the royalist Mackenzies had, on behalf of the king, besieged his castle of Ardvreck as a Covenanter stronghold and though Macleod himself had not taken the field against Montrose many of his clansmen are known to have done so. So it would appear that Montrose had every reason to consider him one of his enemies and had no reason to seek his protection. What one would like to know is: did Macleod capture the enemy general and most properly hand him over to authority, accepting the advertised reward, or did he offer shelter and safety to a fugitive and then betray him? Family tradition says the former, local tradition claims the latter. One must remember, however, that the taking of blood money is always repulsive and nowhere more so than in the Highlands where, later, the poorest peasant could be, and was, trusted with the £30,000 secret of Prince Charles Edward's movements. Such reward, however fairly earned, was hated, so his neighbours would have undoubtedly been prejudiced. And so the mystery remains.

Some claim that from the day Montrose left the Castle of Ardvreck as a prisoner the castle began to disintegrate of itself, as if the very walls could not bear the shame of the deed which they had witnessed, and that it soon fell into ruins. But another and more curious story tells how Niall Macleod, anxious at a later date to prove his loyalty to the Crown, held great rejoicings with much revelry at the Restoration, including a Ball on a Saturday night. This went on well into the Sabbath morning but, that his Covenanting neighbours should not realise the hour and break up the party, he had had all the windows blacked out that the dawn might not be noticed and all the local cocks' tongues cut out so that they could not crow. There was, however, one whom he could not deceive. The Devil in person attended his relative's ball and it was he who, when the music struck up for a dance after what should have been cock-crow on the Sabbath morning, caused the castle he had built to fall to ruin in fire and smoke. Others say that scandalised Covenanting neighbours set fire to what they believed to be a house of evil. One thing *is* certain: the Castle of Ardvreck is now a ruin.

On the shore of Loch Assynt not far from the Castle stands another ruin, that of Caldra House which is said to have been destroyed by the Mackenzies of Kintail, rather than allow it to fall into the hands of the Sutherland family, in the late eighteenth century when feeling was very bitter.

After Loch Assynt the road passes by Inchnadamph and runs on to where Ben More and Suilven form a striking background for little Loch Borralan, with its beds of graciously waving reeds and its waterhorse which is reputed to be an unusually beautiful one. Unlike the Hebridean waterhorses, who invariably carried off girls, those in Sutherland often removed men also, usually those who presumed to interfere with their fishing. Two men were fishing in Loch Borralan when they saw the Loch's horse. Instead of hastily putting running water between it and them, as any wise man would, they stayed to admire its beauty and were never, either of them, seen again. Only their rods and the fish they had taken were found, and near them the hoof-prints of a huge horse.

The road then follows the River Oykell for a time, a lovely brown peat burn and a happy hunting ground for many small birds including the stonechat, of whom it is told that there is something queer about his ancestry. Indeed he is referred to as 'the waddling stonechat, the frog's grandchild'. It can never stop chattering since by its hopeless efforts to keep the disciples awake in the Garden of Gethsemane it disturbed Christ by its chitter-chatter. It is an omen of an unlucky year to

> See a stone-chitter on a broken dyke,
> A snail on a bare ledge,
> A snipe on top of a grass tuft;
> To hear the cuckoo before having food;
> To see a foal with its back to me.   (Gaelic rhyme)

Near here the River Oykell, and so also the road, run for a short distance through a curious point of Ross-shire. The reason for this is said to be that the Rosses of Balnagown claimed this piece of land as theirs and a part of Ross-shire although it was obvious that the land in dispute was geographically a part of Sutherland. The matter went to arbitration but when the arbiter arrived on the scene the Ross of the day had a large number of witnesses waiting, their brogues filled with Balnagown earth. They all walked along the disputed boundary, swearing at intervals that they stood on Balnagown soil, and so the land was awarded to Balnagown and is still a part of Ross-shire.

In due course the road reaches Bridge of Oykell, with a gracious old bridge, and then runs down the pleasant Strath Oykell and eventually back to Lairg.

Setting out from Lairg once more, this time on the road to Tongue, we find that it too starts along Loch Shin but soon branches off to the right to run for many miles through beautiful but utterly lonely moors. Indeed what strikes most people most when they first visit Sutherland is its loneliness—you may drive ten, or perhaps even twenty, miles and not pass a house. The Brahan Seer noted this in his 'stone' three and a half centuries ago and left a strange prophecy which has, at least in part, been fulfilled. 'The day will come when the jaw-bone of the big sheep (caoirich mhora) will put the plough on the rafters.' The bleating of sheep will cover the Highlands, good prices will be got, then they will go back until 'a man finding the jaw-bone of a sheep in a cairn will not recognise or be able to tell what animal it belonged to. The ancient proprietors of the land shall give place to strange merchant proprietors.' Then the country is to be given over to deer and not a man left. 'The crow of a cock shall not be heard north of Druim-Uachdair; the people will emigrate to Islands now unknown but which shall yet be discovered in the boundless oceans, after which the deer and other wild animals in the huge wilderness shall be exterminated and drowned by a horrid black rain' (radio-active fall-out?). 'The people will then return and take possession of the land of their ancestors.' A shorter version of it which I used to hear in my childhood was: 'Sheep shall eat men: men will eat sheep: the Black Rain will eat all things: in the latter end old men will return from new lands.'

The sheep have certainly driven out men to the 'new Islands'
—let us hope we never see the 'horrid black rain', but it is com-
forting to know that if we do, people of our blood will come
back to the Highlands. Another form of the prophecy, 'The teeth
of the sheep shall lay the plough on the shelf' is said to have been
uttered by Thomas the Rhymer long before the Brahan Seer's
time.

How bitter feeling was about the 'sheep' clearances all over
the Highlands is illustrated by this story from Skye. A minister
had in his sermon been praising Heaven and enumerating its joys.
He finished: 'No evil thing can enter the Blessed Kingdom so we
may rest assured there will be no Big Sheep there.'

In the summer the moorland is a sea of purple heather, in the
autumn it is gold-red with deer grass, in the winter white with
snow. Which is the most beautiful? Who can say? But one
thing stands out during most of the year, and that is a collection
of rather flat-topped green hillocks. These are 'Lord Reay's
Green Tables'. He called them up out of the peat when, by a
piece of reckless folly, he had let himself in for giving a dinner
party for the Devil. As I have never, to my knowledge, dined
with His Satanic Majesty I do not know the 'drill' or the dangers
to avoid. But it was certainly a matter of the first importance in
Lord Reay's opinion that the Devil should not be allowed to take
the first place at the function when presumably, as host, he would
'own' all who came to eat bread and salt with him (not, of course,
that he himself would touch salt), nor yet be offered second place
and thereby be insulted. Neither would Lord Reay invite the
Devil to dine in his castle. He solved the problem by offering
each guest his own separate and private table beneath the open
sky, so no one dined with Satan yet no insult was offered to him.

In due course the road reaches a point from which an excellent
view of Strath Naver and its lochs is to be obtained. Very beautiful and smiling the Strath looks today, yet it is one of those tragic
places which, once thickly populated, was turned into a desert at
the time of the Clearances; houses and often belongings, such as
they were, were burned to drive the people out. Many of the
people were shipped overseas, some willingly some not, others

were driven down on to the shore to live on shell-fish and dulse (a kind of seaweed) or die. Not all the owners of the land were heartless but some were and many were absentees. Bettyhill, for instance, owes its name to Elizabeth, Countess of Stafford, later Duchess of Sutherland, who had pity and, it is said, sold her jewels to build a township here for some of the refugees, supply them with boats for the fishing and provide other help.

In Strath Naver is a tiny loch called in Gaelic Loch mo Naire whose waters have healing powers for any who bathe in it on the first Monday in May or the first Monday in August. But only, repeat *only*, if they are not of Gordon blood. If a Gordon bathes in the water he will not only receive no benefit but will acquire all the ills the water has taken from previous bathers. So let visitors named Gordon beware! The reason is this. There was once a woman who owned some marvellous white stones which had such potent healing powers that water in which they had been dipped would cure any sickness. Naturally, such precious things were greatly coveted. One day a man of the name of Gordon saw her returning from a house where she had been visiting a sick child, carrying the precious stones. He tried to grab them from her. She ran and he gave chase. Realising that he was overtaking her and determined that he should never have the stones, she flung them from her into the loch, exclaiming as she did so 'Mo Naire! Mo Naire!' (My shame! My shame!) and the loch absorbed the healing power of the stones.

Strath Naver is not far from Ben Loyal, an unusual mountain, both in appearance and in reputation, being magnetic and so having the property of distorting compass readings. This was blamed by some for the accident in which the Duke of Kent was killed in 1942. The reason given for this curious attribute of Ben Loyal's is that not only is it full of iron ore but that at its heart is one of the largest of smelting furnaces. This is run by the dwarfs. There is a stone not far off which used to be known in Gaelic as the Stone of the Little Men. Leave there a silver coin and a model or drawing of any metal thing you need and return on that day week, and you will find a perfect one awaiting you.

Some say that the dwarfs are the children of Adam, born before the creation of Eve when he had to wife a forest demon called Lilith. But others hold that Eve had many children after she and Adam were driven out of the Garden and did not care very well for them, being too busy lamenting the easy life she had lost, and that the Lord God was annoyed and rebuked her, saying that he would send an angel in a month's time to see how she did. Eve still did not bother until just before the angel was due, when she drove all her children before her like a flock of sheep to the River Naver and began hurriedly washing them and their clothes. She had dealt with about half of them when she heard her name called, not, as she had expected, in the voice of an angel but in the voice of the Lord God himself. Terrified to show him how little she had heeded his words, she ordered the unwashed children to hide in a cave in the side of Ben Loyal and took the clean ones with her to show to the Lord God. The poor little dirty ones have had to remain hidden from the Lord's sight in the mountain's heart ever since. They only leave it after dark.

Others again, however, say the dwarfs were once a race of very small men who dwelt on earth like others. In those days the Norse Thunder God, Thor, was very young and very large and very 'jolly' and he loved bouncing about and making a noise. He didn't generally mean any harm, just didn't know his strength. Both men and gods grew tired of his ways and snubbed him and told him it was time he grew up, but the dwarfs were terrified and he, discovering this, loved to throw his great hammer (thunder) at them and watch them run. He was most careful never to squash one but they, poor little things, were frightened almost beyond endurance by the noise so they took refuge in the heart of the mountains where Thor could not follow. And though later, when they became artisans, he was their special god and tried hard both to be friends with them and to befriend them, it was no good. They remained terrified. Even today, if they leave their hills for any purpose and hear a cow 'moo' or a stag 'roar' they shake with fear. The only noise they don't mind is the noise of their own hammers, for they are all smiths or smelters and very good ones. It is said that when the first railway train ran through Sutherland the dwarfs, fascinated by this new manifestation of their special medium, metal, came out in huge numbers to watch, but unfortunately the engine driver was from the south and did not know their terror of noise so, anxious to impress, let off steam. No dwarfs have been seen in Sutherland since.

It is told that when the 'Good' St. Lawrence came to Sutherland in olden times to preach the gospel he felt that his first requisite was a church, but having as yet no congregation he saw difficulties in the way of obtaining one. Then he remembered the giants and the dwarfs. Perhaps they could help for some small reward; they were reputed helpful and, the giants at least, not too clever. So he toiled off over the moors to Ben Loyal to visit them. Everyone knew of the Little Men's stone upon which any tool placed with a piece of money would be repaired or altered as directed. So to the stone he went and there awaited the arrival of the dwarfs after dark. In due course they came and he agreed with them to do all the carpentry and metal work necessary for a small sum. Then they directed him to the giant's cave on the mountain above, and there St. Lawrence went, to find the giant at home, busily engaged in pegging out the skin of a deer to dry, his baby daughter kicking and chortling at his feet while her mother prepared the deer's meat for their evening meal. The saint explained what he had come about and the giant agreed that he could build a church and would be willing to do so. Only the price remained to be fixed. 'I cannot pay much' explained the saint. 'I don't want gold,' said the giant, 'that's what dwarfs want. Funny little people. My price is three souls, a soul for my wife, a soul for my daughter and one for me.' 'That's too much,' said St. Lawrence automatically, 'I'll give you two.' 'One for my wife and one for the baby . . .' began the giant, but suddenly a furious whirlwind intervened. It was his wife. 'You'll do nothing of the kind; we'll all have souls or all perish together,' she said, then, turning on the astonished saint, she exclaimed. 'How dare you try to separate a family, you wicked old man!' 'Good' St. Lawrence was deeply shocked. No one had called him a wicked old man before. But he was not so shocked as to give in without a fight. Now, every giant had a 'secret' name, known only to his family, so the saint offered three souls as the price of the building of his church unless he could 'name' the giant before the last stone was put in its place. Certain that his name really was a secret, the giant agreed.

The church grew apace for the giant was a good and steady worker and every day as he placed the heavy stones in position he had to face the saint addressing him by a new name. 'Good day, Garth', 'Good morning, Caenn', 'A fine morning, Rhitho', and so on. The giant worked in silence. But one day most unfortunately, in stepping back to line up a stone, he stepped on the foot of a dwarf whom he had not noticed behind him. The giant, a kindly if clumsy young man, apologised at once. But he tactlessly added, 'I never saw you. You're so small.' This further peeved the already footsore dwarf and he exclaimed that he was not so small as all that and that he was sure (which he was not!) that the giant had done it on purpose. 'I'll do it on purpose if you like; then you'll feel the difference,' said the giant in amiable tones, and went off whistling. This greatly angered the dwarf. Everyone knew of the giant's bargain with the saint and that night the dwarf called upon 'Good' St. Lawrence and said to him: 'If you want to know the giant's name, why don't you hide in his cave when he is away and hear what his wife calls him when she hushes their child?' 'But he never is far away,' said the saint nervously. 'Send him to the hills of Alba for a special stone for the altar,' said the dwarf and departed. 'Good' St. Lawrence thought it over and then did as the dwarf had suggested. Hidden in bushes close to the cave's mouth he watched the giant's wife prepare a meal for herself and her baby and then sit down by the fire and, rocking the child in her arms, begin to sing:

> Sleep, my little one, sleep free from sin
> Tomorrow will come your father Finn
> Tomorrow our souls for us he'll win.

'Good' St. Lawrence went home happy. Next day the giant had just placed the last stone on edge preparatory to slipping it into its place when the saint said, 'Stop, Finn.' Then 'Good' St. Lawrence called Finn's wife and bade her bring her baby and he turned them all three into pillars of stone to ornament his churchyard.

The giants always seem to have had a rather hard time in the North where they were a race of friendly, rather slow and clumsy people, not to be confused with the giant Feinn of the West who might well claim the title of supermen in a good sense, still less with the very evil giants of the fairy tales who usually had many hands and heads and no virtues at all. These northern giants seem often to have come into conflict with the early saints too, which was a pity. All the same, I wonder whether there was ever an historic St. Lawrence in Britain at all, for R. Thurston Hopkins in his book *Kipling's Sussex* mentions an 'Old Lawrence, a kind of imaginary saint or fairy' who made people slothful. The life work of St. Lawrence (not 'Old Lawrence') was supposed, in legend, to have been touring the North, compelling dwarfs and giants and trolls to build churches for him. Some have even confused him with the saintly Archbishop of Dublin, that Lawrence who saved 300 children in a famine, giving his all to feed them. The confusion seems only to have been because the Archbishop helped to build the cathedral in Dublin.

Leaving Strath Naver to the right, the road passes through Altnaharra and along the shores of Loch Loyal below the striking mass and cliffs of Ben Loyal and so down a steep hill to the wooded valley where Tongue lies on the sea-loch of that name, once called Kirkiboil but known in Gaelic as 'The Head of Mackay's Salt Water'. Much use has always been made of this fertile spot. In the time of Clan Mackay the old and now ruined Castle of Varrich stood guard on its promontory. In 1678 a Lord Reay built Tongue House to be his seat. It now belongs to the Duke of Sutherland but the Mackay motto 'Manu Forti' can still be seen on a carved shield. Tongue has, too, an old church, and at the mouth of the Kyles are several islands, including 'Rabbit Island'. It was on the sands near this island that the French sloop *Hazard* ran aground and was held fast when she came to Scotland carrying gold for the Jacobite cause.

The road east and north from Tongue goes over the neck of the next headland by a route of lonely moors and tiny lochs, many full of reeds, water-lilies and less-known flowers. Birds are plentiful, especially hawks; two or three at a time can be seen hovering against the sky. The blue falcon (the peregrine), famous in Highland stories, may here not be quite what she seems: she may be only a lovely streak of blue in the sky, death to mice and their kin or she may be the great goddess Frigga in her dress of falcon's feathers watching over the best laid schemes of mice and men.

In the North that attractive insect the Ladybird, also, is not
what she seems. It is all very well to sing:

> Ladybird, ladybird, fly away home,
> Your house in on fire and your children all gone,

but she was once a most important person, no less than the
personal messenger of the goddess Frigga, sent by her to earth to
collect men's prayers and carry them back direct to the goddess.
That is why it is lucky if a ladybird settles on your hand or dress.
Later she became 'Our Lady's bird', her five black spots typifying
the five wounds of Christ.

Later, the road returns to the coast with its fine mixture of
wild cliff scenery and peaceful sandy bays. It passes through
Bettyhill and Melvich and on over the moors to Caithness.
Suddenly, as it tops a small rise, there in the far distance is a
gleaming ball—like a balloon; it is Dounreay. A palace fit for
the Queen of the Little People it looks, and is suitably able to
grant wishes and make dreams come true—we hope.

Back to Lairg again, but this time to go south-east to Dornoch
by the east coast. First down to Invershin and Bonar Bridge past
Carbisdale, where Montrose met defeat after his landing from the
Orkneys; round the shore of the Kyles of Sutherland and the
Dornoch Firth by Spinningdale with its ruined cotton mill, burnt
down in 1808 and looking now like the ruins of some historic
castle; near Skibo Castle rebuilt by Mr Carnegie of library fame;
and at length to Dornoch itself. Dornoch is a town with a history
and also with one of Scotland's better golf courses; no upstart
growth, this course, for it is first mentioned in 1616. Dornoch,
the county town of Sutherland, was once the seat of the Bishop
of Sutherland and Caithness; it has been suggested that its name
means Holy Place. The old pre-Reformation cathedral, which
contains the tombs of the Sutherland family, is now the Parish
Church though still always called the Cathedral, and Dornoch
Castle, once the Bishop's Palace, has become a quite charming
hotel with a genuine and unspoilt fifteenth-century 'smoking
room' and cellars which go back to the thirteenth century. Dornoch was made the seat of the Bishopric about 1223 by Gilbert
de Moray who, claims Sutherland, was 'the last Scot to be canon-

ised'. But this distinction may soon end, for Fanny Macdonnell of Keppoch, under her religious title of Madame Frances Xavier, Mother Superior of the Order of the Assumption, was given the first steps towards canonisation between the wars.

A strange story is told in the *Landnahambok* of how, in the wars between Sigurd, Earl of Orkneys, and Thorstein the Red on the one hand and the Maormors (Earls or Lords) of Northern Scotland on the other, two of the maormors were killed. One of them was Melbrigda Tonn, believed to have been the Maormor of Moray, who got his nickname of Tonn from possessing a large buck tooth. Sigurd slew him in single combat in battle on the slopes of the Grampians and, cutting off his head, rode proudly off with his horrid trophy dangling from his saddle bow. But Melbrigda was soon avenged, for his buck tooth was jolted against Sigurd's leg and, entering his thigh, caused a poisoned wound from which he died. Tradition says he got almost as far as Dornoch in an attempt to return to the Orkneys but could go no further and died there at what is now Cyderhall but which was Sywardhoth, i.e. Sigurd's howe, as late as 1230. The sagas state that he was buried at Ekkialsbakki (Oykell Bridge) in A.D. 890. A burial mound near the river long bore his name.

Dornoch can claim to be the place where the last legal witch-burning in Scotland took place and also, I believe, the first conviction of anyone in Scotland for falsely accusing an old woman of witchcraft. But, witchcraft or no, Dornoch long counted among its treasures the bridle of a waterhorse, said by some to be the bridle of the sea god Manannan's own steed. For it is said that on one occasion Manannan was riding from his home in the Isle of Man to Tir-nan-og in the West and, for reasons unknown to any but himself, came by Dornoch. Here he was invited ashore and hospitably entertained. At dawn, when he desired to leave, he called for his horse, the famous Embarr of the Flowing Mane who was 'swift as the cold clear wind of spring' and travelled, as became the horse of a god, with equal ease over land and sea. No rider on her back could ever be killed. Not being as observant as he might have been, Manannan did not notice that when the superb creature with its curling white mane was led up its bridle was not the same one as it had worn on arrival. To own

Manannan's bridle was a very great thing: all sea and water creatures must obey it and also, if the bridle were held over a pool or bath of pure, clean water it would disclose the face of any worker of evil who had ill designs against the holder. It could also, some claimed, confer invisibility.

After leaving Dornoch the road runs through, not round, Loch Fleet on an embankment which carries it across this stretch of water. This is known as The Mound and the railway station near by as The Mound Station. Every stranger who comes looks, I think, at the three fair-sized hills near by and wonders which of them is *the* mound and why. Overlooking the loch stand the ruins of Skelbo Castle where the Commissioners of Scotland received the fatal news of the death of The Maid of Norway. Dornoch has beautiful sands and these continue round the coast for some miles, indeed as far as Brora. On this coast wherever a river comes down to the sea there is a town or village and generally a ruined castle. Golspie, the next place on the road, however, is more fortunate. Its castle is Dunrobin, still the seat of the Dukes of Sutherland and, since the gale of 1953 blew down much of its famous woods, easily seen from the road. Though most of Dunrobin was built in the nineteenth century some traces of the original thirteenth-century castle still remain. The 'Gaelic Stone' in the old bridge on the Mill Brae is the rallying point of Clan Sutherland, 'Ceann na Drochaide Bige' (top of the little bridge) being the Clan's slogan. Above the village towers Ben Bhraggie with, on its summit, a huge statue of the first Duke of Sutherland. Further round the coast at Lothbeg there is a stone marking the spot where the last wolf was killed. A young and pretty visitor to Sutherland was shown both and was later heard pointing out the Duke's statue to a friend and saying: 'They must have thought an awful lot of wolves here once, because that statue was put up to the memory of one that was killed.'

Next comes Golspie, a pleasant holiday resort with a good golf course, bathing etc. and then Brora which also has beautiful sands. Here too there is a golf course, many hotels and, curiously enough, a coal mine first worked in 1598 to provide fuel for the production of salt, for Brora then as now was Sutherland's industrial centre. Also, if stories be true, her chief battle ground where

Mackays, Sutherlands and Sinclairs destroyed each other with happy abandon. Once Brora's harbour was an important one and it is thought to have been from here that the first Highland settlers for New Zealand set sail.

The next place of importance we come to is Helmsdale at the mouth of the river of that name, nearly but not quite on the borders of Caithness. Like most of this district it is closely associated with the Sutherland family, those of its streets which run east and west bearing names from the Duke's Scottish estates and those which run north and south from his English ones. The ruins of Helmsdale Castle overlook the town from the river's mouth, of which castle it is told that Isobel Sinclair here entertained the Earl and Countess of Sutherland in 1567 and, in a quiet and workman-like manner, set about to poison them both so that her son, the Earl of Caithness, might succeed to the Earldom of Sutherland. She was too successful. Her chosen victims duly died but her son accidentally drank of the poison and died also. It was said that this tragedy turned Isobel's brain and that she cursed the Castle and all who lived in it before killing herself. Certainly the castle must shortly have deteriorated greatly as we hear that it required reconstruction in 1616. Soon it was once more a ruin.

Helmsdale has also always had a close connection with salmon. A lovely sight it is to see the nets drawn from the mouth of the Helmsdale weighed down with their haul of living silver. It was in the Helmsdale river, it is believed, that certain particularly rude little salmon fry lived. Here is the sad tale of the salmon fry, who are by no means as handsome or as dignified as their elders, for these are always courteous and good-mannered while the number of slightly foolish young heroes they have rescued from trouble is enormous. But, fine fish as they are, their fry are not well behaved. When the Devil fell from heaven they mocked him, popping up whenever he approached a river and crying: 'Yah! Sooty nose!' and other rude remarks. It was the Helmsdale fry who started this game. Now, the Devil has always been excessively sensitive about his nose, no one knows why, and at that time he was feeling sore and angry so he turned and roundly cursed them. That is why one in every ten is born with twin tails, two heads, or some other deformity which invariably results in

their being promptly eaten by their cannibalistic brothers and
sisters. The tragedy is that the Devil cursed sea-trout fry at the
same time, and they were quite innocent.

Not many miles from Helmsdale is that great headland the
Ord of Caithness, 747 feet high, and just beyond it the famous
Berriedale Hill, for so long a test hill for cars. On a Monday in
the year 1513 the Earl of Caithness with 300 men crossed the Ord
on his way to Flodden Field. Not one man returned. Local
superstition holds it unlucky, therefore, to cross the Ord on a
Monday, especially if you are a Sinclair and/or wearing green.

A road runs up Strath Ullie from Helmsdale into the heart
of Sutherland, past Kildonan and Forsinard and down Strath
Halladale to Melvich. Once this strath too was thickly populated,
now it stands empty and bleak. But not forgotten, for New
Kildonan was founded on the Red River in Canada by the evicted
and later became Winnipeg. In 1869 Kildonan and Suisgill burns
were the site of a gold rush! Would-be smelters came in ever-
increasing numbers, for both burns held gold. But when, in 1911,
an expert surveyed the area he reported the gold dust too fine to
be commercially practicable. 'That's the dwarfs,' was the local
comment, 'of course we might have known they'd carry off the
gold or do something about it.'

Kildonan commemorates St. Donan, saint and martyr of the
seventh century, probably that same St. Donan who was burnt to
death in the cave of Eigg. All this part of Sutherland contains
traces of many ancient Celtic churches; indeed it must once have
been full of them. A sad story is told of the first attempt to build
a church in this region, not far from Forsinard. On a small island
in a loch in the heart of the Sutherland moors near that place there
dwelt a giant and his wife Guru. They had fled from Norway
when the old gods fled before the coming of Christianity. They
dwelt alone together, safe and happy in each other's company for,
being soul-less, there was no place for them in the new Christian
world. But one day they learned that St. Olaf had sent saints to
Scotland also, for one appeared on the shores of their loch and
announced it as his intent to build a church on their island. They
begged him to go elsewhere but he would not. So the giant
waded into the water, seized the prow of his boat and lifted it and

him both ashore. The saint was very angry and immediately turned the giant into a pillar of stone. His wife Guru sobbed bitterly, telling the saint of her husband's goodness to her and to their small human neighbours. The neighbours came also and begged the saint to lift his spell. At last he agreed to make one concession. The giant, he said, might come to life again on Yule Eve for that one night each year if he was embraced by one of his own race who would give a hundred years of his or her own life to do so. So Guru remained on the island alone with her stone, the saint having gone elsewhere to build his church. Every Yule Eve she embraced her husband, he came to life, and they had one night of happiness together. Then one day a young couple came to the island and begged shelter. So Guru shared her home with them, on one condition; they must leave every Yuletide. They agreed. But one Christmas Eve a baby was born to the young wife and Guru could not turn them out. However, they swore they would not peep beyond the door nor say the Holy Name, but Astog forgot and hushed her baby with a blessing—whereupon the giant was changed into stone forever and Guru became an outcast, a wanderer on the face of the earth. Before leaving she gave her house to the remorseful young couple, bidding them only to teach other humans to be kind to the little hill dwarfs.

St. Olaf's disciple never could understand why his preaching of God's love and charity had so little success in this district.

III

WEST FROM INVERNESS

My heart is filled with longing for the hills
 of grey and brown,
And the scent o' pines and seawrack and the
 sight of warring seas.
W. CAMPBELL GALBRAITH

13

LOCH NESS

From reining of the Water horse
That bounded till the waves were foaming,
Watching the infant tempest's course,
Chasing the sea-snake in his roaming

     *   *   *   *   *

Children of wild Thule, we.
Sir Walter Scott

'NESS' is believed to be an early Pictish word, its meaning unknown. It probably first belonged to the River Ness and may have been the name of some ancient goddess. There are, however, many tales purporting to explain or account for it.

In the very early days, it is said, there was no loch in the Great Glen; instead, the land now under water held many farms and homesteads, for the Glen was then a dry and fertile valley, a giver of plenty to its inhabitants. In the middle of the valley was a spring of magic virtue guarded by a strict taboo. Whoever came to draw water from this well must remove the stone, draw water and *immediately* replace the stone, no matter how long a queue of would-be water drawers might be waiting, 'or else—!' One day a woman went alone to the well for water and as she removed the stone she heard her child scream as if in agony or great fear. She dropped the stone and ran. After her ran the water, for the well instantly overflowed and shortly filled the long valley. The people of the valley fled to the hills, crying as they ran: 'Tha loch nis ann, tha loch nis ann' (There is a loch there now). Hence its name.

The western side of Inverness is in the old 'parish' of Bona. This is said to have taken its name from the ferry across the River Ness near Dochfour, soon after the river leaves the loch. The ferry was called Ban-àth or white ford and Dr Watson believes it was named from the white stones in the water there. There is still a small white beach close by. Local tradition makes it one of these white stones that St. Columba is related in Adamnan's *Life of St. Columba* to have sent to King Brude. In the *Life* it is told how Broichan, the Druid and the foster-father of King Brude, held a maidservant captive and how St. Columba had pity on the girl and ordered him to free her, but Broichan refused. Then the saint said: 'Know, Broichan, know that if you refuse to deliver to me this captive stranger before I leave this Province you will surely die.' And this he said in the presence of Brude the King. Then St. Columba departed and began his journey home to Iona. When he came to the River Ness he lifted from the water a white pebble and, holding it up in the clear sunlight, he told all who were with him to look well at it for it was a stone which should cure many. Then he told them that Broichan was 'smitten by an angel and severely ill and would soon free the maid'. Two horsemen, riding hard, soon overtook St. Columba's party, bringing the news which the saint had foretold. Broichan, they said, was willing to free the girl and Brude had sent them to beg that the saint would return to the aid of the King's foster-father who was very ill. But St. Columba would not, saying the time had now come when he must leave that place. However, he sent two of his monks to the king, with the stone and with the word: 'If Broichan is willing first to free the girl, let this stone be dipped in water and give him to drink and he will recover. But if he opposes the freeing of the slave-girl he will die immediately.'

The two monks, very frightened, went to the king. The Druid immediately freed the girl, drank water in which the stone was dipped, and recovered. The stone floated on the water 'contrary to its nature'. The stone was preserved by the king and cured many, but when a man's time came to die the stone could never be found although it was kept, carefully guarded, among the king's treasures. Thus it was sought in vain on the day of the death of King Brude in 583.

St. Columba visited Brude on more than one occasion but, not unnaturally after this matter of the slave girl, both he and his visits were far from popular with the king's foster-father. Broichan felt that the saint had made him lose face and he planned to regain his old ascendancy. He asked St. Columba on one occasion when he proposed to journey home. 'On the third day, God willing and life remaining, we propose to begin our voyage,' answered the saint. 'You will not be able to do so,' replied the Druid, 'for I can make the wind contrary for you and bring clouds upon you.' The saint replied that God rules all things and they will do as He directs. On the third day St. Columba and his monks, with a large crowd following them, set out for Loch Ness but when they reached the water's edge 'a great darkness descended upon the water with contrary winds and tempest'. St. Columba called upon God and entered the boat which awaited him and as the sailors hesitated in fear, knowing well the Loch's treacheries, he bade them make sail. Then the watching crowd saw the boat borne rapidly in the right direction against the contrary winds and then the winds themselves veering round to the direction desired by the saint. So he and his monks reached the further end of the Loch swiftly and without mishap.

To traverse the Great Glen is to make in a sense a pilgrimage for it was by this chain of lochs—Loch Linnhe, Loch Lochy, Loch Oich, Loch Ness—that St. Columba and his monks came to visit King Brude, or, as one might say, by this chain of lochs Christianity came to the Highlands. It is told how they once stopped to rest and eat not far from what is now Foyers. As they rested they saw a party of evil men approaching and St. Columba, knowing that they were searching for him to kill him, bade his monks raise their voices in a hymn he had composed, known since as the Hymn of the Deer. They obeyed and God deafened the ears of his enemies so that the hymn appeared to them as herds of deer calling. 'Where deer call, men are not,' said the leader and he and his men paddled away from that shore. Legend says, however, that St. Columba had supernatural aid of another sort also on his first journey. Here is the story.

Since there were then no roads St. Columba and his monks had to journey over heather-clad hills and through a part of the Caledonian Forest as best they could, carrying their coracles. Thankful indeed were they when they reached each loch in turn and were able to sail down it. But the weather was stormy and by the time they arrived at Loch Ness, that 30-mile long sheet of water covered with white-capped waves looked anything but inviting to the tired men. Suddenly among the tossing white wave crests appeared a black head—it was the Waterhorse of Loch Ness come to pay his duty to St. Columba, and a handsome great stallion he was though not unduly wise. He swam up to the saint to offer his service, but it was some time before he understood what the monks' boats were for or that they were attempting to row themselves down the length of the great loch against the wind. Once he had grasped the situation, however, he took charge in a most practical manner. Explaining that he needed hands, he assumed the form of an athletic young man, seized the painters of each coracle and strung them together on to one large withy, then, resuming horse form, he took the withy between his strong teeth and swam rapidly off. Almost before they knew it the saint and his party were landing in comfort on the little white sheltered beach at the eastern end of the loch. Here St. Columba blessed the Each Uisge and gave him the freedom of Loch Ness for ever.

But it was not only the help and blessing of a Saint that this waterhorse coveted; he is also reputed to have made a pact with the Devil. But the Devil got the better of him. The waterhorse was very much worried by the belief that as the River Ness ran through Loch Ness and as no waterhorse can cross over running water he could never pass from one side of his own loch to the other. The Devil promised him that if he would give him one ride every year over any water he (the Devil) might choose to name, he in return would ensure that every drop of water the river brought into the loch it would carry out again, and not a drop more. To do this the river water must flow strictly in its own path on the loch surface and the Each Uisge could dive under it in safety. What the Devil did not tell, and the waterhorse did not know, was that this was in any case the law enforced on all Highland rivers from olden times when what might perhaps be described as The Amalgamated Union of Waterhorses and Waterbulls had made just such a pact with the Evil One to cover all rivers that passed through a loch, that running waters might not trouble the loch creatures. And it had been made with no promise of service to the Devil in return. It is certainly curious that these waterhorses, lords not only of many a loch but also of many a river pool, should not dare to cross a river, and even more curious that the Devil should be supposed to have power over all rivers. But running water has strange powers. It is not only waterhorses which dare not cross it. No witch may cross running water either, neither may the fairies (anyhow, not when pursuing mortals), nor a ghost, though ghosts may go as far across a river that is bridged as the keystone of the bridge but no further. The sea, however, is evidently quite crossable by ghosts, for 'Big Donald of the Ghosts' fled from his besetting spectre to America and found his ghost already there awaiting his arrival. 'How did you come here?' he cried in amaze. 'Oh, I came round about; the ghost's trick,' replied the imperturbable spectre.

Everyone knows that 'He will have no luck who takes a cat across a stream.'

From time immemorial Loch Ness has been a 'queer' loch with 'queer' stories of its inhabitants. There are stories of a Something, very old and evil, which once lived in its depths and to whom sacrifices were made—sacrifices generally of cattle, sometimes in the dim past of children, flung in withy baskets into its waters. I used to hear in my childhood, when we often visited Glen Urquhart, that this 'thing' was still sometimes seen, a great dark shapeless mass, brooding over the waters, dreaming of evil. And its dreams worked, for if it was seen, however faint and form-less an apparition, shortly afterwards someone would be drowned and their body would never be found. There were several schools of thought about this last fact, for fact it apparently is that a body lost in Loch Ness is never, or very rarely, seen again. In olden times, 'it' claimed them; later came the idea that Loch Ness had a central hole which went deeper than anything else in Scotland, perhaps in the world, and into this bottomless pit all lost things were drawn. Dr Johnson records that on his visit he was told that the loch was 140 fathoms deep. Some said the 'deep' had an outlet to the sea, others that it connected with an equally deep hole in Lough Long in Ireland. The great cavern, said others, contained a Monster, or many Monsters, slimy white eyeless creatures that never saw the light. When Loch Ness was being sounded for the building of the Caledonian Canal the ship's sounding line ran right out somewhere between Invermoriston and Drumnadrochit and did not reach bottom. This at once revived the belief in the bottomless abyss there. In vain the engineers concerned explained that the line they were using was of no great length, they having only wished to ascertain that ships of a draught suitable for the Canal could be sure of enough water in Loch Ness; how much more depth there was did not concern them. However, as considerable interest was aroused a longer sea-sounding line was borrowed and let down. It too failed to reach bottom it was said, and so the old belief in the bottomless pit was reinforced with a story that it had proved deeper than anything known in the ocean. I am told it has now been exactly charted and is 'deep for a loch'.

Tales of the great eyeless monsters also persist. We have 'Nessie' of course, who has been seen and described by too many reliable witnesses whose testimony cannot be ignored for her existence to be doubted but who, alas!, has also been seen and described by so many unreliable witnesses that she has become an impossible joke to the general public. One of the nicest of the stories of this kind came from an excited family from a Lancashire town who in the days before the Second World War claimed to have seen 'Nessie' leave the water and conceal herself in the bracken 'to await her prey'. She was a terrible creature covered with red hair, with fearsome horns and chewing something from which blood dripped as she chewed. A brave policeman returned with them to beard her in her lair and found it not such a bad description, if you leave out the dripping blood, of a rather nice red Highland cow chewing the cud in a bracken bed.

A more horrible origin for the 'eyeless ones' seems to be great eels. That these live and grow to an exceptionally large size in Loch Ness is not disputed. Many years ago, before 'Nessie' had been heard of, a visitor was drowned in the Loch and her husband, determined to recover her body, hired a diver. After one descent the diver refused to return to the water, saying that the eels made the risk too great. The husband said he was 'a local man and just superstitious' and appealed to the Navy at Invergordon. A naval diving party was sent and the first man down signalled to come up almost at once and said the eels were too dangerous; he could not protect his air line. The husband repeated 'superstition' and, being both rich and obstinate, got a diving party up from the London docks and met them at the station to avoid their hearing 'eel gossip'. They also refused to remain in the water because of 'the great eels trying to foul their air lines and wrap themselves round them'. They were reputed to have said that they never before saw such creatures and that to remain in their company was suicide and to send divers down among them was murder. What there really is or is not in the depths beneath the waters of Scotland's largest loch is still a question, but from time immemorial 'it', whatever 'it' is, has had an evil and terrifying reputation very different from that enjoyed by the ordinary waterhorse. No doubt the facts that storms rise to a dangerous pitch with little warning on such a long, narrow piece of water and that the Great Glen has always been a weak point for earth tremors may have added to its reputation both for evil and for beauty. On a still day it is *very* beautiful, especially in spring and autumn, and on a wild day magnificent.

The Feinn also have a connection with the Glen. Once Fionn put himself under promise to the Big Lad that if the Big Lad would serve him for a year and a day Fionn would accompany him to a feast to be held in the palace of the King of Lochlann and that 'he would not take with him a dog or a man, a calf or a child, a weapon or an adversary, but would go himself alone'. When the day came for them to go Fionn was heavy of heart for he saw well that it was a trap. He bade the Feinn seek him in Lochlann in a year and a day and told them 'to hold one great day on the strand of Lochlann' to avenge him if he had not returned. These things they promised. But as he made ready to start his fool spoke to him and asked if he would take the advice of a fool. 'What is that?' enquired Fionn courteously. 'Take Bran's gold chain with you,' said the fool, 'for it is not a dog or a man, a calf or a child, a weapon or an adversary.' Fionn, saying fools are often wise, agreed. At great speed he and the Big Lad travelled to the palace of the King of Lochlann and by the time they arrived Fionn was weary. The King and his lords were all seated, discussing how best to put Fionn to death. 'What,' asked the King, 'is the most shameful death a Fiann can die?' 'Let us hang him,' cried some. 'No, burn him,' said others. 'Drown him,' advised another. Then one rose and said: 'The most disgraceful death a Fiann can die is to be killed by a cur of a dog. Let us send him unarmed into Glen More where the Grey Dog will kill him.' And all cried: 'To face the Grey Dog, that is the death for Fionn.'

Now Grey Dog was blood-brother to Fionn's dog Bran and he belonged to the Brave Young Hero. But a chief of the men of Lochlann had once found the Brave Young Hero alone by the sea-shore and he and his crew had captured him and claimed the dog as his ransom. The chief took the dog to the King of Lochlann but the animal went mad for grief at the loss of his master. So he was sent back to Scotland and was turned loose to run wild in the Great Glen.

The men of Lochlann took Fionn to the mouth of the Glen and there, when they could hear the howling of Grey Dog, they left him. Grey Dog came down the glen howling and foaming, with his tongue out to one side of his mouth and his eyes glaring, like the mad thing he was. So hot was his breath that each snort of his nostrils burned everything, trees, heather, creatures, for three miles on either side of him and for three miles before him. He looked at Fionn and snorted. The heat tormented Fionn. It was unbearable. He plunged into Loch Ness and hid in its waters. Then, as Grey Dog drew near, he raised one arm out of the water and shook Bran's gold chain towards Grey Dog. Grey Dog saw the chain and knew it. He wagged his tail and came to Fionn. Fionn left the water and caressed Grey Dog, and Grey Dog licked Fionn's burns that he had made with his breath 'from top of head to sole of foot'. Then Fionn put Bran's gold chain round his neck and together they walked down the Glen. Near the Glen's mouth was a little house where dwelt an old man and an old woman who used to feed Grey Dog. They saw Fionn coming with Grey Dog and the old man said: 'Though the people of Lochlann and of Ireland were assembled, among them all there would not be a man who could do that but Fionn, King of the Feinn and Bran's chain of gold with him.' They offered Fionn hospitality. Fionn told the old man his tale and he told the old woman and it pleased her, so that she said Fionn might rest in her house till the end of the year and a day, and Grey Dog with him. This they did. On the last day of the year and a day an 'innumerable host' appeared on the strand. It was the Feinn come to search for or to avenge their King. Fionn and Grey Dog strode to meet them. Very great joy was theirs in the host when they met Fionn and very great joy of meeting between Bran and Grey Dog. They took vengeance on the men of Lochlann. Indeed 'They began at one end of Lochlann and stopped not till they came out at the other.' Then they went home to the hall of Fionn and 'held a merry feast for a day and a year'.

Castle Urquhart

14

INVERNESS
TO FORT AUGUSTUS

From the ruined castle wall
That nods to the darkened moon,
'Tis an old time song comes faintly along
Like the sough of a fairy's croon.
MURDOCH MACLEAN

THE GREAT GLEN has had the honour to be classified in
the U.S.A. guides as one of the four things which every
visitor to Britain must see, and it is certainly worthy of
note. It is definitely more satisfying to travel through it by
water if possible because the two roads which run one on either
side of the Loch show only the opposite shore. The hills are too
close and too steep to be seen from directly below.

The Glen has always had a rather sinister reputation and this
is hardly to be wondered at perhaps in view of its history, for it
has seen much fighting and for many centuries. Indeed, if tradition is to be believed, from Roman times until the '45 there can
scarcely have been a single month in which it did not see a fight,
a murder or a cattle-raid. A line of ancient forts protected it,
some vitrified, others of the 'dun' type. These still await scientific
excavation, so their exact age is not known, but all are believed
to date back at least to the bronze age and some may be older.

The first road down the north shore of Loch Ness from Inverness to Drumnadrochit was made by Sir James Grant when
wheeled vehicles appeared in the North in the middle of the
eighteenth century. He was known as 'the good Sir James'. The
present road was engineered in the early nineteenth century by
Telford, the builder of the Caledonian Canal, whose name and
work are commemorated in Telford Street and Telford Road in
Inverness. This road was an enormous boon to the county but

it was very narrow, and twisty beyond belief. There was a stretch of ten miles between Drumnadrochit and Invermoriston on which two cars could not pass, and fifteen miles of it had to have a speed limit of 12 miles per hour. So the present wider road was blasted out of the rock face, a big undertaking most fortunately finished just before the last war. Before 'good Sir James' there was nothing but the old grass road across the hills by Abriachan which may well go back to the stone age but is simply a drove road.

The present road crosses the Canal to the west of Inverness, passing close to Tom-na-hurich and then on beneath the shadow of Torbhean—one of the old vitrified forts and a wonderful sight when the trees have their autumn colouring; indeed the whole road should be seen then. It passes Craig Dunain, the tragically large mental hospital which yet is not large enough, and then Dunain itself where once an old dun could be seen and where an evil hag keeps watch, hoping for chances to destroy any of the name of MacDougall, and on to the end of the River Ness where the Castle of Bona once guarded the pass.

The rich lands and, especially, herds of the Glen were a great temptation to the clans of the West with their poor pasture land, so cattle-lifting raids were common. When Hector Buie Maclean became Warden of Bona and Urquhart Castles for Alexander, Lord of the Isles, he determined to put an end to the raids by raiding Lochaber in return. This he did while Lochiel was absent in Ireland with his men. Maclean killed and plundered without mercy, then retreated along the south shore of the Loch to Castle Bona with his plunder and his captives. Lochiel, on his return from Ireland, at once pursued him with a large force of the western clans. Hector threatened to kill his prisoners if Lochiel did not retreat; Lochiel, who had by this time captured Hector's two sons and several of his followers, offered to exchange prisoners. Maclean refused and at once carried out his threat to kill all the prisoners in his hands. The furious Camerons replied by hanging his two sons and the other Urquhart men in front of the Castle. In the ensuing battle Hector Maclean was killed. The ghosts of both sets of prisoners were supposed to haunt the Castle, joined together in hatred of their human murderers, and it became known no longer as Castle Bona but as Caisteal Spioradan, Castle of the Ghosts or Spirits. Soon, no one could be found willing to garrison it and it fell into ruins. The ghosts then took to venting their spite on any passing traveller, however innocent of murder he might be, and there was general relief in the neighbourhood when the ruins were demolished to make way for the Caledonian Canal.

In Commonwealth days it was from Bona that the first frigate to sail Loch Ness set out. Cromwell, when he built his Citadel in Inverness, intended it to be the centre of a peaceful and well-ordered countryside and proceeded, as was his wont, to make it so. The memory of the law and order which he enforced still lingers in pleasant contrast to the murder and rape of Cumberland's 'Hanoverian occupation'. Cromwell found all the clans in arms, many making use of the disorders of the day to plunder their neighbours. His troops found the country difficult and complained that marauders constantly escaped across the loch in small boats they had hidden in the reeds or even on blown-up sheep skins. So the order was given: 'Put a frigate on the lake.' Just like that! The ship was brought to Inverness under sail, there she was dismantled as far as possible and a sort of wooden cage was built round her to hold her upright; this was then set on rollers made of pines felled for the purpose and three companies of troops manhandled her, on these clumsy rollers, from Inverness to Bona (there was no road then, remember!) where she was refitted and put to 'sea'. Few things can ever have created such excitement in the Glen or indeed throughout the North, and a lovely sight she must have been flying down the Loch, her white sails against the green of the woods and blue of the hills. It is recorded of her that she carried 60 men in all, and stores, from one end of the loch to the other 'in a few hours'.

To return to the road. This next passes Dochfour with its small lakes and lovely gardens. This part is well worth a visit in spring, just to see the masses of daffodils, and later of flowering shrubs, running down to the water. After Dochfour great Loch Ness herself bursts upon the view and from there on the scenery is indescribably beautiful at almost any season and in most weather. This stretch of road and hillside used to be a great haunt of snakes,

not only the harmless grass snake but also the poisonous viper.
On any warm day one could count on seeing at least half a dozen
sunning themselves on the rocks beside the road. Then Baroness
Burton decided to keep goats and a flock of beautiful silky white
ones appeared. The fashion spread and soon goats of all sizes and
colours wandered about the hillside and now there appear to be
no snakes, or, to be fair, few goats either. It has long been held
by serious farmers that goats do rid a countryside of snakes, and
legend has it that goats like eating snakes. They are said, when
they find one, to put a hoof on its head and then begin to eat it

". . . used to be a great haunt of snakes . . ."

from the tail up, uttering plaintive, unhappy little cries all the
time as though they found the wriggling of the snake unpleasant.
They may well do so. Goats are queer creatures. So of course
are snakes. It is most unlucky not to kill every snake you meet.
If you don't, it may later kill or bewitch you. But, no matter
what you do, no snake will die till the sun sets. Goats' milk was
highly prized in the Highlands: we hear,

> Garlic with May butter
> Cureth all disease
> But drink of goats' white milk
> At the same time as these,

and also,

Wash thy face with a lotion of goats' milk and sweet violets and there's
not a King's son but will then run after thee.

The road passes Temple Pier where the little loch steamer
called regularly on its way to and from Inverness and Fort
William. Above the pier there is a crag and a hollow, both believed to have been sacred spots in the old pagan days. In the

hollow was a healing spring, once the abode of a god or goddess. When St. Columba brought Christianity to the Highlands he is reputed to have dealt gently (and wisely) with old pagan gods and demons who were worshipped in groves and springs and lakes throughout the glens. He explained to his converts that these spirits were under One God, just creatures as we are. If a spring could heal the sick, let us thank God for this blessing He has sent us and build a church or cell near by in which to give continued thanks. If an evil spirit troubled certain waters, the saint would bless them and drive away the evil in God's name and, once again, build a church to protect men. So here the pagan sacred spot was blessed and a tiny church was built in honour of St. Finan. This St. Finan was a contemporary and companion of Columba and became the chief saint of this district. Later again, a bigger church was built on the site, this time in honour of St. Ninian. The healing well held pride of place beside each in turn and each seems to have been known as Teampuill St. So-and-so, but which gave its name to Temple Pier is not clear.

The story is told that St. Finan, as an old man, desired to ride from Temple Hollow to his church on Loch Lochy. He set out alone and most unfortunately his horse caught its foot in a rabbit hole and came down, breaking its leg. The old saint was helpless. He was too far from either church to reach them on foot and no one knew his whereabouts. He knelt down to pray and await death but his prayers were disturbed by a soft nose nuzzling his ear. He looked and, behold, a red deer stag stood by him. Breviary in hand, he mounted his new steed and was soon delivered safely at his church on Loch Lochy side.

Not far from Temple Pier the Glen Urquhart road takes off to the right in the middle of Drumnadrochit while the main road turns round a small bay and passes over the headland on which the ruins of Castle Urquhart are to be seen, down by the water's edge. Once a great stronghold with a fleet of galleys which controlled the Loch, the Castle has now fallen upon evil days. Where once its owners grew rich on tolls from every boat which passed up or down this, the main waterway of a roadless Highlands, tourists now pay a small entrance fee to the Board of Ancient Monuments. But perhaps it is poetic justice, for the Castle galleys

were supposed, in return for prompt payment of tolls, to ensure
safe passage for all boats traversing the loch, and fear of robbers,
outlaws and pirates made boat owners willing to pay for protection, but it was said that under these conditions piracy ceased to
be worth while and that then the Castle galleys had to do a bit of
it themselves on the side to keep the tolls going. Others said
bitterly that the Castle was nothing better than a pirate stronghold
and never had been. It was subsidised competition that drove the
'free' pirates off the water!

Actually the Castle has a history of wars and sieges second to
none in Scotland. It was an important stronghold because it
controlled the Great Glen, a main route between East and West,
and between the years 1160 and 1398 it changed hands at least
sixteen times, although several of the different holders claimed
to 'hold it for the King'. It ceased to be a royal fortress in 1509
when the King made a gift of it to the Grant of the day, known
as the Red Bard. According to tradition the Castle was built by
an Irishman, Conachar (or O'Chonachar) MacNessa, a prince of
Ulster, in the twelfth century. Conachar himself is a half-legendary
figure reputed, on the one hand, to have received the land and the
dun which preceded the Castle on that headland from King
Malcolm IV as a reward for his help in the war of 1160 against the
Highlanders and to have immediately enlarged the dun into a
Castle and greatly strengthened it, and on the other hand to be
the son of an Irish goddess Nessa who, according to this story,
gave her name to Loch Ness. In this version Conachar called
upon the witches of the Glen to help him build his castle and the
witches hewed and carried every block of stone used for the walls.
They brought it in part from Abriachan and in part from Caiplich
but they were very angry indeed at the task. How Conachar
forced them into it is not known, but the spot from which they
first sighted the castle on each heavily-laden journey was known
as Cragan nam Mallachd, the Rock of the Curses, within living
memory. The witches of the Glen were both numerous and
powerful—it was a famous witch centre—and they used to meet
and hold their 'Sabbaths' on An Clairach, the Harp, a rock on the
shore of Loch Ness near the farm of Tychat. Here Satan used to
sit and play for them every 12th of May (old May Day) that they

might dance for his pleasure; hence the rock's name. The witches' curses on Castle Urquhart seem to have been fulfilled, judging from its subsequent history.

Conachar of Castle Urquhart possessed a great dog which grew old and stiff and he decided to kill it but was prevented by a woman who approached him as he went out to hunt and said: 'Let the dog live: his own day awaits him', and disappeared. Realising that it is never wise to ignore old women, Conachar took her advice. One day, as he set out to hunt, the old dog left its place by the hall fire and 'gambolling nimbly as a puppy' accompanied him. At this time the country round was being ravished by an enormous boar. This creature attacked Conachar, his spear and his sword slid off its tough hide and it was his old dog who saved him, killed the boar and was itself killed in the act. Conachar had three sons it is said, John who received land in Aberdeenshire from William the Lion and founded the family of Forbes, Alexander who was sent by the King to Caithness to repel the Danes and whose success was rewarded with their lands after which he founded the family of Mackay, and a third who took the name of Urquhart from the Castle which he inherited. All three were proud to be known as 'Son of the Killer of the Beast' and all adopted a boar's head as their arms in their father's honour. No one seems to have honoured the great hound.

The two strong towers on the landward side of Castle Urquhart were added by Sir William Fitzwarren when he held the castle for Edward I of England during his wars with Scotland. There are many stories of the Castle. Of how the Forbes who held it for Robert the Bruce were starved out by the English troops and how, at the end, they made a last desperate sortie and were all killed. Of how first, however, Forbes' wife, disguised as a serving maid, was allowed safely through the English lines and reached her home in safety, there, in Ireland, to bear his child, and of how later that child regained the Castle. Of how Thomas Randolph, Keeper of the Castle for the Bruce and later guardian of his infant son, King David, administered such justice during the child's minority 'that a man might tie his horse to the Inn rail or leave his plough by the furrow without fear of theft throughout the length and breadth of the land'. His method was simple

and direct. He made each sheriff responsible for law and order
in his own sheriffdom. If aught was stolen and not recovered, the
sheriff must pay its full value out of his own pocket to the bereft
owner.

Randolph even stood up to the Pope. A murderer was brought
before him in Inverness. He admitted murdering a priest but
produced the Pope's absolution—a trick which was growing
common. 'The Pope may absolve you from the spiritual consequences of your sin,' said Randolph, 'but of the crime you have
committed against the law of this land I am your judge.' The
man was executed. But enforcing the law without fear or favour
was a dangerous occupation in those days and the 'Good Sir
Thomas' was poisoned by 'an infamous friar hired for the purpose'.

There was Lady Mary Ogilvie, the widow of a Laird of Grant,
who was Lady of Urquhart and came to a bad end, a refugee,
penniless and forlorn, because she refused her support to the
Covenanters. Later, there was Mary Grant, daughter of Grant of
Castle Urquhart. She loved Donald Donn, the poet son of Macdonald of Bohuntin in Brae Lochaber. Unfortunately Donald
looked on cattle lifting as legitimate warfare and the reiver's life
as a gentleman's calling. Mary's father did not, and the lovers
were forbidden to meet. Nevertheless, meet they did. Donald
was an unusual reiver for the place and time, a sort of Robin
Hood, killing no one if he could conveniently avoid it and being
kind and generous to the poor. It is told of him that one day
when driving stolen cattle he saw a strange shadow among them
which proved to be an old woman clinging to a cow. He spoke
to her and she told him that the cow was hers and all she had.
If she lost it she would starve to death, so she might as well die
here. 'If you hold like that to one cow what would you do with
two?' exclaimed Donald and sent her home with two cows.

One day Donald stopped to see Mary on his way back from
a raid. His pursuers were thus able to catch up with the herd he
had lifted, though Donald himself escaped. They reported what
had happened to the Laird of Grant, who, furious that the stolen
cattle had been found on his land, swore to capture and hang
Donald. Donald, now well hunted, hid in a cave on the loch-side
to be near Mary. His hiding place was discovered and a message,

purporting to be from her, was sent to him, entreating him to meet her at the house of a friend. He obeyed and was captured. When Donald had first heard that the Laird of Grant had sworn to hang him he had exclaimed: 'The Devil will take the Laird of Grant out of his shoes and Donald Donn shall not be hanged.' When he was condemned he appealed to be beheaded as a gentleman, not hanged like a felon. This request was granted and he is reputed to have been led away repeating: 'The Devil will take the Laird of Grant out of his shoes and Donald Donn shall not be hanged.' Legend tells how as his severed head rolled from the block it spoke and said: 'Mary lift ye my head.' Some of his poems in Gaelic have survived, including one of which the last verse is:

> Tomorrow I shall be on a hill, without a head.
> Have you no compassion for my sorrowful maiden,
> My Mary, the fair and tender eyed?

The Castle was last occupied by the troops of William of Orange and Mary his Queen. In 1692 they left, blowing up the main fortifications and the towers when they did so. By 1708 all slates and timber had been stolen to build houses, and Castle Urquhart was a ruin as we see it today. Beneath the castle are two huge dungeons. One is filled with treasure, the other with the plague.

The next place of any size is Invermoriston village. Invermoriston House itself was burnt to the ground in 1930. No one ever knew how the fire started, except that it was in the roof. Lightning perhaps. But its gardens and the family burying ground can still be seen between the road and the loch. This was not the first time Invermoriston House was burnt, however. The first stone house on the site was built in the middle of the sixteenth century by a Thane of Cawdor for his much-loved daughter when she married Partick Grant of Glenmoriston. Cawdor is said to have visited the young couple and been horrified to find his daughter living in a wattle house, so, by way of encouraging his son-in-law to allow him to build them a house of stone, he set fire to the old one. No one had seen a stone house in the Glen before and the workmen had all to be brought from Cawdor.

This Patrick Grant was succeeded by his son John, noted for

great size, wit and strength. He visited London in 1631-32 and
was much teased as a wild Highlander. One day an acquaintance
sneered in his presence at the 'fir candles' of his native glen, 'Glen
Moriston the smooth, where the dogs cannot eat the candles'.
John bet his tormentor that he could not produce in London a
finer candlestick or more brilliant lights than he could bring from
his Highland estate. The bet was accepted. 'Glenmoriston' des-
patched a servant to the North to bring him Iain MacEobhain
Bhain, the Glenmoriston bard, noted alike for wit and good looks.
At the appointed time the scoffer produced a very fine wrought
silver candelabrum holding the best candles. All praised their
light. Then, at a signal, the Bard stepped into the chamber in full
Highland dress, holding aloft blazing torches cut from the richest
pines of Glenmoriston and then steeped in resin. In the blaze of
light they produced the candle flames were all but invisible and
the astonished spectators adjudged 'Glenmoriston' an easy winner.

Invermoriston House was burnt down yet another time, this
time in 1716 by the King's troops as Grant of Glenmoriston was
among those who refused to seek pardon and lay down their arms
after the Rising.

There are many stories about Invermoriston and the surrounding hills. One tells how a Grant 'of that ilk' had an only and
adored son. One day as old Grant sat at breakfast a man in the
last stages of exhaustion stumbled into the room, and, grabbing
bread and salt from the table, swallowed some, then panted that
he was a hunted man and could go no further. He claimed hospitality, the protection of bread and salt. 'I have no choice,' said
the Chief, 'you have eaten my bread. Who hunts you and why?'
'I killed a man in a quarrel,' was the answer, 'and his friends are
pursuing me.' Grant showed him a safe place to sleep and left him.
A few minutes later his pursuers appeared, led, to the horror of
the old Chief, by his son's foster-brothers. They told him that
his son had been foully murdered and that the murderer, whom
they were pursuing, had been seen coming towards the house.
'No one has passed here,' replied the Chief without hesitation,
'try up the Glen.' So they departed and he went to see his son's
murderer. He found him sleeping peacefully, unarmed, certain
of safety under his enemy's protection. At dusk Grant roused the

fugitive, gave him food and wine and bade him go. 'You have till dawn,' he told him, 'then we will hunt and kill you. Go!' And he went.

The old law of hospitality in the Highlands was said to be: 'No guest may be asked his business for one year and one day.' It was also felt that the best must be set before an invited guest. At a dinner given to Argyll by MacEachin in Cantyre the table groaned under one each of every available creature, roasted whole and set on the table 'standing on its stumps'. Ox, goat, sheep, stag, roe, hares, rabbits and innumerable varieties of poultry were said to have been so displayed.

A road to the West takes off from Invermoriston and runs through Glenmoriston, Glenshiel and Kintail to the western sea and Kyle of Lochalsh. Six miles further along the main road from Invermoriston is Fort Augustus, at the head of the Loch, where the road from the Loch's southern shore joins it and where there is also a fine 'stair' of locks connecting the Loch with the next stretch of the canal. Fort Augustus was so named by General Wade about 1730 in honour of His Royal Highness William Augustus, Duke of Cumberland, better known in the North as Stinking Willie and Butcher Cumberland. The old Gaelic name for the village was Cilchumen (or Kiltcheumein), the Church of Cummin, St. Cummein the Fair who wrote a biography of St. Columba about 650 being the saint in question.

The story goes that St. Cummein founded an abbey or some form of religious house here long before the present Benedictine abbey was born or thought of. The country round was wild and uncultivated and the saint, seeing the need both to grow grain for the making of meal and also to spread knowledge of agriculture among the primitive inhabitants, bade his monks clear and plough a parcel of land round their holy house. At first all went well but it was desperately hard work and some of the monks began to grumble. It was for them to lead a leisured life teaching and preaching, they said; let others clear the ground and plough. God could not mean *them* to do it. At last matters came to a head and one monk, bolder than the rest, faced the saint and told him that if God had need of ploughed land He must provide it; they would not. 'So be it, my son,' replied the saint, 'but you may not eat of the fruits thereof', and he went to his cell to pray while the monks, half joyful, half fearful, took a holiday and went fishing. When they rose next morning, rather late for none had rung the abbot's bell, they saw the saint standing by the disputed land and talking to a team of red deer harnessed to the monks' plough. Already some land was ploughed. All day the deer ploughed and the saint watched. Frightened and shamefaced, the monks did their daily tasks and brought food to the saint, who refused it, and fodder to the stags, who ate daintily. As evening fell, the saint stopped the tired beasts and, thanking them for their work, for they had done much, sent them back to their hills with his blessing. That night two monks arose and went quietly out to see the deer's furrows. It was their intention to plough till dawn now that they knew it to be the will of God. But the plough was gone from its shed by the water's edge and there, ploughing at speed in the quiet moonlight, was an enormous black stallion, the waterhorse of Loch Ness. By dawn all the land lay ploughed in the sun's rays and the great horse had returned to his own place, but on his back had gone a rider, the monk who tried to teach the Lord.

It is interesting to note in this old story that even from the beginning the Iona Church tried to teach agriculture and civilised ways to a very primitive and backward people. Later, improving education and way of life was one of their great tasks. Another was the encouraging of all men to come and pray in the tiny churches at any time they felt the desire, that they might learn for themselves the power of prayer. This was one of the main differences between Celtic and Roman Churches in the early days in the Highlands. The Roman Catholic priests held prayer in their own hands to a far greater extent, the Celtic Church held it out as God's gift to every man.

The second of the Great Glen roads runs along the south shore of Loch Ness. Leaving Inverness at the foot of Bridge Street it passes the War Memorial and the Islands and then runs parallel with the River Ness almost as far as the village of Dores. On the left a few miles from Inverness is Ness Castle, at the moment a hotel. Of it McBain in his *Place Names* says its 'old name was Borlum, meaning Bordlands, whence the infamous and notorious

Borlum family got its name'. It would be interesting to know what this 'infamous' family was and what it did. Unfortunately it seems to be no longer notorious. Next comes Aldourie, now turned into flats, with a lovely position on the Loch, and then, about a mile further on, the village of Dores, before we reach which there is a fine view down the length of Loch Ness. The chief claim of Dores to fame today is that her inn is kept by a retired lady's maid of the Queen Mother.

> If you'd seen this road
> Before it was made
> You'd hold up your hand
> And bless General Wade.

Few truer rhymes have ever been remembered, for General Wade made the first road through the Great Glen, *circa* 1726, where this one now runs. His reputation for fair dealing, justice and hard work remains a very live memory, as do the many roads he made, most of which, like this one, are still in use. It was down this road that Johnson and Boswell travelled and Dr Johnson much admired the Loch, adding two pieces of information about it that he obtained at Fort Augustus. One was that 'its water is imagined by the natives to be medicinal', an idea long since extinct, and the other that it was said to remain open in the hardest winters. It is certainly a fact that I have seen the Beauly Firth frozen almost across and the Cromarty Firth completely frozen and able to bear a cart, both of these being salt-water lochs, when Loch Ness had only a little thin ice round the shore. Whether it ever has been known to freeze, however, I don't know.

Beyond Dores the road becomes unimaginably beautiful, both for scenery and for the more homely things such as birch woods yellow with primroses, the young green of the birches themselves, the flaming scarlet of rowan trees standing out amid the guinea gold of birches in autumn, warm old gold of oak woods studded here and there with the living green of firs, and, loveliest of all, in the winter the birches again, grey and purple against the snow. In the woods on this side of the Loch there were once herds of wild horses, creatures rather of the hill pony type; shaggy and sure-footed, they roamed about the hills from Moray to Suther-land but these woods were one of their favourite haunts. In the

Loch Ness

woods, too, was an enormous yellow horse, some say more than one, who carried off boys and young men. Two young brothers once went to fish in Loch Ness. Before they set out their father warned them to beware of 'the Horse'. Sure enough, the horse came down to the loch-side to drink and both boys were overwhelmed with admiration for its beauty. Never before had they seen such a stallion. Its coat glowed like some fine silk cloth, finer than either boy had ever imagined, its mane was like the silken floss of a maiden's hair and its eyes were sad. Surely so fine a creature could not be evil. The boys did not try to escape and when it approached and offered them a ride the elder boy could not resist. He sprang on its back and instantly found himself glued on, unable to move. He tried to cry a warning to his young brother, but too late; the boy had raised his hand to stroke the arching neck and as he touched the glossy skin his hand stuck fast. Realising their danger, the younger boy drew his knife and cut off his own fingers, then, as at sight of steel the horse fled, bound up his hand with the healing leaves of figwort and followed its track through the woods, stopping only as he passed their home to take his brother's sword. All day he followed the horse's track and just as night fell he came upon it resting by a burn, his brother still fast on its back. Creeping up, the boy lifted the sword and managed to cut off the beautiful golden head. To his amazement, he had hardly done so when there stood before him not only his brother freed from the spell but another and very handsome young man with white skin and golden hair. In his hand the youth held the boy's fingers. 'How can I thank you for freeing me?' he asked, adding, 'Show me your hand.' The boy removed the bandage and the youth replaced his fingers and his hand grew whole once more. The golden youth told them of how he had fallen under the spell of a magician which could only be broken if his head was cut off by one who had never before held a sword. The three young men strolled happily home together but the brothers were lucky, for many a boy or man who met a yellow horse was never seen again.

The black stallion of Loch Ness and the yellow horses of the woods were not the only equine inhabitants of the Great Glen. There was also the White Mare of Corri-Dho, who dwelt in the hills between Glenmoriston and Glen Urquhart. She was a creature of such overwhelming charm that no horse could resist her. Any horse turned out to graze anywhere in the Great Glen would immediately seek her and would never be seen again. At last the men of the district determined to intervene. They made a cordon round her in her favourite haunt and slowly the lines drew closer till it seemed that she could not escape. But one of them, Alexander Cutach (or the Short), conceited as small men so often are, thought he could capture the beauty single-handed and seized her by the tail. Infuriated, she broke through the cordon with Alexander attached, for his hand was stuck fast. Later, his mangled body was found on the moor, but of the White Mare there was no trace; she had returned to wherever she belonged.

Close to Dores village three large stones can be seen in the waters of the loch. The centre one of these is known as 'The Thieves' Stone' because cattle raiders could tell by the height of the water on its side whether or not the 'lifted' cattle could safely cross the ford at Bona. A little farther along the road is the Well of the Outstretched Hand which was said to be the abode of some large-sized spirit whose phantom hand would often be seen stretched out over the heads of those about to drink the well water. Many thirsty travellers were terrified but I never heard of one being harmed and no one seems to know the origin or purpose of the apparition. The well was marked with a name stone in 1922. A little farther yet on the road is a crossing of a deep burn on whose banks two fugitives from Culloden died of their wounds and a stone carved with the date 1746 can still be found in the ravine. Burns, big and small, are almost as plentiful as corners on this road and near the next bridge, the witch's bridge, there lived a witch with a very evil eye as late as 1881 when she invited herself, like the witches in the fairy tales, to the wedding of the then Fraser Tytler of Aldourie, bringing with her, in a cooking pot, a highly magic potion of a gruel-like nature.

Further on again we pass the site of General Wade's camp and later, near a small piece of arable land, are the outlines of an ancient cottage. Here a tiny 'change house' or posting inn stood at the time of Culloden. Its owner had recently died and the inn was in the hands of his old and crippled mother and pretty young daughter. One of Cumberland's officers saw and admired the girl and assaulted her. The old grandmother tried to protect her, whereupon the officer throttled the old woman in her chair and turned once more to the girl. But she had used the moment to escape and made her way to a settlement known as 'the town of the freebooters' on the loch side. The men of the township returned with her, made the officer a prisoner and took both him and the old woman's body to the Duke at Fort Augustus. He expressed anger and ordered the officer to 'mend his manners and pay blood money'. It was at this same cottage that Dr Johnson and Mr Boswell called and were surprised to find an old woman alone in the house and obviously afraid of them. But the inn was not, perhaps, as innocent as it appeared, for a little later the pay-master of the troops at Fort Augustus stopped there for the night after a visit to Inverness to collect a large bag of gold coin. Neither he nor his horse, its harness or the gold were ever seen again. Some claimed that he was murdered and his body thrown into Loch Ness, others that this was what he wished to be believed.

The next point of interest is where the road to Inverfarigaig takes off to the left, with its precipitous river valley and its slopes starry with grass of Parnassus and scabious. This is not a road to take lightly; to get round the bend into it many cars must reverse. However, one gets good warning for the start of the road is an avenue of cypress-like trees. Not far from the Inverfarigaig turning comes the pleasant little Foyers Hotel and then Foyers itself with its Falls, its aluminium works and its monster, for the favourite sporting ground of 'Nessie' lies between Foyers and Fort Augustus. Foyers had the honour of being bombed in the war, not by mistake but of intent.

Beyond Foyers lies Camus Mharbh Dhaoine, The Bay of the Dead Men, so called because of a fierce fight there between the galleys of Portclair (who had come to avenge a slight to his young bride) and the men of Grant who rowed out to meet him. Needless to say, the galleys defeated the small boats with much slaughter and the Grants lost Foyers. But who Gruer Mor of Portclair was and how or why his bride was slighted in Foyers I should hate to guess. What was she doing in Foyers anyway?

Portclair is on the other shore. Traditionally she came there to collect bride gifts, but this seems a little unusual.

From there the road runs on, beautifully, down to Fort Augustus.

15

FORT AUGUSTUS
TO BALLACHULISH

Bannocks o' bear meal,
Bannocks o' barley,
Here's to the Highlandman's
Bannocks o' barley.

ROBERT BURNS

AFTER FORT AUGUSTUS the road follows the line of the Canal and the shores of Loch Oich and Loch Lochy to Fort William. It first passes through some flat land, probably once water meadows, which has always been a popular gathering place for the clans and camping place of armies. There are not, when you look around, very many possible camping grounds to be found in this part of the Highlands; the high ground is too high and the low too marshy. It was here that the Earls of Mar and of Caithness camped with the troops of King James I of Scotland before the fatal battle of Inverlochy, when Caithness was killed on the field and Mar escaped alone and on foot into the Great Glen. The Highlanders had won a signal victory. Severely wounded, Mar wandered in the hills till at last he was saved by a herd-woman who found him dying of hunger and exhaustion. Having neither cup nor platter, she took off his shoe, mixed barley meal and water in it and gave it to him. Later he composed a verse in Gaelic of which the following is a translation:

Hunger is a cook right good
Woe to him that sneers at food—
Barley crowdie in my shoe
The sweetest food I ever knew.

Another army to camp here was that of Claverhouse, 'Bonny Dundee'. He was more fortunate than the two earls for he left it to win a noted victory, the Battle of Killiecrankie. Among others with him was Lochiel, who was credited with possessing

second sight. Before the battle Dundee enquired from him which
side would be victorious and he replied 'the Army which first
sheds blood'. The two armies were already drawn up facing one
another and Locheil's words ran like wildfire through the troops
till they reached young Grant of Glenmoriston who called an
accomplished Glenmoriston deer-stalker to him, repeated the
prophecy and at the same time pointed out an officer mounted
on a white horse in front of the enemy's lines as being 'most con-
spicuous'. The stalker took aim and ensured victory for Dundee.
General Monk passed here too, en route for Glengarry, but he is
reputed not to have camped; only delayed long enough to burn
all the houses of Glen Roy. The Duke of Cumberland spent
seven weeks in Fort Augustus, itself a misfortune for any district.

Little Loch Oich is the first in the chain of lochs after Loch
Ness. It is a slim, narrow piece of water between high fir-covered
hillsides, very attractive but not unsuited to its name if, as some
say, it means The Place of Awe. Long before 'Nessie' stole the
limelight Loch Oich had its own monster, a waterhorse with a
difference, for its head was said to be flat rather than horse-shaped;
it took no interest in human beings but was reputed to watch for
sheep or deer coming to drink from the loch; these it would seize
and, dragging them into the water, sit on their heads until they
drowned. Some claimed to have seen the creature behaving as
described; others, however, held that she was too convenient an
alibi for deer poachers and sheep stealers to be entirely credible,
especially as sheep do not drink. Also, her manner of killing was
queer. Actually, I once knew a dog, an elderly spaniel, who did
just that. He would drive his master's sheep, one at a time, into
the sea and then, deliberately and of malice aforethought, sit on
its head till it died. At that point he would lose all interest in it,
come quietly ashore and start again with another one.

On the north shore of Loch Oich stand the ruins of the old
Macdonald Castle of Glengarry, three times burnt. The huge
Macdonald Clan, with its many leading families, has a queer
history of marriage and inter-marriage, even marriage in Scotland
not recognised in England and vice-versa. At last their descents
became such a tangle that a case was brought before the House of
Lords, that the Law Lords might sift the evidence and decide who

was in fact the Chief of the Clan. The House did its best but had finally to decide that on present evidence no decision was possible as between the three leading families, Clanranald, Glengarry and Sleat, and that they could only suggest that these three take the Chieftainship in rotation. The history and adventures of Clan Donald would fill many tomes but on one thing all are agreed— Macdonald pride. Once, it is said, a woman in Lochaber went to Confession and admitted that her besetting sin was pride. The priest reproved her for it and gave her advice on how to subdue it. She listened reverently and then said: 'God and men know I have a right to be proud. I was born a Macdonald.'

Once Glengarry House, which stands not far from the ruins of the Castle, had a brownie but the unfortunate little creature was accidentally scalded while helping in the kitchen. He promptly left, taking, it is believed, the luck of the house with him. The road to the West by Glengarry and Tomdoun takes off to the right here and nearby is the famous Well of the Heads, where Iain Lom, the Gaelic Poet Laureate to Charles II, washed the heads of the seven murderers of Macdonald of Keppoch before presenting them to 'Glengarry'. He is said to have carried them on his saddle bow, strung together by a withy through their ears. An odd way for a poet to behave, perhaps, but he was of the Keppoch family and felt strongly on clan matters, as some of his verses show. For instance:

> Up the green slope of Cuil-Eachhaidh
> Came Clan Donald, marching stoutly;
> Churls who laid my home in ashes
> Now shall pay the fine devoutly.
>
> ★ ★ ★ ★ ★
>
> On the wings of eager rumour
> Far and wide the tale is flying,
> How the slippery knaves, the Campbells,
> With their cloven skulls are lying.'
> (From his 'Battle of Inverlochy')

After Loch Oich comes Loch Lochy, the home of a water goddess and, most strange to relate, she is black. All this was St. Finan's country and he had once a small church near the loch, presumably to control her. The hillsides beside the loch have been forested, with excellent results. The road is now almost always usable whereas in the years before the planting heavy rain, snow and frost were all liable to bring down a landslide of loose stone and shale, burying the roadway. I can remember in 1922 or 1923 my father's car being caught between two such falls. We got out by driving along the loch's narrow and stony beach with two wheels in the water part of the way. The result was four punctures and one broken spring, but we got through.

Not far to the north-west of this loch lies Loch Arkaig where it has long been believed Prince Charles's French treasure was hidden. Its exact whereabouts (if it really existed) are not known and though many have searched no trace has ever been found. By tradition three men knew the secret and all died without revealing it.

With Loch Lochy the 'real' lochs end and the road rises over some higher ground between it and the sea-loch, Loch Linnhe, on which Fort William stands. The Canal, too, crosses the high ground to Banavie by the Giant's Staircase (also called Neptune's Staircase), a very fine sequence of locks but uneconomical in use. In the days when MacBrayne's ran a steamer service between Inverness and Oban, one steamer stopped below the locks and another took on at Fort William, the connecting link being supplied by a bus. The road from Loch Lochy by Spean Bridge to Fort William runs by moor and riverside. It is a lonely, rather bare country full of sad tales and much overshadowed by the enormous bulk of Ben Nevis looking squarely down on it all. It was here that in the last war most of our Commando troops were trained. A striking monument to them has been erected in a dominating position hard by the road. Much of this Glen became the Great Glen Cattle Ranch, where great herds wander over the hills. It was a pioneer scheme and may do much for the Highlands. The original owners of the Ranch are now the owners of the present Inverlochy Castle where Queen Victoria once stayed. The old Castle of Inverlochy was in its heyday the palace of the Kings of Scots and is supposed to date from A.D. 600 or 700.

Once a Glaistic (a sort of fairy woman) inhabited the slopes above Inverlochy. She was up to many a trick and her presence was not at all popular with the local people. One day Big

The Commando Monument

Kennedy of Lianachan saw her near his farm and managed to seize her. He heated a ploughshare red hot, then let it cool to black and said to her: 'If you will swear on this ploughshare that you will trouble the people of the Glen no more, I will set you free.' The Glaistic placed 'her lovely little hand' on the ploughshare and it was burnt to the bone. She fled screaming up the hillside and there 'the blood of her heart burst forth' and she died. As she was dying she said:

> Growth like fern to them
> Wasting like rushes to them,
> And as unlasting as the mist of the hill.

and that curse has been on Big Kennedy's descendants ever since, while the vegetation round the spot where she died is still russet hued, stained by her heart's blood.

One of the stories told of this bleak moor is of a party of soldiers, who, marching back to Fort Augustus after the massacre of Glencoe, heard the sound of piping in the hills. Believing that

a Macdonald piper must have been among those who had escaped
the massacre and that he was now using his pipes to collect
stragglers, the officer in charge ordered his men on to the moor
in search of him. The piping soon grew louder and clearer but
ever kept ahead of them until at last the music led the party to a
small hill loch and vanished into the water. It was a piper of the
Little People that they followed and he gladly led them astray.
Hungry, footsore and angry, the party began their struggle back
through the snow to the valley below. As they went, another
sound broke the stillness of the snow-clad hills—the crying of a
young child. The officer called up one of his men. 'Find that
child and wring its neck,' he ordered angrily, 'then follow our
tracks down.' The soldier went off as bidden, with as bad a grace
as he dared, for he too was tired and hungry. Led by the baby's
crying he began to climb again. Then the sound stopped. Instead
came the loveliest singing he had ever heard. Soon he came upon
the singer. It was a young mother, an escaped fugitive, utterly
exhausted, lulling her baby to the sleep of death in the snow.
When she saw the soldier, sword in hand, she did not move. She
was too tired. He looked down at mother and child but could
not speak to them for they had no English and he no Gaelic.
But he remembered how he had left his own wife with their baby
in her arms, took what little food he had and offered it to the
woman, then took off his greatcoat to wrap round the child.
Then he turned and ran. On his way down he passed another
woman who had also escaped the massacre but this one was less
fortunate; the wolf that had killed her was still at his feast. The
soldier slew the wolf and when he rejoined his party and was
asked by the officer: 'Did you get the child?', replied: 'I found it'
and held up his sword, stained with the wolf's blood. The officer
grunted and the party marched on. It is pleasant to know that
the woman and child survived and their descendants are said to
be in Lochaber today.

This same moor was once the favourite hunting ground of a
young hunter, Donald Cameron. One day he shot at a hind and
wounded it but though he followed her for some time the deer
escaped. Months later Donald was overtaken by darkness and
decided to spend the night on the moor. He found shelter beneath

a boulder and soon fell asleep, but his sleep was disturbed by the appearance of a most beautiful woman who approached him and offered him an arrow. 'Never did I believe you would harm me, Donald,' she said reproachfully, 'after the many hours we have wandered together over the hill.' 'But,' said the perplexed Donald, 'I never saw you before and I certainly never harmed you or any woman, and where did you get my arrow?' 'I am the hind you shot with this arrow,' she answered. 'I am the leader of my herd and many a happy day on the hill have I led you to. I am under Fith Fath (enchantment).' The young man did not know what to do at all but accepted the arrow and promised in future only to shoot at stags, not hinds. Then the maiden moved away with her deer and he heard her singing:

> I would not let my herd of deer,
> My herd of deer, my herd of deer,
> I would not let my herd of deer
> Go seek grey shells upon the strand.
>
> They had rather the cresses green,
> The cresses green, the cresses green,
> They had rather the cresses green
> That grow on the mead of the glorious springs.

Slowly the singing died away among the hills.

A mile or two before Fort William is reached a road takes off to Banavie (the Canal mouth) and Corpach, the Place of Bodies. This name goes back to the days when kings and chiefs were taken to Iona for burial. If, as frequently happened, the sea was not calm enough for the funeral barge to sail, the whole party remained with the body at Corpach until it was safe to set out. Funerals to Iona went in great state.

And this is the manner in which a Lord of the Isles would die. His fair body was brought to Iona of Colum-cille. And the Abbot and the monks and the vicars came forth to meet the King of the Isles; and his service and waking were honourably performed during eight days and eight nights; after which his full, noble body was laid in the same grave with his fathers, in the Reilig of Oran.

This account is of the burying of Donald, King of the Isles, who received his Sceptre of the Isles from his brother Ranald. 'He was the son of Good John, son of Angus Og, son of Angus Mor, son

of Donald, son of Ranald, son of Somerled, the noble and renowned High Chief of the Hebrides.' He made a reliquary or
covering of gold and silver for the hand of St. Columba.

To this day lights are seen on the waters of Loch Leven,
shimmering where the funeral barges passed carrying Kings and
Chiefs to their burial.

St. Columba and his monks often visited this part of the mainland and it was said to be near here that St. Columba was once
approached by a beggar. The Saint did not approve of begging
and said so in no uncertain terms. The man explained that he was
a hunter to trade but such a bad one that he was rarely successful
and now that he was too weak from hunger to follow the deer
on the hills his wife and children would starve. St. Columba then
took pity on him and gave him a 'blessed pike' which would hunt
for him by killing any animal at which it was pointed. The man
went home happy and soon he and his family were sleek and
well-liking, with open door for every neighbour. But the day
came when Columba returned to the district and found the man
again a beggar. He explained that his wife had taken a dislike to
the blessed pike, fearing it might harm the children, and had
made him destroy it.

Near Loch Eil, at the head of Loch Linnhe, lived a poor man
who once gave St. Columba a night's hospitality. In the morning
the Saint asked him how many cows he had. 'Five,' was the reply.
'A hundred and five they shall become, neither more nor less,
answered the Saint, and so it came to pass. No matter how many
he used or gave to the needy, his herd grew no less, and no matter
how hard he tried to increase the number his herd grew no larger.

Fort William itself was built close to the village of Auchintore
and was called after William of Orange, while the village had its
name changed to Maryburgh in honour of Mary his wife. Later,
both names were changed to Gordonsburgh by a Duke of Gordon
who did not love the House of Orange, and later again, with the
'passing' of the Gordons, it became Duncanburgh to please Sir
Duncan Cameron of Fossfearn who had no love for the House
of Gordon. Now, and one hopes finally, it has reverted to being
Fort William.

Beyond Fort William the road follows the lochside through

Onich to North Ballachulish and the ferry to Argyll, or round
Loch Leven on the Inverness-shire shore to Kinlochleven with
its aluminium works. A most lovely drive. Once Sir Ewen
Cameron of Locheil was going along the ferry road in peace
when he was overtaken by a noted witch, Great Gormul of Moy,
who had followed him all the way from Inverness.

'Step on, beloved Ewen,' she greeted him, but he, knowing
well that she did not love him, answered,

'Step on thyself, Carlin. And if it be necessary to take the
step, a step beyond thee for Ewen.'

'Step on, beloved Ewen,' she said again, and he answered
much as before,

'Step to step with thee, old one, and the odd step to Ewen.'

And so they went on down to the loch shore. When they
reached the ferry Sir Ewen was still one step ahead. He hailed
the ferry and stepped quickly on board. Great Gormul made to
follow him but the ferryman, knowing who she was, would not
take her. Then she said farewell to Sir Ewen, adding, 'And the
wish of my heart to thee, thou best beloved of men, Ewen.'

'The wish of thy heart be upon yonder grey stone, Carlin,'
he retorted. And instantly the stone split in two.

16

GLEN URQUHART

Gloom and silence and spell,
Spell and silence and gloom,
And the weird death-light burns dim in the night
And the dead men rise from the tomb.
MURDOCH MACLEAN

GLEN URQUHART is the only place I ever heard of
that recognises three Devils, the Black Devil, the Speckled
Devil and the White Devil, and the last of these three,
because he was able to assume the appearance of an angel or other
good spirit and so deceive men, was by far the most deadly.

Glen Urquhart first appears in written history in Adamnan's
Life of St. Columba. Once, while the saint and his monks were
journeying down Loch Ness, it was revealed to St. Columba that
he must hurry to Glen Urquhart (Airchart-Dan) where he would
find an old man named Emchath on his death-bed and should
baptise him. 'For he is a man who has always preserved his
natural goodness and angels are already on their way for his soul.'
St. Columba did as directed and duly found Emchath. The saint
preached the word of God to him and he believed and was baptised, then 'safe and joyfully with the angels who met him he
passed away to the Lord'.

A somewhat similar summons came to one of the 'Men' as
Glen Urquhart called certain virtuous Elders, many centuries
later. He too was summoned to a dying man to pray with him.
It was a dark and stormy night when, wrapping himself in a
cloak, he set out. As he passed along the wooded bank of the
Meiklie Burn he heard a whimpering and found a baby lying
under a bush, cold and wet. Wrapping the shivering child in his
cloak he hoisted it on to his back and continued his way, but the
child grew heavier and heavier until at last he felt he must rest.
When he would have risen again to go on he found himself being

held down by a hideous monster whose horrible hairy hands were already round his neck. He fought fiercely to free himself, then, realising it must be a creature of evil, he called aloud on God for help and the creature—who is believed to have been undoubtedly the White Devil—disappeared, leaving him free to visit and pray with the dying man, which obviously it had hoped to prevent.

Glen Urquhart is the only district, too, where as far as I know, the Devil in person has beaten and kicked men to death. In other places he is content to incite others to such deeds. It is, I believe, usually the Speckled Devil who behaves in this manner. But the power of evil in this Glen has always seemed stronger and a more sentient thing than anywhere else in Scotland. It is a glen both larger and longer than it appears at its mouth; now a route which even tour buses take, it was until well into this century completely remote. No public transport of any sort connected it with the outside world until the 1920's. The consequence was that the Glen was famed alike for its Gaelic (Glen Urquhart Gaelic was said to be the purest in Scotland) and for its witches—real 'black' ones. When Gaelic came from Ireland to Scotland it naturally changed considerably over the ages till now a man speaking Erse and one speaking Gaelic have considerable difficulty in understanding one another. But Gaelic in Scotland itself also changed very much in different districts. In the time of St. Columba and his Church it was the language in which his monks preached, so it slowly ousted the old Pictish tongue and became universal in the Highlands. But geographical features such as sea and mountains separated the different localities, as also did such long-lasting Clan feuds as that between the Campbells of Argyll and the Macdonalds of the Isles, with the result that various dialects of Gaelic grew up in different places, differing greatly, and each claiming itself to be the true Gaelic. Finally they have boiled down to three: Argyllshire Gaelic which is the best known and the one most closely akin to Erse, containing many Irish words and forms I am told; Island Gaelic, to some extent contaminated by Norse words and forms of speech; and Glen Urquhart Gaelic, said to be the purest of them all. No doubt B.B.C. Gaelic will soon supplant all three.

Witches are a different matter. As a child I used to stay with an aunt at Kilmartin on Loch Meiklie, well up the Glen. In those days there was no public transport at all. Letters for the 'Big Houses' were sent out by horse from Inverness in locked letter bags, one bag for each house. Each owner had his key, emptied out the incoming post and replaced it with the outgoing mail, if any, and that was that. My cousin had many small friends round about who showed us birds' nests and other joys. One day, two of them told me they had something special to show me—my cousin, being older, was still at lessons—and took me to a little burn which came tumbling down the hillside not far from Hazel Brae. Here, hidden and held fast by two stones, was a queer little wax doll. It had a few strands of real hair on its head, nail parings stood out like fingers from the ends of its arms, its eyes were tiny bits of coal, horribly shiny and alive-looking. 'Don't touch; it might do things,' I was warned. I didn't understand, but in some queer way I was very frightened, not so much of the image as of the whole feel of things. Perhaps the other children were frightened (they were certainly awed) and this frightened me. One of them told me who had made the image and whose image it was, and explained that the woman in question was a witch. If a witch made an image and put it in the burn, the burn would wear it away very slowly but surely, and the man whose image it was would equally slowly but surely die. Anyone could make an image but only a witch knew the proper things to say to it. They had found this one because they had seen the farmer whose image it was, turning the witch's cows out of his corn and so they were sure she would make an image of him and he would die. All this was explained by the same child who had explained butter-making to me a few days before, and in the same matter-of-fact tone, and I found it much the more natural and the easier to believe of the two. After all, why *should* milk turn into butter? Or, for that matter, why should anyone in love entering the dairy disturb the butter and prevent its 'coming' as I was told it did?

Needless to say, I was sworn to secrecy and we waited for what we regarded as the certain result. Then I went home and soon forgot, till my aunt came to stay a few months later and mentioned in my hearing how sorry she was for this farmer's wife and children as he had just died, quite young. The doctors

did not know why or of what. I kept the secret for many years
and with it a fear and horror of witchcraft. Even yet I sometimes
wonder whether evil and hatred let loose by anyone in any con-
centrated form such as 'over-looking' or cursing may not do
harm beyond our comprehension, just as blessings may do good.

Some years later my mother engaged that witch's daughter
as housemaid, and a very good and well trained one she was. At
first all went well, her work was well done, she was tidy and
pleasant, but on several occasions my mother found the other
maids doing things which were her work; however, a kitchen in
which one obliges another (within limits) is usually a happy
kitchen. But one winter morning my mother, taking a short cut
down the back stairs, came upon a procession. In front walked
Peggy, a lady of leisure; behind her came the tablemaid with
brush and dustpan; last but not least came Cook in person, carrying kindling for the fires. The resultant enquiries elicited the fact
that Peggy did not like to spoil her hands doing grates or dusting,
nor did she like to tire herself with a broom, and: 'We wouldn't
wish to offend her mother so we just do it ourselves. . . . Oh, no,
M'm, please you mustn't say anything. We couldn't stay if you
did. Indeed we wouldn't be safe from bad luck *anywhere* if her
mother thought we had grudged the work or complained. . . .
No, you *can't* make a change, M'm, anything might happen.'
Having satisfied herself that nothing would be done which could
offend Peggy's redoubtable mother, Cook, who belonged to an
older generation and had been a noted player of the 'proverb
game' in the Ceilidhs of her youth, added with scorn: 'But the
laziness of her! Yon would be "a good messenger to send for
death", but there, "Clean bird never left kite's nest." '

In the end, as my mother saw no point in paying Peggy for
doing practically nothing, and as it was obvious that no one local
would dare to come to us if we contrived to annoy Peggy's
mother, we had to close the house for a time, dismiss the whole
staff (officially) and start fresh on our return. 'I could wait and
come back to you,' Peggy offered when she heard, and it was felt
it would be tactless to reply: 'No, thank you, we don't believe in
witches but we won't re-engage a witch's child.'

Between the wars a Yorkshire man who had bought a place

in the Glen decided to rear pigs and brought up his pig-man from Yorkshire to superintend. This swineherd quarrelled with a woman in the Glen reputed to be the possessor of the Evil Eye. She was seen to walk past the piggeries and eighty-three young pigs were dead next day. 'Over-looking' said everyone, including (it was believed) the young and rather scared policeman. But the owner himself said: 'Poison', and announced that if any more of his animals died he would call in Scotland Yard. No more died.

The Little People lived in Glen Urquhart also. An Gobha Mor —the Big Smith or Armourer—knew all about that. He and his seven sons were noted alike in their day for their strength and their skill. The fame of their cold-iron swords spread throughout Scotland. In making these much-prized weapons the iron was heated and shaped by heavy and repeated hammer blows, without the use of fire. The smith's herd of cattle on his farm at Polmaily were also famous for their perfections. One morning the smith, visiting his byre, found his cattle looking lean and hungry and no matter what he did they grew scraggier and scraggier. Near Polmaily was the fairy hillock of Tornashee and one of the fairies from it was the smith's 'fairy-love', a relationship not very un-common in those parts in his time. She told him the fairies had carried off and eaten his cattle. Furious, he took his axe and rushed to the byre to kill the fairy kine, but when they saw him coming they all slipped their heads out of their head-ropes and escaped. The smith caught the last by its tail and was carried with it, willy nilly, over grassland and moorland, over bog and rock, till they came to Carn-an-Rath in Ben-an Gharbhlaich near Achnababan. As they approached this hill or dun it opened to admit them. No sooner were they within than the cattle turned back into some of the Little People. The smith, looking round, found himself in a fine hall, full of rare jewels, gold and silver. The fairy chief politely apologised for his rough ride and also for 'lifting' his cattle and asked him to take any one thing he saw as recompense. Many of the fine jewels were of far greater value than his herd but the smith noticed in a far corner a small shaggy pony and, remembering something his fairy-love had once told him of the powers and strength of this horse, he avoided the jewels (which would most likely have turned to dead leaves anyway) and chose the filly. 'A tooth out of your informant's mouth' cried the angry Little People but they gave him the pony, only warning him never to harness it to anything but the plough,

Highland Ponies in snow

and let him go. Wise indeed was his choice, for never so strong a horse was seen in the Highlands.

> Achnababan she could plough,
> And Lurgamore from east to west
> Likewise Gorstan-Keppagach
> And still plough on without a rest.

But one day the smith harnessed her to a cart and her powers left her.

Once the Urquhart men drove their cattle to feed in Corri Dho, but two supernatural beings there drove them out, crying:

> Mine are Doire-Dhamb and Doire-Dhailbhidh
> And yellow Borrisgidh of the streams
> And wide Ceanacroc, with its woods and pasturage.
> Ye black and singed carles, take yourselves away.

Glen Urquhart was the scene of many a Clan fight and many a cattle-lifting and its consequences. There is hardly a stone or a hollow that is not known by some such name as 'The Hollow of the Dead Men', 'The Stone of the Slaying' and so on. But despite the horror of its past it is a very beautiful valley, especially perhaps in winter with its birches purple against the snow, Loch Meiklie reflecting the cold clear blue of the sky and Corrimony woods white with the white purity of snowdrops. It looks more a country for angels than witches and wars. Yet it is close to these very woods that those with 'the sight' may receive warning of horrors to come, in the form of vast shadowy hosts battling over the Corrimony moors. What their coming portends no man knows, except that it is a sight of unimaginable evil.

The road crosses Corrimony and runs over the moors and then down a steep hill with beautiful views to the River Cannich. To go by Glen Urquhart to Glen Affric, returning by way of Glen Cannich and Chisholm's Tooth, makes a most memorable drive. It is not quite so good if done in reverse as one then misses the views running down the long hill from Glen Urquhart to Cannich.

Between Corrimony and Invermoriston lies a piece of very wild country once occupied by a Cailleach a'Chrathaich or Hag of the Cràach as that part was called. She had a grievance against the MacMillans and used to accost every wayfarer to discover his name and, if it was MacMillan, engage his attention in the most pleasing manner and quietly steal his bonnet and then leave him. She would seat herself and begin to rub the bonnet between two stones—as it wore thin the man began to tire and when at length a hole came he dropped down dead. Once Donald MacMillan of Balmacaan saw her steal his cap, a fierce struggle ensued, he escaped with it unharmed, but as he went she hissed after him that he would die at nine of the clock three nights thence. As the clock struck the fatal hour he fell back in his chair dead. Not far off, near Tornashee, lived a good and gentle spirit who did what she could to warn and protect travellers from the Hag. She had a passion for riding and once asked Donald Macrae of Lochletter for a lift. He placed her before him on his horse then, binding her with the horse rope, took her home a prisoner and tied her to his

door-post. Instantly the place was surrounded by crowds of
furious Little People who, shouting and screaming curses upon
him, stripped the building of every bit of roof. Thoroughly
frightened, Macrae offered to let her go if she would rebuild his
house. To this she agreed and called:

> Speed wood and sod
> To the house of Macrae
> Except honeysuckle and bird-cherry.

Instantly, timber and turf came flying in through the air and soon
the house was restored as it had been and the good fairy was freed.
Macrae had better luck than he deserved that time.

17

GLENMORISTON
AND GLENGARRY

O'er the moor at midnight
The wee folk pass,
They whisper 'mong the rushes
And o'er the green grass;
All through the marshy places
They glint and pass away,
The light folk, the lone folk
    the folk that will not stay.

   ★   ★   ★   ★   ★

O never wrong the wee folk,
The red folk and the green,
The fierce folk, the angry folk,
    the folk that steal and slay.
DONALD A. MACKENZIE

THE MAIN ROAD to Glenelg, Lochalsh and Skye, when it turns off the Loch Ness road, first runs beside the River Moriston. Moriston is said to come from an old Pictish word meaning waterfall, and certainly for many centuries Glenmoriston Falls were worthy of note. They are beautiful even now, though two hydro-electric dams between them and Loch Cluanie have greatly reduced their perfection.

Glenmoriston has always been a main route to the West and tradition speaks of the Lords of the Isles and other important chiefs passing through it with considerable pomp. A number of Macdonalds had once settled here and it is said that whenever Macdonald of the Isles passed through 'in state' he formally exchanged shirts with the chief of the Glenmoriston Macdonalds as a pledge of 'mutual friendship and fidelity'. There were five septs of these Macdonalds in Glenmoriston and four of them were descended from four sons of Iain Mor Ruigh-nan-Stop (Great

Iain of the Liquor-Pot!). Iain Mor had sixteen fine sons; one day
returning from Glen Urquhart with their father they sat down
to rest near the Raven's Rock at Fasadh-an-Fitheach. A raven
flew over and dropped a bone. Twelve of the sons handled
it with curiosity, then, as the thirteenth put out his hand for it, his
father prevented him, saying, 'If it augurs good fortune we have
enough; if evil, we have too much.' Before the end of a year and
a day the twelve who touched the bone were dead.

The remaining four, Iain Ruadh (Red John), Iain Caol (Slen-
der John), Eobhan Ban (Fair Ewen), and Gilleasbuig (Archibald),
were the founders of four of the five septs of the Macdonalds in
the Glen. These four septs were by custom always buried feet to
the east and on their backs, that they might have their faces towards Our Lord when at the Last Day He comes from the East.
But the fifth sept, Slioched Alasdair Choire-Dho, though buried
in the same old churchyard of Clachan Mercheird, were always
buried feet to the west, that their first sight when waking at the
Last Day may be their beloved Corri-Dho. The posture of burial
must once have been held of great importance in the Celtic world.
Egghan, King of Connaught, when dying of his wounds during
war with the men of Ulster commanded that he should be buried
upright, his red javelin in his hand and his face turned towards
Ulster, as if still fighting his foes. As long as he so remained
Connaught prevailed and Ulster lost. But the men of Ulster
discovered the reason, dug him up and re-buried him facing the
opposite way as if in retreat. It is recorded that Ulster was then
victorious.

This old church of Merchard, of which the burial ground is
all that remains, has a strange history. St. Erchard, more often
called Merchard from Mo Erchard, My Erchard, a term of affection, was one of the very early Saints and went with two disciples
to preach the Gospel in Strathglass. His attention was there drawn
to a white cow which stood, day after day, gazing at a certain
tree. She never 'bent her neck to the grass' yet always had plenty
of milk and looked plump and well-liking. Puzzled, the saint
decided to dig at the foot of the tree and there he found three
bells, 'new and burnished as if fresh from their makers' hands'.
He gave one each to his disciples and took one himself. It was

HTL R

then revealed to him that they must all three set out, each going his own way, and each must build a church where his bell rang for the third time. So they started. One went eastward and built the church of Glenconvinth, another westward and erected his church at Broadford in Skye; Merchard himself travelled southward in the direction of Glenmoriston. When he reached the hill called Suidh Merchard, Merchard's Seat, his bell rang its first ring and he rested there awhile, whence its name. It next rang at Ballintombuie and the saint stopped and drank from a spring there, since known as Fuaran Mhercheird, Merchard's Well; then he came down to the River Moriston and his bell rang for the third time, so there, near the river where the old graveyard still is, he built his church, Clachan Mhercheird. There he taught and preached and eventually died. He became the Glen's patron saint and has been known to intervene in its affairs repeatedly. Dr W. Mackay in his *Urquhart and Glenmoriston* tells how in olden times when a tenant died the proprietor had a right to his horse as a heriot. If the man left no horse, sheep or cattle to a horse's value could be taken instead. On one occasion, more than a thousand years after the Saint's death, a tenant died leaving no horse and his widow's sheep were taken by the law officer. That same night as the officer lay in bed, an unearthly voice spoke to him: 'I am great Merchard of the miracles, passing homeward in the night. Declare thou unto MacPhatrick (the proprietor) that the widow's sheep will never bring him any good.' The frightened officer hastened to the laird as early as he dared in the morning and the sheep were at once returned to the widow. Nor did the laird ever again demand a heriot.

The wonder bell remained in the church, curing all those sick or infirm who touched it in faith, until the old church began to crumble and fall into ruin. It was then moved out into the churchyard and placed upon a tombstone specially set aside for the purpose. From here it was stolen about 1870. This bell rang of itself when a funeral was approaching the church or a dead man was carried near it. On one occasion it was heard ringing urgently in the night. Alarmed, various men got together and went to see the cause. They found a dead man lying a few yards from the church, obviously murdered. A search was immediately

begun for the murderer, who, thanks to the bell's timely warning,
was quickly caught, his clothes still wet with his victim's blood.

At the further end of Glenmoriston comes Dun Dreggan, said
to mean the dun of the great beast or dragon, and the Dun itself
to take its name from the field (or place) of the Dragon nearby.
There are various tales to account for the name. Very possibly
the skeleton of some huge prehistoric animal really was found
buried here. This Glen, as legend recounts, may well have once
been such a swamp as these creatures are believed to have inhabited, and peat is a fine preservative. Others tell that a dragon
(some say 'Grey Dog') dwelt here into human times and was
ultimately slain by Fionn and his men after an epic battle and
buried where it fell. Fionn then built a dun near his fallen foe to
reassure the people of the valley who feared that dragon cubs
might have survived their parent. In due course the dun naturally
became a dwelling place of the Little People and the 'Wee Folk'
of Glenmoriston were reputed very active. The particular clan
or tribe who lived in Dundreggan were always very anxious to
carry off the mothers of new-born babies to be wet nurses to
their fairy children. They were more interested in doing this
than in stealing the babies themselves. Ewen Macdonald of Dundreggan was out attending to his beasts on the night when his
wife had her first-born son. A sudden gust of wind passed him
and as it shook him he heard his wife's sigh in it. She sighed as
she had sighed before her child was born and he, recognising the
sound, flung his knife into the wind in the name of the Trinity,
and his wife dropped safely to the ground beside him.

If a fairy child had a mortal foster-mother it gained a 'something' it could obtain no other way, so the Glenmoriston fairies
believed. And more than once they successfully stole and kept a
wife. As, in the words written by John M. Hay, one bereft
husband sighed:

> The fairy folk have lured your face away
> Unto the land where one grows never old,
> Beyond the hollow hills and doors of day.

One night a man out late upon the hill heard the sound of singing
—very sad and plaintive—coming out of the knoll of Dundreggan.

He bent to listen and heard a woman's voice chanting over and over again:

> I am the wife of the Laird of Balnain
> The Folk have stolen me over again.

He hurried to the house in question and there found that the owner was absent and his wife and baby son missing. Much worried, he sought out a priest who came back to the fairy knoll with him, blessed it and sprinkled it with holy water. Suddenly the night grew dark and there was a loud noise as of thunder; then the moon came out from behind a cloud and there was the woman, lying on the grass with her baby in her arms. She was exhausted as if she had travelled a long distance and could not tell how she got there.

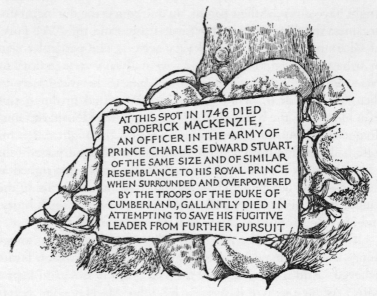

AT THIS SPOT IN 1746 DIED RODERICK MACKENZIE, AN OFFICER IN THE ARMY OF PRINCE CHARLES EDWARD STUART. OF THE SAME SIZE AND OF SIMILAR RESEMBLANCE TO HIS ROYAL PRINCE WHEN SURROUNDED AND OVERPOWERED BY THE TROOPS OF THE DUKE OF CUMBERLAND, GALLANTLY DIED IN ATTEMPTING TO SAVE HIS FUGITIVE LEADER FROM FURTHER PURSUIT

Some miles further, near Cean-na-Croc, the grave of one Roderick Mackenzie is to be seen. At least it is his grave in part, as one might say, his head being elsewhere. Why he has not become famous in song and story it is hard to see, for he undoubtedly gave his life that Prince Charles Edward might have the better chance of escape. He was a young officer of the Prince's army. After Culloden he, like others, escaped and went into hiding, in his case in Glenmoriston. Now Roderick excessively resembled the Prince in appearance. It is said that he heard a rumour that the Prince was in hiding in this district; no one knows how much he knew but what is known is that after lying safely hidden for some time he came out into the open and allowed the Government troops, who were searching the Glen, a good sight of his face. He was mistaken for Prince Charles Edward and the chase was on. In the end he was overtaken at Cean-na-Croc and turned at bay. He fought hard and bravely but at last fell dying of multiple wounds. As he died he cried clearly: 'Alas, you have slain your Prince.' The troops who had chased and killed him had no doubt at all but that he was Prince Charles Edward. One is even supposed to have expressed some anxiety as to the consequences of killing Royalty. They cut off Roderick Mackenzie's head, buried his body where it lay and carried the head in haste to Fort Augustus. There was no one there who knew the Prince well by sight so the head passed as his and was hastily pickled in a brine tub and sent south, and it was some time before the truth was discovered. Meanwhile pursuit of the Prince slackened; indeed in some districts it ceased altogether, and this gave him the chance to escape to France which he might otherwise have found impossible. A cairn marks the grave of Roderick Mackenzie. After he got safely away from Skye, Prince Charles Edward with three friends did make for Glenmoriston, there to be helped and sheltered and fed for three weeks by the 'Seven Men of Glenmoriston', themselves fugitives on his account. Two things are recorded of this time. When he left them the Prince gave each of them three guineas to remember him by—a curious gift to men who could have had £30,000 for his head by strolling down the Glen, but all he had to give. He also shook hands with each man. Two of them vowed never again to allow anyone, man, woman or child, to touch their right hands, and used their left hands for the rest of their lives.

The road through the Glen is very beautiful but also, despite many improvements, very curly. The big dam at Loch Cluanie is itself an interesting sight and its builders have been at much pains to avoid unduly injuring the beauties of the Glen. Through birch woods and oak woods and farm lands the road eventually comes out into some of the loneliest moorland in Scotland. In the days when Scotland had her own Kings this Forest of Cluanie was one of the King's royal forests, and deer still abound, or did a few years ago. But no one knows what numbers can survive the flooding of their old low-lying winter grazing under the hydro-electric scheme. It seems that starvation must drastically reduce the herds. A new road now runs along the hillside above the new loch. The making of this road and the remaking of the old one was an enormous task which occupied many years. Some unfortunates, among whom were my husband and I, had to traverse it frequently at that time and we ended up with an enormous respect for the firm, Watson's, which had the job in hand, and even more for their drivers. Never once were we held up by one of their lorries or machines if it could possibly be avoided, and though the constant traffic must have been infuriating, both to drivers and to road gangs, they were always pleasant and always ready to interrupt their work so as to make a way through for a passing car. It was the more noticeable because some other lorries, and even small cars, will at times hold up everyone behind them on this road for many miles. It is strange what bad driving manners some people have, even people who would be very shocked at the idea of doing an ill-mannered act in ordinary life.

At the western end of Loch Cluanie the road from Invergarry used to come in. The Tomdoun road leaves the main Inverness-Fort William one at Invergarry on the shores of Loch Oich. Passing the attractive Invergarry Hotel and little church, the latter at some times of year almost hidden in blossom, the road runs by the Garry river to Loch Garry itself. Lovely as Highland lochs usually are, Loch Garry has the added beauty in early summer of masses upon masses of rhododendrons, many growing wild in the woods. (Can anyone tell me what the riddle is to which half the answer is: 'And the other rode a dendron'?) The road holds firmly to the loch side till it reaches the pleasant fishing hotel of Tomdoun. The flat ground below the hotel was the scene of a battle between the Macmillans and the Grants. Some of the cairns erected over those killed in the battle may still be found.

At Tomdoun the road divides into two; one arm goes straight on past Loch Quoich to Loch Hourn. Loch Quoich must once have been the heart of a tale now forgotten. All that remains is the saying: 'The black tailor's short cut to Glen Quoich—round the world.' The second arm, the road to the right, has recently been closed to traffic. Instead, a new road now takes off from Loch Garry five miles before Tomdoun is reached and climbs rapidly over the high ground beside the Loch. It is a fine road with the most wonderful views of Loch Garry and, later, Loch Quoich and with many well-placed viewpoints. This road joins the Inverness-Glenshiel one about a mile east of the Cluanie Dam. It is a great time saver for all who come from or go to the West, but some of us regret the old road by Tomdoun which used to come out near Cluanie Inn, just west of the Loch, and was very beautiful. This old road, now closed, turns sharply to the right just beyond Tomdoun Hotel and begins to climb, up and up and up through pine woods and over bare moors to where, in hidden valleys far below, little bare peat lochs reflect the sky. It goes on over the pass which, in winter, is not infrequently blocked by snow or icy road surfaces, but once over it a fine panorama of the old royal Forest of Cluanie lies spread out below. My husband and I were driving from Cluanie to Glengarry one winter. Everything was frozen hard and a recent fall of snow had obliterated all wheel marks in the old snow on the road. The world was virgin white, without trace of life. In spite of our chains we wondered rather anxiously whether we would get over the high ground of the Pass; however, we did and were descending in a completely silent and uninhabited world when we saw a small frozen lochan in the heather to the right of the road and, on it, marks as of cart wheels, clear and unmistakeable in the new-fallen snow which covered the ice. Curious, we stopped and got out to see where they led. No sign or track of living thing was to be seen, we were miles from any house or cultivation and there was no trace of footmark, wheel mark or sledge mark in the snow on the loch shore, either where the wheel marks began on the snow-covered ice or where they ended, or indeed anywhere else. Much puzzled, we searched carefully. Nothing. On return to civilisation we tried to find out if anything could have been there. Nothing. Nothing had been or could have been there. And that was that.

Months later we were told that what we had seen must have been the marks of the Devil's coach wheels. He drives over the moors in winter and his coach wheel marks are often seen on lonely frozen lochs, but never a sign on land nor a sign of the horses that draw his coach. When these wheel marks are seen it is well to stay quiet indoors, for who knows what he seeks? And anyhow those who go prying may be found frozen, for he drives only when the weather is black hard and likely to remain so. But despite the risk his jet-black coach with its jet-black steeds has been seen driving at speed over the moors, both in Rannoch and over the Grampian slopes, leaving wheel tracks on many a small lonely ice-bound loch. It would be very interesting to know the true cause of this phenomenon, these wheel-like tracks, for they certainly do exist and appear to be not uncommon in mountain districts of the Highlands, and the tracks keep the right distance apart for cart or coach wheels. I have been told there are no hoof marks because the Devil's horses are spirits whereas his coach, used to carry mortals, must have earthly substance, but, if so, why do the wheels leave tracks only on ice? And whom does he carry off? And why?

The joint road continues past Cluanie Inn, over open moor and forestry land, to Glen Shiel. In the winter the deer come down from the hills to graze on the low ground between the River Shiel and the road. Hunger makes them so tame that on occasion we have had to get out of the car and drive a herd off the road before we could pass. They don't mind cars in the least. Indeed the smell of the exhaust gas is said to please them. A very sad tale is told of the deer in Glen Shiel. It happened in a deep cattle fold not far from Sgurr Urain. Once there was a girl who daily took her father's cattle out to graze in the Glen. There she met and loved a fairy—a little man who came out of one of the fairy knolls. The whole affair was, they believed, entirely secret and they wished it to remain so. But one day her brother went hunting and when he came home said to her (of course in Gaelic):

> I saw the dearest one yesterday
> Who was asking truly for thee.

at which she eagerly asked:

> How was my love when he remembered me?

only to get her brother's answer:

> I was smiting him sorely,
> To the North and to the South
> With my bright sword and my axe.
> With my left hand and my right.

Indignantly the girl rejoined:

> If thou hast slain the dear Oscar
> Arise and wash thy hands;
> May that be thy last washing
> After which thy body and bones will bleach.
> May there be never a month-old child in thy house.
> May there be no butter on thy milk
> May . . .

But here her mother intervened and said:

> Mayst thou be split like the freshwater salmon
> Between thy two breasts and thy belly,
> May the poisonous serpent be beside thee
> Without thy . . .

At this the girl was very frightened and she repented of her curse and said:

> The ill wish I made for my brother,
> Let it not be on him it rests at all,
> But on the rugged, brindled hills
> And on two thirds of the deer of the Glen.

Next day the rugged brindled hills were riven into fragments through the Glen and two thirds of the deer there were dead.

Glen Shiel is a queer glen, long, twisty, very narrow and steep, and so surrounded by mountains that the sun rarely penetrates it. It is wild and lonely and a little creepy, and in this cold, sunless glen there once lived a woman who spun for the fairies, and a good spinner she was and well the fairies paid her. But one day they fell out, for the Little People said she did not return all their lint, that she had not scraped the distaff tuft. No one had ever heard of such a scraping before and the woman was very angry and offended. However, though they no longer employed her the fairy women used to come to her to borrow her pot. When giving the pot to a fairy the woman would say:

> A pot deserves a bone
> And to be brought home whole;
> A smith deserves coal
> To heat cold iron.

and every day the pot would come home and something in it. But one day she forgot to say the spell on the pot and it did not come home. The woman was very angry for she had no other cooking pot. She went to the fairy mound to seek it and, seeing it, she seized it and, without speaking, carried it away. Then the fairy, gazing after her, said:

> Thou dumb woman there, thou dumb woman
> Who art come to us from the land of the cormorants,
> She seized the pot with her evil claw;
> Loose the noose and let slip the Fierce.

That was done and a great dog leapt after the woman and seized her by the leg. She screamed and was dead.

All this area is Fiann country and a giant suddenly appearing from among the rocks and clefts of the barren hills would not be surprising. It could easily have been they, not heavy rain, that started the landslide which cut the road here a few years ago, for instance. The scar it left on the hill side and some of the boulders it brought down are still to be seen. So too is the big stone in whose shelter Prince Charles Edward and his two guides are reputed to have slept peacefully through a raging storm.

Once my husband and I had to drive from Skye to Inverness on a wet and stormy winter night, arriving about midnight. From the outskirts of Kyle of Lochalsh to Dochfour (some 80 miles) we saw no living thing or sign of one; no car, no man, no sheep, no dog, no deer, no cow, not even a house showing a light (Cluanie Inn was closed), not even a hunting cat or the white tail of a rabbit. No sound but lashing rain in sheets and the wind howling in the hills. It was the eeriest and loneliest thing I have ever seen. *Anything* might have been about. We did not even see the spectre warriors fighting a ghostly battle in the Glen itself, though this is said to be not infrequently visible. There was once a Battle of Glen Shiel. It was fought as late as 1719, between the King's troops under General Wrightman and a force of Spaniards who had landed in the West to help the 'Old Chevalier'. Probably this was the last foreign invasion of Britain and the King's troops were completely victorious. Nothing more was ever heard of the Spanish invaders but it is said that on nights of low cloud when the mist whirls and twists around the mountains they can be seen busy as they were in life, not only fighting the King's men but marching wearily up the Pass. The men of both armies are there too, burying their dead.

Glen Shiel ends in some lovely country with the hills reflected in a reed-covered loch near Shiel Bridge. Here the road divides; that to the left crosses Mamratagan to Glenelg and that to the right runs along Loch Duich to Kyle of Lochalsh. Both roads end with a ferry to Skye.

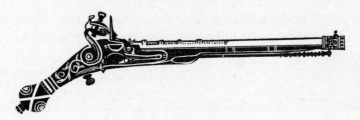

Highland Pistol

18

SHIEL BRIDGE
TO KYLE OF LOCHALSH

Farewell to MacKenneth, Great Earl of the North,
The Lord of Lochcarron, Glenshiel and Seaforth;

    ★   ★   ★   ★   ★

For a far foreign land he has hoisted his sail,
Farewell to Mackenzie, High Chief of Kintail.
O, swift be the galley and hardy her crew,
May her captain be skilful, her mariners true,

    ★   ★   ★   ★   ★

May he hoist all his canvas from streamer to deck
But, O, crowd it higher when wafting him back,
Till the cliffs of Skooroora and Conan's glad vale
Shall welcome Mackenzie, High Chief of Kintail.
MURDOCH MATHESON; translated by
Sir W. Scott

AFTER SHIEL BRIDGE the road runs through the old
Mackenzie country of Kintail. In later centuries their chief
lived at Brahan Castle near Strathpeffer but in the early
days of the clan Kintail was their homeland. An old riddle asked:
'What are the three curses of a farmer?' to which the answer was:
'May frost, July mist and the Tutor of Kintail.' A 'Tutor' in the
Highlands of olden times meant the regent for an infant Chief,
and in his hands lay the welfare of his Clan. The Tutor of Kintail
did much for the clan but it is said to have been he who condemned
the Castle of Eilean Donnan as too primitive and Kintail as too
remote to be the seat of a Chief. He built Brahan Castle for his
ward and moved the Clan's centre away from Kintail and the
West—hence a certain unpopularity.

Round the head of Loch Duich goes the road and past the
little church of Kintail on its hillock overlooking the water. A
man once committed suicide in Loch Duich and was buried in

this little churchyard, to the north of the church, buried with his head, not his feet, to the east as is becoming for a suicide. But as a result of his act the herring left Loch Duich. The fishers waited for two years but the fish did not return. (Seven years is the usual length of the herring's absence after a murder or a suicide in their water.) Then the fishermen grew tired of waiting and one dark night they dug up the suicide's body from the churchyard and carried it to the top of a high hill where Inverness-shire and Ross-shire meet; here they buried it again, hoping to appease the herring. The herring were duly appeased and returned to the loch. A similar burial and for the same reason is said to have taken place on the summit of Aird Dhubh.

Loch Duich herring seem easily perturbed, for they are said to have been absent from duty when, disabled by storm, a 'foreign vessel' came into the Loch. By the custom of the time MacRae of Inverinate might have treated both the vessel and its cargo as his by right, but instead he helped the crew to make and fit a new mast from his woods and allowed them to depart in peace. Before leaving, the captain, to show his gratitude, presented MacRae with a small silver herring. This highly magic little fish had only to be laid in the waters of the loch to attract herring in shoals from far and near. It proved, as may be imagined, a most valuable possession.

The road runs through the Inverinate woods, then up and up, past mountain burns and through fields of the wild iris, to a high summit looking down on the sea-lochs below. There are few views to equal this one in Scotland. To the south-east the Five Sisters of Kintail lift their blue heads above their scarves of mist, to the west lies Eilean Donnan Castle on its rock (perhaps the most photographed spot in the Highlands) guarding the blue Kyles; and in the distance stand the hills of Skye.

Loch Duich is a loch of many stories. Once there lived in Kintail an old man who had seven beautiful daughters. He was much worried, for he felt that they were so beautiful that they should marry well but his farm was in a lonely glen on the shore of Loch Duich and he really did not see how or whom they were to marry at all. Every day they grew more beautiful and desirable and every day the old man worried more. One night, how-

ever, there was a great storm and into the Loch for shelter came
a fine ship. Once she had been very fair indeed but now she was
battered by the waves and with her sails in shreds. Her owners,
two young brothers, thankfully accepted the old man's offer of
help and of timber to refit her. The youths were very handsome,
with red-gold hair and with eyes blue-grey like the sea; they were
tall, too, and stronger than any in the glen. Needless to say, the
seven sisters saw and loved them. Needless also to say, the brothers were enchanted by the beauty of their young hostesses. For
many months work on the ship continued. Everything a ship
could need was done. She was careened on the shore and scraped,
fresh sails were sewn by the sisters and fitted, and so forth. But
at last the day came when they could find no further excuse to
linger in the Loch and the two brothers took their courage in
their hands and, coming to the old farmer, asked for his two
youngest daughters in marriage. The old man went to consult the
seven. The two youngest were delighted; they were very willing
to sail happily away with their lovers, they declared. But the five
elder sisters wept and at last the eldest daughter said to their
father: 'We do not think it right that our youngest sisters should
be married before us; let the suitors choose according to age as is
proper.' The old man brought back this answer to the young
sea-captains. The younger looked very dismayed but the elder
replied: 'What your daughters say is right and wise and we do
not deny it but we, my brother and I, are ourselves younger
brothers, having five brothers older, handsomer and richer than
ourselves. When they see our wives they will most certainly
desire to wed your elder daughters. It would not, therefore, be
proper for us to ask the hands of the two eldest sisters.' And so
it was agreed, the two young men married the two youngest
sisters and sailed away with them to Ireland, first making firm
and solemn promise that their five brothers would come soon
out of Ireland to woo and win their brides.

Winter passed and summer passed and winter came again but
no ship sailed in from Ireland with five eager bridegrooms on
board. Meanwhile the fame of the girls' beauty spread throughout Kintail and many a young man found business which led
him to the farm, there to offer for the hand of one of the re-

maining five daughters. But the girls would have none of them.

'His hair is not like spun gold but mere mouse-colour,' said one.

'I will marry no man under whose arm I cannot walk,' said another when a small but rich young farmer proposed for her hand.

And so it went on while their father grew older and more worried. One day he went out, killed a stag and carried it to the Grey Magician of Coire Dhuinid who was famed for his wisdom. The Wise Man listened and promised to come and talk to the sisters. He came and told them of how he had gazed into the black pool of the corrie and had learned there that no such young men as their brother-in-law had described existed. They were waiting only for shadows, he said. Let them therefore be wise in time and marry while they could, for that way happiness and safety lay. But the sisters would not.

'Are we to be farmers' wives while our sisters are queens in Ireland?' asked the eldest.

'Are we to live and die in Kintail,' cried the second, 'while our sisters sail out into the world?'

'Are we to be poor, and our sisters rich?' asked the third angrily.

'I have seen him in dreams and I love him,' sobbed the fourth, 'I will marry no man but him.'

'I have seen my lover's face in the loch water,' said the youngest firmly, 'and I will be faithful to him until death.'

So the magician left and the years passed and the old farmer grew aged and feeble and *very* worried. He sent again to the Grey Magician, who came and for long they sat over the peat fire talking; then the magician left. Next day the old man died and the five daughters found themselves alone in the world. But with night came the magician.

'Yesterday,' he said, 'I talked with your father and promised him to hold you in my protection. It is time you married.'

'No,' said five voices.

'Do you wish to wait for ever for your dream bridegrooms?' asked the wizard. 'Think well before you answer,' he added, 'for in your answers lies your fate.'

'We will wait and watch forever,' they replied.

'In that case,' said the magician in practical tones, 'I will turn you into five mountains and place you at the head of Loch Duich so that you can wait and watch forever as you desire, safe from the evils and dangers of the world.'

So the sisters became five hills, the beauty that was theirs in life remains theirs still and as 'The Five Sisters of Kintail' they wait and watch for the sails of the ship which never comes, the ship they even yet believe will still come and bring their lovers.

It is to Loch Duich, too, that seal-people come of an evening and it has been known even to tempt mermen into the shallows. The seals are a gentle, kindly folk but very unhappy. You have only to look at their eyes to see that. They do not fear humans half as much as most wild creatures do, and if you go down to the shore and there locate a seal swimming along with its bullet head above water like a dog, and you stand on the shore and bark to it it will, after the first moment of surprise, answer you. Then a lengthy if limited conversation can be carried on as it will remain near as long as you will bark. It is an unkind thing to do though, for it encourages that particular seal to look on humans as pleasant, barking creatures and makes it more vulnerable in consequence to the seal-hunters who want its liver to make seal oil. Seal oil in the highlands was, and in some places still is, what cod liver oil is to the South. If properly made—the oil-yielding parts must be melted down over a slow fire but never allowed to boil for if it reaches the boiling point the good will be lost—it is extremely effective for the colds and coughs of winter or for the child that does not thrive. But few nowadays have the patience to make it properly. The Health Service will provide, so why bother?

It has long been believed that seals were human beings under enchantment and that they are allowed to resume their human forms for short periods, 'to keep them unhappy' think some. When the time for the seals to assume human shape arrives they come ashore, slough their seal skins and hide them carefully beneath a rock or in a convenient cave. There are many stories of men finding and hiding a skin. If this happens, the seal concerned is unable to rejoin the others when their human time is up but must remain on shore, utterly helpless, the slave of the hider of the skin. Usually it is a beautiful maiden whose fur is so concealed, and the seal maidens are very beautiful indeed, with dark hair and large brown eyes. The story is told of three brothers who went down one evening to fish off the rocks in Loch Duich not far from the castle. It was a wonderful moonlight night, no good for the fishing, and as they were looking idly about them they saw a number of seals' heads bobbing along towards the shore. They hid and watched the seals land, slip off their skins, roll them neatly into bundles and hide them beneath the large stones with which the beach was covered. Each seal chose its own stone. Then the seal folk began to run and leap upon the beach or lie stretching in the moonlight, rejoicing in their freedom. Among them were three particularly beautiful girls and the three young men loved them on sight. Animated by a single thought, they crept nearer and nearer to the stones where the skins had been left, carefully hiding behind boulders as they went. At length they were within reach of the skins; each seized the skin of a maiden and fled away with it. They concealed the skins carefully, then returned to the beach to wait. As the grey of dawn began to lighten the sky a curlew called and at this signal each seal made for his or her skin, but the three maidens had no skins. The maidens wrung their hands and wept as the first rays of the rising sun struck the beach and the seals, all weeping also, slid back into the sea leaving the three frightened girls clinging together at the water's edge, for well they guessed the fate of their skins. The boys, once the seal host had departed, came down on to the shore and spoke to the maidens, explaining how much they admired them and that they wished to marry them. The maidens only wept and begged them to return their skins. The two elder brothers began to tell the girls how much they loved them and what a good life they would have once they were married. A dress of silk, a bed of softest feathers, they promised, butter, too, and cream. But the maidens wept on and trembled as an aspen trembles when no wind stirs it; and the youngest brother said nothing. 'What will you give your bride?' demanded his brothers, 'speak, man, offer her something.' But the youngest brother said nothing, for his heart was stirred with a great love and he knew the gift that he must offer.

HTL S

At length daylight came and the three brothers took each his seal maiden and returned each to his own house and the doors were closed. The youngest brother alone came out again and went to his peat stack. When he returned he bore his bride gift —a seal skin—in his arms. When he opened the door there was his seal maiden crouched by the large box bed, still trembling with great eyes of fear. The boy did not speak, he could not, but he held out to her her seal skin and she grabbed it (there is no other word) and with fingers clumsy with haste she dressed herself in it. Then the young man opened the house door and away she went, slip, slither, down over the grass, into the sea and away. The boy went to milk the cows. When his brothers, each with a good, submissive wife, learned what he had done they started to tease him. But he turned on them so fiercely that they, astonished and afraid, did not mention seals to him again. But on the ninth night they fastened house and door and barn with care. The youngest brother did not trouble. He went down to the sea shore and sat on a stone openly to watch the seals come in, for he felt he could no longer spy on her. The seals came in in hordes, more than he had ever seen before, took human form and hurried off in every direction, searching, searching. His maiden came too and looked shyly at him, then she too began to search, but halfheartedly, until an old man with a fine face spoke to her and together they came to the boy.

'It is my duty to thank you, Sir,' said the man with curious old-world courtesy, 'for liberating my daughter, though not for the fright you gave her.' He spoke coldly. Then he looked up and caught the boy's gaze fixed upon the maiden. His expression changed and he added in warmer tones: 'Should you need us we are your servants. Fionagalla, do your duty.'

The seal maid ran lightly up to the door of the young man's house, opened it and vanished within. The boy rose, bowed to her father (a rather clumsy imitation of the old man's own bow) and followed her. He found bannocks baking and the maiden busy setting the house to rights. He tried to help. Soon she was smiling at his efforts. When the dawn-grey lightened the sky he accompanied her back to the beach. And so it became the custom for the boy to make a tally of a hazel twig and mark off each day till the ninth and for the sea-maiden to make a tally of a razor-shell and mark it also, and every ninth night they spent together in the little house in a happiness nine times greater than was ever in the world before.

Meanwhile the elder brothers grew fat and lazy, their docile wives doing all the work. One day the eldest brother's children were at play in the barn when they explored an old tub and in the bottom lay a brown fur seal skin. They ran in to their mother with their find. One look and the seal woman seized it from them, dressed quickly in it and, with a parting wave to her children, dived back into the sea and was never seen again. The second brother was much concerned, specially when his children asked him what it was that their mother searched for all day while he was out. He thought and thought and at last decided that the only way to hide the skin completely and for ever was to burn it. So he made a fire of straw and laid the skin upon it. There was an instant explosion and the man was thrown to the ground; burning sparks had fired the thatched roof of his house he saw when he rose and hurried over, calling to his wife to bring water. No reply. His wife lay dead within. She had died from burns.

In the long ago days a young girl lived with her father and stepmother on the shore of Loch Duich. They owned a tiny house there. She had the misfortune to have a very evil step-mother and though her father loved her dearly he was no match for his wife who one day in his absence turned the child, for she was little more, out of the house, forbidding her ever to return on pain of cursing. The child went down to the seashore and there, weary and frightened and cold, she sat and wept. A mer-man saw and pitied her; he raised himself from the sea and tried to comfort her and the girl sobbed out her story. 'Come with me to my palace below the sea,' he begged. 'I will care for you.' But she would not, certain that her father would come in search of her. But the night grew wild and cold and her father did not come, for his wife had told him that his daughter had been drowned and the body carried out by the tide. But as the tide rose the girl, exhausted with weeping, decided to wait for it and go where it took her. It was the merman, not the tide, that came for her, however, and he carried her down to his undersea palace.

There she learned that he was a king and rich beyond anything she could imagine. They were married and lived in quiet happiness but in the spring of the year the girl always grew homesick and her husband would rise to the surface and return with news of her father, gathered from the wild duck, the geese and the rock pigeons who were his messengers. One day he told her that her stepmother was dead but that before her death she had ruined her husband who had now neither cow nor sheep, neither a horse to plough with nor seed to sow.

The little earth queen begged eagerly: 'Oh, might I not send him one of my pearls or a golden cup? We have so much and he has nothing.' 'Neither our pearls nor our gold cups would be useful,' he told her, 'but wait.' He summoned a porpoise and spoke to him in a tongue the earth girl had never learnt. 'I have sent to a wreck for earth money,' said the king. Soon the porpoise returned with a bag of gold coins in his mouth, heavier than she could lift, but her husband wrapped it in his tail, took her in his arms and bore her safely back to the shore by her father's house. Leaving the gold hidden under a rock she ran home and great indeed was the happiness in the little farm that night. Her father took some of the gold next day and set out for Dingwall where he bought both grain and beasts. His daughter went down to the shore in search of her husband. He was waiting for her. She asked leave to stay until her father found a wife and the merman agreed, telling her to meet him there each evening. In due course a good wife was found and then, on the ninth day of the ninth month, the little earth wife went down to the sea shore. This time she did not speak, there was no need, for, her task completed, she slid quietly into the grey sea waves by his side and he carried her home, never to be seen on earth again.

From the summit the road runs down an equally steep hill to the village of Dornie at its foot. Here is Dornie Bridge, across the entrance to Loch Long, a great boon to the Isles when opened in 1942, and here, close by the bridge, stands the Castle of Eilean Donnan, a castle with a somewhat chequered history. The first castle on the island, which is believed to have been called after St. Donnan the Martyr of Eigg, was built by Alexander II on, says tradition, the site of a much older fort or dun. It was intended

Eilean Donnan Castle

as a defence against the Danes and Norsemen and the King made one Kenneth Matheson his first Constable of Eilean Donnan. Kenneth's descendants were known as MacKennich, Sons of Kenneth, which soon became Mackenzie. After some centuries, during which the castle had been both destroyed and rebuilt, the Tutor of Kintail, as has been said, made Brahan Castle the new seat of the Clan and the MacRaes became Constables of the Castle for the Mackenzies of Seaforth as they now were.

It would appear that at the time of the Rising of 1715 the
castle was being held for the King. A farmer nearby thought this
was a mistake and offered to place it in the hands of the local
Jacobites. This he did quite simply. On a hot morning he called
on the Garrison Commander and told him that he expected the
weather to break in a few hours, his corn was still out and unless
the Governor would lend him the men to get it in it would be
ruined. Food, as both knew, was scarce and owing to the Troubles
would soon be scarcer. All seemed quiet in the district and the
Governor of the castle led out all his men to help get in the harvest. In his absence the Jacobites seized the fortress. That night
there was great rejoicing in the castle and men were seen dancing
reels on its tower in the moonlight. A few hours later came news
of defeat. Later again the castle was partly demolished by gunfire
from H.M.S. *Worcester* in 1719. After being a ruin for about
200 years it has been rebuilt by Colonel John McRae-Gilstrap to
be as nearly as possible as it was, much of the old walls fortunately
remaining.

There are many stories of the Castle. One is rather curious.
It claims that for long there was enmity between the Macdonnels
of Glengarry and the Mackenzies and that the constant fear of
raids was undermining the morale of both clans. At length the
Wise Raven of Glengarry, having enticed Macdonnell's heir into
the hills, spoke to him very seriously on the subject. Acting on
the Raven's advice, young Glengarry got a contingent of fighting
men from his father and successfully attacked and captured Eilean
Donnan Castle and the heir to the Chief of Clan Mackenzie with
it. Now in a strong position, he was able to dictate terms. These
were laid down by the Wise Raven and led to a lasting peace
between the clans.

Serpents (adders) were very common in this part of the Highlands. They were believed to sleep through the winter and appear
on Bride's Day (February 1st), and this should be their greeting:

> Early on the Feast of Bride
> The daughter of Ivor will come from her hole
> I will not harm the daughter of Ivor
> And the daughter of Ivor will not harm me.

Some of the charms addressed to the serpent hail her as 'noble

Queen', which is comprehensible, but no one seems to know why 'daughter of Ivor'. Legend in this district, however, says that in the very early days of Eilean Donnan a Constable of the Castle married a Russian wife who was a very powerful witch and her father, whose name was Ivor, was an even more potent wizard. The snakes were her familiars and on occasion she herself would take snake form. That is why there were so many snakes in this district. No one dared to harm them in case they should accidentally kill the daughter of Ivor and her father or husband would avenge her. On the other hand it is said that Mrs Macleod of Stein (Flora Macdonald's eldest daughter) filled a stocking with peat every St. Bride's Day and stamped it flat as a symbol of bruising the serpent's head.

The road continues by the side of Loch Alsh as far as Ardelve. Near here is a cave in the cliffs, said to be an old 'Pict's House' for it is lined and roofed with slabs of stone and although the entrance is narrow and unimportant-looking the cave itself is of considerable size.

After Ardelve come Balmacarra, now a National Trust property, and Balmacarra House, now a school, and then the road turns slightly inland over the base of a peninsula to Kyle of Lochalsh.* The road soon passes a lovely small loch with tiny islands. Tradition, but a very shaky tradition, claims this as the site of a battle between, perhaps, Mathesons, whose country this was, and a Sutherland raiding party. Both chiefs were killed and were buried together in harmony on this tiny island.

The road, through very beautiful country and views, runs down to Kyle of Lochalsh—a village of roses where the sun, one feels, always shines. From here the main car ferry to Skye functions. Not quite fifty years ago this ferry was a rowing boat with two planks across it. The car drove on to the planks (if it could) and was then lashed on. If seas rose while crossing, the lashings would be cast off, leaving the car free and ready to slide over the side if the boat began to roll, thus leaving the boat safe. Changed days!

* During the post-war housing shortage, a cave close to the roadside just after Balmacarra was occupied by a family who lived there for some years for want of better accommodation.

It has long been held in the Highlands that she who borrows or steals a burning peat from her neighbour's fire can then, should she wish, drain the milk from her neighbour's cow or the cream from her milk and have it herself. Indeed she can, if she wishes, take the substance out of all that the unfortunate neighbour possesses. Apparently such a belief is not only widespread but also old. Once there were two giants; they were brothers, Akin and Rhea, living near one another in two strong castles on the slopes above the Kyles, and were such great friends that they were almost inseparable. Being giants, they had no difficulty in leaping over to Skye when need arose. One day the younger brother, Rhea, returning from a deer hunt in the Island, found his fire out and his castle cold and comfortless. He passed on to Akin's castle where the fire had been well smoored and he soon blew it into flames and warmed himself at it. Then he prepared to go home, taking with him a smouldering peat ember to re-start his own fire. Unfortunately at that moment Akin returned and, finding his brother taking fire and with it, if he so willed, the substance of all he possessed, was furious, for he was a somewhat hasty-tempered young giant, and he began to fling rocks and boulders after him. The size and number that he threw can be judged by those still to be seen peppering the low ground today and testifying both to his strength and excessively wild aim and to the heinousness of the offence. But unfortunately his aim really *was* wild. He meant to frighten his brother, show his displeasure and teach him a lesson. But, alas!, one of the larger boulders caught Rhea between the shoulders; he tripped, fell, and, half stunned, rolled into the sea and was drowned. Kylerhea has ever since borne his name. Akin was desperately unhappy without him. Rhea was equally unhappy without Akin. One evening Akin returned cold and miserable from hunting, no longer for pleasure but only for food. He found the fire in his castle a cheerful blaze and, kneeling by it and blowing up the flames, the spirit of Rhea. Realising that he was forgiven and that Rhea had come for him, he immediately drowned himself in the Kyle which now bears his name, and the two spirits departed together in perfect happiness for the Blessed Isles.

19

SHIEL BRIDGE TO GLENELG

*The door of Fionn is always open and the name of his hall
is the stranger's home. None ever went sad from Fionn*
(Old saying)

THE ROAD over Mamratagan to the Glenelg-Kylerhea
ferry was a very popular one before the opening of Dornie
Bridge in 1942 as it enabled cars to reach Skye without
crossing a second ferry. Also, Mamratagan is no mean hill, even
for the West Coast, and from the road over it there is a series of
wonderful views, although the hillside is now forested and as the
trees grow taller views will grow fewer. 'Mam' is very common
in the names of swelling, rounded hills in the West Highlands
but was also used in the Isles to describe a swelling of the body
of any kind, including mumps. So, by a natural association of
ideas, in the olden days the local 'wise' man or woman would
banish such an ill to the nearest hill of the same name.

Mamratagan was one of the favourite hills for this practice
and must be positively alive with mumps germs and other bac-
teria in banishment there. The procedure was complicated. First
a suitable hill must be chosen and it must be known to the patient;
then the swellings must be divided into three imaginary sections,
a basin of pure water must be at hand and a needle and an axe be
dipped in it. The needle is then placed against one of the three
parts of the swelling and the axe brought down as if to fall upon
it and drive it in with great force, but at the last moment the axe
is diverted to a piece of wood. This is done to each of the three
parts in turn. While striking, the 'wise one' recites an appropriate
charm. In the case of Mamratagan it was:

Be this stroke upon the Mam of Domhaillean,
Be this stroke upon the Mam of Gleann Eilg,
Be this stroke upon the Mam of Ratagan,
In the name of the Father and the Son and the Holy Spirit.

All present must reply: 'Amen. Thy pang be in the ground, thy pain be in the earth.' Within three days the patient should recover. I never heard tell of a mountain that was any the worse.

The connection here between the disease and the cure is easy to see but some of the most attractive of the charms from this part of the world seem to have very little connection at all with the cure desired. For instance, to cure toothache one must repeat the Charm Against Toothache, as follows:

> The charm placed by Columba
> About the right knee of Maol Iodha
> Against pain, against sting, against poison,
> Against tooth disease, against bodily disease.
>
> Said Peter unto James
> 'I get no rest from the toothache,
> It is with me lying down and rising up
> And leaping on my two soles.'
>
> Said Christ, answering the problem,
> 'The toothache and the rune
> Shall not henceforth abide in the same head.'*
> (Of course, in Gaelic the verses rhyme)

Kylerhea in Skye and Glenelg on the mainland were much beloved of the Feinn and they were believed to have lived in Glenelg. At a place called (according to A. R. Forbes in his *Place Names of Skye*) Imir nam Fear Mora, Field of the Big Men, in Glenelg, there were some large burial mounds, traditionally the graves of the Feinn. Macpherson's *Ossian* and the controversy to which it gave rise resulted in a revival of interest in such matters and one day in the early nineteenth century two of these grave mounds were opened in the presence of 'a number of local gentlemen of repute' including a parish minister. In them are said to have been found stone coffins enclosing skeletons of two men and a woman, all considerably larger than life size as it is known today. It is believed that a doctor examined the two best preserved skeletons and estimated their heights when alive as having been, one approximately $8\frac{1}{2}$ feet and the other almost 11 feet and said that they appeared strong-boned and well proportioned.

* These Translations from *Carmina Gadelica*.

These are not by any means the only 'Fiann graves' known in the North. Fionn himself was, in tradition, buried near Killin in Perthshire, although some have claimed the honour for a mound near the shore of little Loch Killin in Inverness-shire. Grainne, Fionn's wife, lies beneath a cairn on the summit of Ben na Cailleach in Skye, just across the water from Glenelg. Ossian

An ancient Dun, Glenelg

had many different endings, going direct to Heaven or to the Isle of the Blest, or living still, asleep beneath a mountain. But Perthshire says that he was buried just like any other man of his rank and time, in a stone coffin in the Sma' Glen, and that here his bones would be resting still but for General Wade. At this point we come into history. When Wade's men were preparing the foundations of his road to the North, they came upon an old stone cist or coffin of great age. This was opened and seen to contain a very large skeleton. But the men of the Highland clans who were working on the road became much upset when they

saw what had been done, and explained that these were the bones
of the great Ossian and should not have been disturbed nor his
grave opened. The consequences might be appalling. Indeed, so
angry and frightened were they that the young engineer in charge
of that section thought it unwise to proceed without new and
exact orders, and so sent a message to General Wade. He replied
that all work on that sector was to cease until he himself arrived;
he would ride over next day. In the night the bones and the heavy
stone coffin which had held them disappeared and next day the
workmen denied all knowledge of them. It appeared that none
of them had ever seen a coffin or bones, nor heard of Ossian. In
fact, no one knew anything about anything. But some soldiers
in camp nearby had had sentries out and one of these had reported
large numbers of men on the move. The sentry claimed to have
seen a long procession of torches moving through the gloom of
the night mist and to have heard wild, unearthly chanting sweeping by on the wind. Where Ossian's bones, if his they were, now
lie, no one knows. But it does appear from these large skeletons
and from the old songs and stories that there must once have been
in the Highlands a tribe or clan of men larger and perhaps more
civilised than their neighbours. That there are such large races
has just been demonstrated by the discovery of a tribe in Africa
considerably above normal height, and the Maharajah of Mysore
always had giants as his State doorkeepers, men about 8 feet tall,
at least as lately as 1943.

Traditionally the Feinn were fair and very tall, not quite
'giants' in the fairy tale sense but larger than men, say 9 to 10 feet
in height; 'his fault is the fault of Fionn' was said in Gaelic of a
little man, because Fionn's only fault is believed to have been his
small size. He was smaller than his men, only 8 feet high or so
some claim. But others say 'as long in the head as Fionn was in
the leg'. The Feinn were strong and swift of foot, great fighters
and hunters, and above all brave, courteous and just. They came
to Scotland from Ireland. Their Chief was Fionn and under him
were several families or clans, each with its own title to fame.
Their six great assets were said to be: The Luck (or Wisdom) of
Fionn, the Hand of Gaul, Oscar's rapid blows, Ossian's quickness
at play, Caoilte's hard running, and Comal's planning of the

battle. It was said, too, that 'their banner never went back though the grey earth trembled'. Like other heroes, they had their butt; this was 'the Mischief of the Feinn, quick-tempered, rash and meddlesome Conon, who was always in trouble. He once spied upon the wives of the Feinn as they went about their own concerns on the slopes of Mamratagan. The women, determined on revenge, laid a trap for him, into which he walked and lost all his hair. Poor bald Conon was much teased, so, sore and angry, he decided to leave Glenelg for a time and visit those of his friends who had died and whom he believed he would find in Ifrinn (Hell). They, he felt sure, would be glad to see him and would know nothing of the jokes being made at his expense. But he forgot the fiends who guard and rule Ifrinn and soon found himself engaged in single combat with their Chief. Walter Scott describes the fight as: ' "Claw to claw," as Conon said to Satan, "and the Devil take the shortest nails." '

The Feinn came to protect Scotland, and the little men there, from the raiders from Lochlann and they possessed certain magic gifts, chief of which was Fionn's Tooth of Wisdom which, if he pressed it, both could and would tell him all he needed to know. Stories of the Feinn are as widespread throughout the Highlands as are stories of King Arthur and his knights in England, but Argyll and Inverness-shire, including Skye, seem to have been their main haunts. Mamratagan, as has been already said, was very much their country. Here they hunted the deer and the wild boar, here the Yellow Magician turned Grainne, Fionn's wife, into a white hind. Here, too, it is said that Bran the great hound found Fionn's son Ossian and protected him from the hound pack who mistook him for a deer like his mother.

There are very many versions of the story of Grainne's enchantment and the birth of her son Ossian or his finding by his father Fionn. Campbell of Islay, the gatherer of a famous collection of old Highland stories, is reputed to have known fourteen. Indeed the tale of the white hind may well have as many forms as the rhyme about the Missionary who ate (or was eaten by) the Cassowary. In it, only three things were constant—a missionary, a cassowary and Timbuctoo. So all versions of the White Hind tale contain Fionn, his wife Grainne (who is changed to a white hind) and their son Ossian. Here is one which I have heard of Mamratagan.

At one time the Feinn lived in Glenelg and hunted on Mamratagan and it was here that Grainne's old nurse came to Fionn to beg his aid for her nursling. From here too Fionn set out to save Grainne from the clutches of a many-headed giant. Before this he had had, as was the fashion of the time, a fairy-love from a dun nearby. This fairy maid was lovely and charming but, like all the fairy people, she could not grow old. 'Grow old along with me, The best is yet to be' could never be applied to a fairy love affair. And as Fionn matured from youth to manhood he slowly and unconsciously outgrew his fairy love. Her youthful naiveté and sweetness began to irritate him and as his own wider understanding developed his need of a more responsible helpmeet grew greater. When he was thrown into the company of Grainne on their long and dangerous journey back from the giant's castle and she risked her life to save his, he found in her all he sought in a wife, and they were married. Usually, fairy loves accepted the position but Fionn's did not and on the day when Grainne's baby son was born she waited nearby and, in the temporary absence of Grainne's women, laid a spell upon her that she should become a white hind. And so she did. But, not realising what had happened, Grainne licked her baby's face, deer fashion, and on his forehead sprouted a patch of deer's hair. Horrified, she fled. When Fionn returned from hunting and found her missing, he pressed his Tooth of Wisdom which showed him what had happened.

Against the power of the spell which his discarded fairy love had bought at great cost from the Yellow Magician he was powerless. Nevertheless, he constantly sought for the white hind but never found her until she lay dying. Meanwhile her little son Ossian grew up with the Feinn and above all things loved to accompany them on their hunting trips. On one of these occasions he became separated from his companions and, just as he realised that he was lost, he saw a very beautiful white hind. What a prize to bring back to his teachers! Knowing nothing of his mother's story, he flung his spear at the hind but most fortunately, being both young and excited, missed her. To his surprise the hind did not gallop off but stood looking at him with lovely sad eyes and said: 'Don't harm me, Ossian, I am thy mother under the Fith-Fath (enchantment). Thou art weary, hungry and thirsty; come home with me, fawn of my heart.' Ossian went with her and she led him to a solid-seeming rock face on the mountain side where she pressed the stone, a door slid open and they entered. As soon as the door closed behind them she resumed human form and Ossian saw before him the loveliest woman he could imagine. The house was brightly lit, though not by sun or moon or stars, and well furnished. Grainne told him her story as she prepared food and drink for him. Then, while soft music played, he ate 'his seven full satisfactions'. At last he said he must rejoin the Feinn hunting on the hills near by. His mother gave him three kisses and let him go. When he looked back no sign of the rock door could he see, or ever again find.

Ossian thought he had spent three days with his mother but on earth it was three years. It was then and for her that Ossian made his first song—a song to warn her against the men and the hounds of the Feinn.

> If thou be my mother and thou a deer,
> Arise ere the sun rises on thee.
> Travel the hills ere the heat of the hunt,
> Beware thou the men of the Feinn
> Beware thou the hounds of the Feinn,
> Avoid the bitch of the black tail,
> Avoid Bran, son of Buidheag, foe of deer.
> (and so on for many verses)

Then he left the rock wall, outside which he had sung, and went to tell Fionn. And it is said that the Feinn never again hunted on that hillside so long as the white hind lived. But Fionn, with Bran on leash, searched it inch by inch and day by day, but Grainne he never saw for the evil of his fairy love sent her to other pastures.

Ossian is perhaps the most famous of all the Feinn, better remembered than even Fionn himself, for he was their bard and poet, and so lived on. One story tells how he outlived his beloved only son Oscar, and Fionn himself, and then agreed to go to the Islands of the Blest with the beautiful Niam, daughter of the King of the Land of the Living.

Redder was her cheek than the rose,
Fairer her face than swan upon the wave,
More sweet the taste of her balsam lips
Than honey mingled with red wine.

She carried Ossian on her horse across the western sea waves to
where, she promised him, 'Fleeting time shall not bend thee nor
death nor decay shalt thou see,' and the Feinn raised three shouts
of mourning as he went. But after some 300 years of living the
life of a lotus eater in the Islands of perpetual spring and perpetual
sunshine, where all flowers always bloomed, where trees bore
fruit and flower on one branch, where birds ever sang, he grew
homesick for the Highlands, his old haunts and friends and, above
all, for mist and rain. Niam, knowing all was changed, bade an
eagle carry him low over the land, wherever he would. He
returned to Tir-nan-Og horrified by what he had seen. Men,
he said, had become small and wizened and weak; women were
no longer lovely but pitiful, and they had lost all the knowledge
of older times. He begged Niam to let him return to earth and
teach them. This, she told him, was not possible. Should he
touch the earth he would grow old and blind and wizened and
vanish in dust. At last, however, she agreed to give him a horse
which would carry him over the sea to Scotland and, so long as
he did not dismount nor touch earth, he would be safe. Ossian
promised only to teach men how to build houses, kindle fire,
cook food and so on, and not himself to dismount even for a
moment. He rode across the sea to a beach and soon had a number
of men gathering stones to build themselves a house. But they
could not lift what seemed to Ossian such little, light rocks. At
last he could bear it no longer and leaned from his horse to give
a push to a recalcitrant stone. As he touched it he turned to dust.

Another and more widely spread version of Ossian's end,
however, makes him outlive all the Feinn. In this story he finally
enters a hill with his mother and sleeps for 300 years. He is
awakened by the sound of St. Patrick's bell, though his hill, so
far as I know, is never described as being in Ireland. But then in
legend St. Patrick came first to Scotland and only fled to Ireland
when the witches of Scotland drove him out, throwing Dunbarton
Rock after him. During his sleep Ossian was in 'cold Elphin' but

he now becomes a resident in one of St. Patrick's monasteries and does not like it at all. He comments sadly on the dreariness of monastic life. 'Too much fast, and drowsy sound of bell,' he says. Ossian ran nine skewers into his stomach to restrain his appetite, but even then he was getting the food of fifteen men and was still hungry. He came out of his cell to help some builders and lifted a lintel-stone above a door which fifteen warriors could not handle. 'That was the best feat', said they. 'If the people inside gave me the food of sixteen men that were no feat', answered Ossian. Finally he obtained an interview with St. Patrick, with whom he held a disputation. According to the *Dialogue of the Ancients* (eleventh century) St. Patrick having said that Fionn must be in Hell, Ossian replied: Fionn, King of Feinn, the Generous One, was without blemish. All the qualities which you and your clerics say are according to the rule of the King of the Stars, Fionn's Fenians had them all; and if they are in pain, great would be the shame, for if God Himself would be in bonds, my Chief would fight on His behalf. Fionn never suffered anyone to be in pain or difficulty and can his doom be Hell, in the House of Cold?' (Fionn, it seems, was threatened with the cold hell of the Northern gods, a place of ice and wind and darkness ruled over by Hel herself, and not with our Eastern hell of fire and brimstone.)

Ossian then bitterly laments the passing of Fionn and his times. The *Lament of Ossian in his Old Age* has been preserved in the *Book of the Dean of Lismore* (sixteenth century) and translated by Dr Douglas Hyde. Here is an extract:

> Long was last night in cold Elphin,
> More long is tonight on its weary way.
> Though yesterday seemed to me long and ill,
> Yet longer still was this weary day.
>
> And long for me is each hour new-born,
> Stricken, forlorn and smit with grief
> For the hunting lands and the Fenian bands
> And the long-haired, generous Fenian Chief.
>
> I hear no music, I find no feast,
> I slay no beast from a bounding steed.
> I bestow no gold, I am poor and old,
> I am sick and cold, without wine or mead.

I court no more, I hunt no more,
These were before my strong delight,
I cannot slay, and I take no prey,
Weary the day and long the night.

No heroes come in their war array,
No game I play, there is naught to win,
I swim no stream with my men of might,
Long is the night in cold Elphin.

Ask, O Patrick, thy God of Grace
To tell me the place he will place me in,
And save my soul from the Ill One's might
For long is tonight in cold Elphin.

St. Patrick offers Ossian baptism and Heaven but he decides he does not want to be saved and go alone to Heaven but to rejoin Fionn and the Feinn at the Last Day. This is his prayer. St. Patrick at last assures him that he will after all meet Fionn and his Feinn in Heaven, their good deeds having saved them. Ossian then agrees to be baptised for them all and as the holy water touches him he dies.

On every New Year's Eve, at that moment between the years when there is no time and no man can be born or die, the Feinn meet again on the top of Mamratagan. But for them the moment lasts until the first dawn flash comes up over the hills to the east. This is their reward for never turning their backs on an enemy in battle, never harming a woman, never betraying a man. For this they are allowed to leave cold Elphin where some say, being pagans, they have to spend the time between their own deaths and the world's end. Others, however, think that St. Patrick kept his promise to Ossian and they are all in Heaven, but that even there they are homesick for the Highlands.

From the top of Mamratagan the road winds down a long steep hill into the green valley of Glenelg. And anyone who looks across the water to Skye and at the other views which open out to east and west as one descends the hill will realise why those who belong to the Highlands will always be homesick for them, wheresoever they may be.

INDEX

All Birds, Castles, Churches, Fish, Lochs, Markets, Priories, Rivers, Saints, Stones and Wells are listed under those words and not under their individual names

★ Several forms are known for the word Feinn: Fian, Fienne, the Fians.